T0000220

PENGUIN BOOKS

THOSE WE THROW AWAY ARE DIAMONDS

Mondiant Nshimiyimana Dogon is an author, human rights activist, and refugee ambassador. Born into a Congolese Tutsi family in Bagogwe tribe in North Kivu province, at age three he was forced to leave his home village, Bikenke, because of the Rwandan genocide against Tutsis that spilled over into the Democratic Republic of Congo. Since 1996 he has lived in refugee camps. Dogon holds a BA from the University of Rwanda and an MA in international education from New York University.

Jenna Krajeski is a reporter for *The Fuller Project* whose writing has appeared in *The New Yorker*, *The New York Times*, and *The Nation*, among other publications. She is the coauthor of Nobel laureate Nadia Murad's memoir, *The Last Girl*, and was a Knight-Wallace Fellow at the University of Michigan.

THOSE WE THROW AWAY

ARE DIAMONDS

A Refugee's Search for Home

MONDIANT DOGON

with Jenna Krajeski

PENGUIN BOOKS

For all refugees

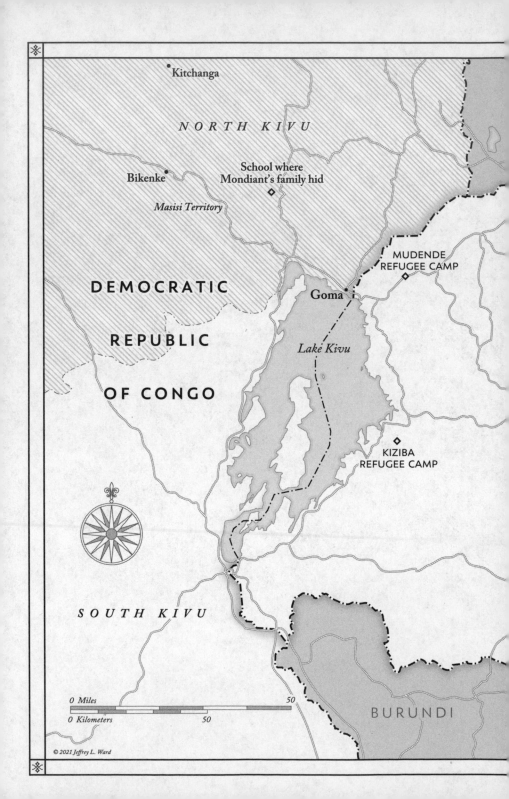

Kitchanga

NORTH KIVU

Bikenke

School where
Mondiant's family hid

Masisi Territory

MUDENDE
REFUGEE CAMP

DEMOCRATIC

Goma

REPUBLIC

Lake Kivu

OF CONGO

KIZIBA
REFUGEE CAMP

SOUTH KIVU

0 Miles   50

0 Kilometers   50

BURUNDI

© 2021 Jeffrey L. Ward

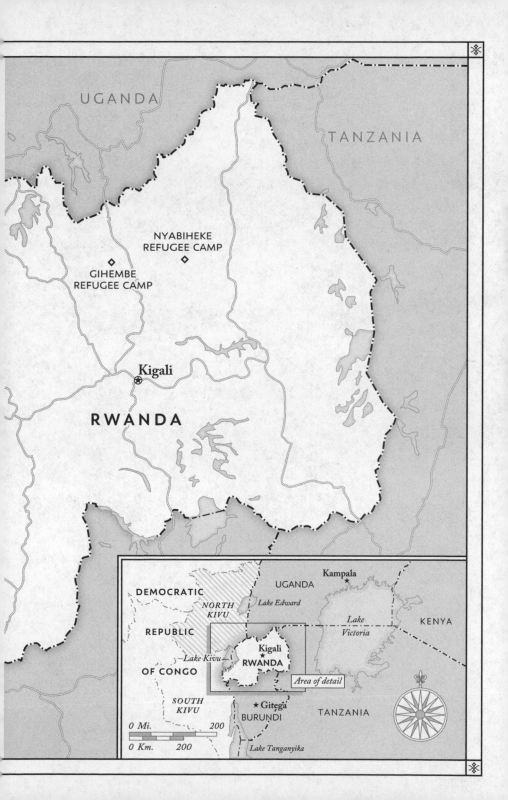

Introduction

Do not keep them away, they need justice to live at least

Do not close your doors, they want to get a little rest

The land has many sinners, the realm needs many priests

To beg almighty God for refugees and migrant's peace

Those we throw away are diamonds

In 2013, when I was still living in Rwanda's Gihembe refugee camp—one of tens of thousands of Congolese Tutsis who had been in the camps since 1997 with little prospect of leaving—to keep my soul from dying, I started writing a book. My book began with a poem, and that poem had a refrain. Each stanza—one about memories of my childhood in rural eastern Congo, another about the massacres that tore us from that home, others about the resilience of refugees all around the world—ended with a single line: Those we throw away are diamonds.

"We are thousands of youth on this mountain," I wrote. "We are conquerors, we quell earthquakes."

We are the Congolese refugees who have lived in the Gihembe refugee camp for years. Don't throw us away.

"We were weaned from school due to funds," the poem continues. "It's a burden, it's a border against our bright future / Bear this in mind: we no longer play for fun / Those we throw away are diamonds."

Diamonds, to a Congolese person, bring to mind colonialism, theft, and slavery. Refugees make others think of war, poverty, famine. In my writing, I wanted to reimagine everything. I wanted to wipe everything clean. I wanted readers to know that the real wealth in Congo isn't what was hidden in the ground, exploited by white colonizers. Congo is full of real people. Many of them, like me, have been forced from their homes because of violence, and live without a way to have their voices heard. Every refugee, from Rwanda to Syria to Guatemala, has a story. Every refugee is a diamond.

For years, I wrote whenever I could, a sentence at night in my home that I shared with my family in Gihembe, a paragraph between classes in my dorm at the Rwandan high school I fought to get into; at the University of Rwanda in Kigali, when I could afford to be there. When it rained and soaked my pages I started again, and years later when someone lent me a laptop, I typed so slowly that I worried it would take me decades to finish. But I wrote because my life and the lives of all the refugees around me were a series of untold stories, unheard by a world that too quickly forgot about us.

Some of those stories are nightmares. We ran from massacres and watched from a hill while my aunt and her family, who had stayed on the farm too long, were burned alive inside their home. My mother fed us the gluey mess of a boiled blanket. We walked for hours searching for the firewood and water that would keep us alive, and were beaten by local security forces if we strayed too far. The land we lived on would never be ours; we prayed that one day we would be embraced by any country. I wrote because I wanted to find meaning in these tragedies.

There are many stories of hope. Refugees built lives in the camp in spite of the restrictions. We opened stores and planted gardens. We studied day and night in order to continue going to school, and then the luckiest among us walked for days to get to that school. We had weddings and graduations, festivals in which we sang the songs of our Bagogwe heritage. If you closed your eyes, it was as though you were home in

Congo. Babies were born to ecstatic mothers and fathers. Some of us were able to leave and start lives elsewhere. I was helped by a miracle. For many, just enduring Gihembe is a triumph worth telling over and over.

I wrote to feel connected to the tens of millions of refugees searching the world for a home. Sometimes we heard stories about them on our radio. Refugees were fleeing from the Middle East, Central America, and East Africa—a "refugee crisis," the reporters called it. In so many ways their lives were exotic to me. I had never been to Syria or Myanmar. But in other ways, their journeys were identical to the one I took in 1995, when I fled violence in eastern Congo with my family. By writing about what came after that flight, after the gates to a refugee camp close and the journalists leave, I hoped to remind the world that the refugees' story doesn't end once they arrive in the camp. I hoped that none of these new refugees would be forgotten as we were for decades, forever refugees lost in a permanent impermanence.

I wrote because I wanted to remember. I wanted to remember the sound of the wind in the forest in Congo and the stories my grandmother told me and my siblings before we went to sleep. I worried that unless I wrote them down, I might forget my friends Célestin and Patrick, who died in the massacres in Mudende refugee camp, or my parents' friend Alphonse, who rescued me from a life with the Congolese rebels. My mother's traditional Bagogwe dress, which she wore only on special occasions; my father's laugh as he sat around the fire with friends; even the groan of one of our cows giving birth on a pasture in Congo: these are all remembered in these pages.

But trauma makes a joke out of memory. I fled my home village when I was three years old, and not all of my memories of that time are my own. Much of what I remember was told to me by my parents and older siblings, or my friends, or absorbed through things I read or heard on the radio. Some are impressions I tried my best to translate into language.

Like a wild dog gnawing at a piece of meat, trauma can destroy our understanding of time. When my father appeared at our door in Bikenke, my home village in Congo, with blood running down his face, that was just a single moment in my life. And yet I remember it as though my father stood unmoving in the doorway, bleeding slowly, for hours or even days, before we started running. Sometimes I think he still stands there, wounded, telling us our village is being attacked.

Trauma creates fantasies, it warps real life. I cannot say truthfully that after he died my uncle begged his killers for answers as to why they killed him, and yet I remember him doing so as well as I remember my high school graduation. Sometimes I force myself to remember the worst things that happened as though they were dreams, and other times my mind automatically covers the most grotesque things in a dreamlike veneer, to protect me.

Writing, no matter how imperfect my memory, has given me power. In these pages I tell the story of what happened to my people, the Bagogwe Tutsis of eastern Congo, in the horrible years when the violence from the Rwandan genocide crossed the border into Congo. I tell the story of our lives in the refugee camps, and our dreams of one day getting out. I wrote to remember. But I also hoped that by writing them down I could purge some memories from my mind forever.

Sometimes I used that power to protect. When I want to shield my friends and family, I change their names. Many people I love still live in Gihembe. They deserve as good a life as they can have in the camp, and I would never write anything that would get them into trouble. I changed my own first name in these pages as well, from Dogon—a variation of the nickname given to me by the Congolese rebel group I joined when I was eleven years old, and which I have used on official documents since—to Mondiant, my given name, which has no connection to the rebels. I figured it was my right to do this, as the author, finally, of my own story.

I never imagined that anyone would read my book. Still, as I got older in Rwanda, I never stopped writing. I attended university in Kigali, graduated, and wrote. I began teaching and petitioned the government to increase the pay of refugee teachers, who made less than half what Rwandan teachers did, and I wrote. I founded organizations to help other refugees, particularly women, and traveled from camp to camp, collecting their stories of war and rape—some of them held so tightly for so many years it was like uprooting an ancient tree—and I wrote them down. Each one could turn the world upside down with its sorrow and its hope. I wrote because the world has an obligation to know what is happening to tens of millions of human beings.

I named my book *The Wounds of Dumb*. In Gihembe, silence was as brutal as any attack on our flesh, or any disease. I wanted to help break that silence. I wrote about violence and rape; exile and hopelessness; hatred and fear; all the things my family and neighbors in Gihembe were too frightened or too exhausted or too ashamed to talk about. They were dumb with that fear and mute with that exhaustion, and that silence wounded them just like a machete once had.

When I was finished, I dedicated my book: To all refugees who have been in the camps for too long and have lost hope. To all survivors of mass killings based on race, gender, or nationality. To all forgotten people.

To all the young refugees who have grown up in Rwanda's Gihembe, Kiziba, Nyabiheke, and Kigeme camps, scattered through the small country, hoping for a life they could barely remember. To Iraqi refugees in Turkey and to Syrian refugees in Greece. To Somali refugees making the dangerous trip across the Mediterranean to wherever their boats might land. To Central American refugees caught between death and the US border. To all the refugees who dream of being something other than what you are now: Never give up. The world remembers you. This book is for you.

PART ONE

I was born in an era of bushes, bones cracked into ashes

Lovers hid in the rivers, to save the lives of others

They are not alligators to swim or related to fishes

They are starving; rotten beans and corn are their dishes

Those we throw away are diamonds

One

When I was a child in Bikenke, a village in northeast Congo, my grandmother told terrifying stories in an attempt to teach me about the world. Fierce animals and venomous snakes are waiting in the forest nearby, she told me, so be careful where you walk alone. Don't get close to the fire or a snapping turtle will come out of the flames and bite you. From far away, a chimpanzee looks like a person. Keep your distance from anyone you don't recognize.

Her stories sent me whimpering to bed. But nothing could have prepared me for how scared I was the morning my father showed up at the door to our house, bleeding from the head.

I was a child; I didn't understand what was happening. The mat I sat on, like always, smelled of sharp eucalyptus because it was woven from eucalyptus leaves. Fruit weighed down the branches of the mango tree that grew by our front door; because a year had passed since we last ate them, they were ripe again and would taste sweet. My baby sister, Patience, full of milk, was quiet in my mother's arms. Outside, the rain had turned our roads into pits of mud that came up to our knees if we tried to run on them. Would we have to run now?

My mother turned away from me. She couldn't stop my father from bleeding. "I'll get some herbs," she said. "Wait here." Watching her leave, I felt fear creep into my chest. Would she also be bleeding when she returned?

Would she be gone forever? Soon she came back through our door, carrying some small green plants that were sprouting yellow flowers. Despite feeling as though, at three years old, I had explored all of Congo with my little fingers, I had never seen those plants before. I watched while she pounded the plants into a yellow paste and spread it over my father's face. It mixed with his blood to become a disgusting dark orange. I looked away.

"Last night I was drinking with Mbashagure," my father said. "He warned me that Bagogwe were going to be attacked."

Mbashagure was my father's closest Hutu friend and one of our many Hutu neighbors. His ethnicity, like mine as a Bagogwe, a community of Tutsis who lived in both eastern Congo and western Rwanda, was meaningless to me. I was a child and the fighting in Congo—at the time called Zaire—and across the border in Rwanda wasn't a part of my life, although the adults followed it as closely as was possible in our rural village. They tuned an old radio to Voice of America, where journalists reported attacks on Tutsis—a slaughter near the border, a village burned in the center of the country—in mechanical, unemotional tones. Helicopters sometimes flew overhead. Every weekend Bagogwe adults gathered around a large fire to trade stories and warnings. "This village was attacked," they would say. "That family was killed," another reported, sounding like a more exhausted version of the Voice of America reporters. Because we were Tutsi, we had to keep keenly aware of what was happening so close by. We didn't have a plan, though. Leaving Bikenke was inconceivable. There was nowhere for us to go.

A loud thump at the door made Patience begin to whimper. My father reached for his spear. "I heard you were attacked." Mbashagure stood in the doorway looking stricken, wincing at the sight of my strong father, a leader in the village, sitting weakened on the floor with his face covered in the sickly orange paste. "I am so sorry."

Mbashagure was a good man. His family was like a part of our family, and he told us what was coming. Hutus in northeast Congo—some of whom had escaped or been expelled from Rwanda because of their role in the genocide—had been collecting weapons, intending to attack Tutsis. They considered us strangers in our own home. For generations, we had been told that Belgian colonists, eager to exploit the land for their own wealth and establish a hierarchy that they could control, brought Tutsis to Congo from Ethiopia or Rwanda to manage the land they had stolen. As we farmed the land and took care of the cattle, we tried to ignore the accusation that we didn't belong there. Traditionally Bagogwe were nomadic, traveling between Congo and Rwanda; before colonialism, those geographical differences hadn't mattered. We were Congolese. This was as much our land as anyone's, we thought.

Even before the genocide began in Rwanda, Tutsis were targets of mass killing within Congo. When the genocide began and spilled across the border, the hatred became impossible to ignore. Neighbor turned against neighbor; friend against friend; family member against family member. That genocide is a familiar story now, and by the time it crossed into Congo perhaps people had already grown weary of it. This wave of violence was new—terrifying, spontaneous, life-changing—but our cries fell on a world of deaf ears. Our Hutu neighbors told us that it was time for us to leave and return our land to the people they considered the real Congolese. To me—then as a young child, and still today—the idea of leaving our home was absurd. My family was Congolese and had been for as long as anyone could remember. Where would we go?

By the time my father was attacked, it was too late to try to reason with our neighbors. The people who hated us had already collected weapons of all kinds. I recognized most of these weapons. Some were normally used on the farm. They were the everyday tools that were supposed to help feed us. There were also weapons men carried with them in case they encountered a leopard or a lion, meant to protect us. Then there were weapons people kept in case they were attacked by other men, like guns and grenades. I was a child, but I knew what these objects meant. They filled me with dread. If you had them, it meant you were scared of something.

"I gave them weapons, too." Mbashagure hung his head, ashamed. "I didn't have a choice. You need to leave. They are planning to attack your house at six in the evening." It was late afternoon, almost time for my sister Furaha and my brother, Faustin, to come home from the fields where they were taking care of the cows.

"I'm telling you this because you have been my best friend since we were kids," Mbashagure said to my father. I noticed that he carried a machete in his left hand. "I don't want to see you killed in front of my own eyes."

✦

I THINK THAT EVERY REFUGEE can identify the moment their life changed forever: a final attack that drives you from your home near Damascus, the impossible stab of hunger that causes you to board a rubber dinghy from Libya to Italy, the realization that your religion may force you across the border from Myanmar into Bangladesh. Before I saw my father appear at our front door, bleeding from the head, I was the son of Congolese cattle ranchers, a child content to grow in the shade of our house until I was big enough to help on the farm. After my father was attacked, I became a homeless, displaced person, at the beginning of a long journey to a refugee camp that most of us would never leave. It was one unexpected moment that changed everything, and I have spent the two and a half decades since thinking about it.

As he ran, my father's face swelled and the veins on his neck bulged. Rain, sweat, and blood covered him almost to his waist. In one arm he carried the small amount of food we had grabbed before racing out of our house, and in the other he carried me. My mother, at our side, had Patience strapped to her back in a brightly colored kitenge sling. With every step my cheek banged against my father's wet shoulder. His blood ran onto my head and dripped down my face and neck. I must have looked like I had also been attacked, although I was healthy, fat even, and without a single bruise on my smooth skin. Soon my father's legs began to buckle, and his arm wilted around my back. "I'm weak," he told my mother, putting me down. My mother caught me and ran with me into the forest. My father collapsed on the road behind us.

Once, after my grandmother had finished telling us a story about a disobedient boy who had been attacked by a ferocious animal, I asked her to tell me what a dead person looked like. She didn't think that children should be sheltered from the world, and so she did. A dead person was limp and unmoving, she said. It was just a body, empty of blood and spirit, deflated as though ready to blow away but heavy like butchered meat. It was important to understand that a dead body is no longer a person, and to bury it quickly so that what you remember is the soul of the person who once lived inside.

Lying there, bleeding in the muck of the drenched road, my father looked like the dead person my grandmother had described. He was vanishing, his flesh unmoving except to cough out the last little bits of who he was. Why had my mother left him there? As though sensing my rage, she dashed out of the forest and dragged him to safety. *Oh*, I understood, *she wasn't strong enough to carry all three of us at once*. I felt my little heart soften toward her again.

Crouching in the forest, we heard laughter and talking in the distance. "Keep quiet," my mother said to my father, who was groaning. "People are coming to kill us. Keep quiet." He didn't stop, deaf with pain. With one hand she covered his mouth, and with the other cradled Patience up to her chest, feeding her to keep her from crying. I was so young, but I knew enough about war to know to keep my mouth shut and hold my breath.

"There's blood." A man stopped on the road only a few feet from where we were hiding, pointing at the red stain where my father had been. He walked with a group, all carrying weapons. Some had grenades

strapped to their belts, others carried long guns capped with sharp bayo-
nets. One had a red bandanna tied around his head, and some wore banana tree fronds around their waists. The airy swish of the fronds as they
walked terrified me.

"I smell it," one of his companions said.

"Maybe it was an animal," another said. "Let's look around and see if
we can find it."

"Let me," said the man in the red bandanna. By the tone of his voice
and the way the other men parted to let him through, I could tell that he
was the commander. "I will know whether it's man or animal," he said.

The commander knelt on the road and ran his cupped hands through
the red puddle, then brought them up to his face. Slowly, like someone
taking the first sip of hot tea, he drank. Then he shook the rest of my
father's blood back onto the road. "It's salty," he said. "It belongs to a man.
He must have been bleeding here just a few minutes ago."

"I see a line of blood going into those bushes," another said, pointing
in our direction. They walked toward us and peered through the thick
trees to where we sat. Their eyes were impatient, like mine when I was
begging my mother for something sweet. I was sure that they saw us and
I held my breath to keep it from shaking the leaves and giving us away.
My mother hung her head and closed her eyes, praying, maybe. Patience
cooed and sucked at her breast. My father swallowed his groans.

Every second of my father's life up to this point had been a miracle. He
was born early, a tiny, doomed baby, and his mother died moments after.
Without milk to feed him, his family was forced to contemplate sparing
him the torture of slow starvation. There were impossible but ultimately
merciful decisions that Bagogwe, who didn't have access to formula to
feed their babies or hospitals to incubate them, had to make. But my father was lucky. Word of this tiny, motherless baby spread throughout
Bikenke until a woman—a righteous, aging, childless woman and in-
spired storyteller—heard it and volunteered to take him in.

My grandmother loved my father from the moment she saw him,

producing her own milk to feed him, and as he grew, she gave him opportunities that other boys didn't have. She and my grandfather owned cows and land, and they sent my father to a boarding school until he was sixteen; afterward he got an apprenticeship on a Belgian estate, where he studied veterinary medicine. Once a week he walked for two full days between Bikenke and the Belgian estate, hiding from large animals and eating fruit from trees along with whatever food he brought from home. Congo then was still under Belgian occupation, and although eventually we would all come to celebrate our independence and understand colonialism as slavery, my father knew that the apprenticeship was the best way for him to learn a trade.

As he got older, he acquired more land and more livestock, which he kept healthy on his own, and built a reputation in the region for his skill with animals. By the time I was born, he had become a chief, a leader often called upon to resolve disputes and help make important decisions within Bikenke. He was a person other villagers looked up to. Now it seemed likely he would be killed by these laughing men, a casualty of incomprehensible hatred.

For a reason I could not fathom, the men turned away from the forest that concealed us. Maybe they couldn't make out our faces. Maybe they were daunted by the mess the rain had made, and the hassle of wrestling through the wet plants and deep mud to reach us. That effort, I thought, might take time away from their joyous, murderous spree. For a moment, we felt saved. Then the commander spoke. "Let's go," he said. "I'm sure we can follow this blood to Bikenke. We have orders. We have to find Sedigi and kill him first." Sedigi was my father's name.

◆

MY LIFE HAS OFTEN FELT like a series of stories, half remembered and half told to me. One was about my father's ambition, another about my grandmother's bottomless love. There was a time when I had many brothers and sisters and, because my father had been married before, many half brothers and sisters as well. Our home was sometimes so busy it felt like a village market, but we were mostly joyful, and we lived with purpose. We had jobs to do. Those of us who were old enough took turns working on the farm, taking care of the cattle and tending to vegetables and sugarcane. Young children made a job of absorbing my grandmother's wisdom, listening to her fables and stories and preparing mentally for the rigors of the grown-up world. The children in the middle were asked to gather water and firewood. Both jobs could be risky—children did, as my grandmother warned, fall into the river and drown—but, at the same time, as long as you were careful, you could return home with a hero's cargo.

Other stories were about Bagogwe, who had lived in this part of Congo for as long as anyone in my family could remember and had no intention of leaving. The sloped, green plain was home; the thick, wealthy forest was as well. Our house was strong with mud and covered by an impenetrable straw-and-banana-leaf roof. We knew where to find all the components of a feast of bananas, apples, and avocados. Because we lived among such riches and had access to an endless supply of cow's milk, Bagogwe were known for being strong. It was not unusual to hear about men defeating lions with nothing more than a walking stick. Some people laughed at those stories, calling them ridiculous. But when the men returned home with deep scratches on their arms, waving a walking stick that was nearly severed in two with bite marks and fully, ecstatically alive, it was hard not to believe they had won. We were proud of who we were and where we came from. And we kept each other safe.

What we knew about our history was also filtered through the stories we chose to tell one another, and what we left out. Our parents worshipped Patrice Lumumba, the revolutionary leader and first prime minister of a newly independent Congo, and at first they had a timid appreciation of Mobutu Sese Seko, who deposed Lumumba and his successor; on our farms, we were far from the poverty and disarray caused by the dictator's long, greedy rule. And our father had told us for a long time that before he also turned his back on us, Mobutu said publicly that Tutsis were Congolese. That acknowledgment—whatever Congolese traded for it—held our world together, for a time.

As soon as the violence came to our village, the stories of my childhood faded. Even our story about Mobutu, who would do nothing to protect us, changed. My father appeared at our door, bleeding, and from that moment on, every story was about killing. I stopped being a child, a Bagogwe, a Congolese Tutsi. I stopped having a home. I became a refugee.

Now, as they watched the soldiers walk away from the forest toward our village, my parents started thinking about what had been left behind when we fled. "Furaha and Faustin were with the cows," my mother whispered to my father. She worried that they would retreat to our house, where they would meet the murderers. My aunt and her family were also still in the village, along with countless friends. "We need to get a better look," my mother said.

She suggested we follow the fighters' footsteps toward a hill where we would be able to see into the village and where there were caves in which we could hide from the rain and the fighters. Before walking, my mother wove an umbrella out of wet banana leaves to protect Patience from the rain, which was now pummeling everything. She took my father's hand and pulled him up from where he lay. "Faster," my mother whispered as we started to walk down the road. I was in my father's arms again. The rain seemed to wake him up from near-death, and he began to walk with purpose.

"We should leave the road," he muttered. "The murderers will find us here." Nodding, my mother carried Patience into the sugarcane and banana fields. For what seemed like hours but was only minutes, we trudged through the tall cane. The woody stems rubbed painfully against our arms and legs. I thought about how kids from the village would sometimes sneak into the farms, tipping back on their heels to use their body weight to pull up the grass, then snap open the stalk and suck on the sweet flesh. My old world was quickly retreating.

When we reached the hill, we found a spot underneath a jackalberry tree, the same tree my grandmother had warned concealed lions and jaguars. Where was my grandmother now? I didn't know. Jackalberry trees are enormous—some can grow eighty feet tall, the trunk spanning sixteen feet—with a dark green crown of leaves providing cover for hungry predators. That night it protected us.

For the first time since we had left the house so many hours earlier, my father spoke. "How did I get here?" he asked quietly, looking up at my mother.

She looked at him the way she often looked at me and Patience. Her face was soft with love. That was her moment. She would look at us all that way for decades to come, trying to ease the pain, boredom, and fear that came with being a refugee, remembering when her husband had lain in her lap, asking her to explain the unexplainable. "You came on your own, Sedigi," she replied. "I just held your hand."

Two

That evening, hours after we had fled our home, we began hiding, along with other Tutsis, in a cave near our village. Although it was close to home, the cave was in one of the most dangerous and forbidding parts of eastern Congo, covered in parts by impenetrable forest and in others by the massive scars Belgian colonists had left when they excavated the mountains for material to build their estates. We hoped the dangers would scare away anyone who wanted to hunt us.

Some of the holes were a hundred feet deep or more and obscured by plants. I quickly learned that children were forbidden from leaving the cave at night, in case they tripped into them, and because we had to stay hidden during the day, we couldn't wander when it was light out, either. For the nine months while we hid within shouting distance of home, I only left the cave to go to the bathroom, and even then, I had to be accompanied by an adult. I did what I was told, but I was always frightened. Growing up in Bikenke, I had been warned never to go into the forest alone, where I could be killed by an animal or swallowed up by the thick trees and never seen again. It was hard for me to believe that now the forest would protect me.

From the hill we could see the attackers continue their assault. Some of them had left Rwanda when the Tutsi-led government took power, part of the Interahamwe, the Hutu paramilitary responsible for most of the violence in Rwanda. Others were neighbors who had been persuaded to violence by the rhetoric of the genocide, an extremist movement known as Hutu Power, or manipulated by politicians. I saw Pelagie, who weeks earlier had announced her new hatred of Tutsis by pouring a vat of palm oil over my mother's head, take part in the spree. Mbashagure's children, who had once spent every evening on our veranda, threatened Furaha before she fled. Their hatred of Tutsis, most of whom owned the land and cattle that Hutus took care of, wasn't inevitable; the seed had been planted long ago by Belgian occupiers and watered by power-hungry politicians, even before Hutu Power leaked across the border like a poisonous gas. In Congo it felt like we were all victims of our own history.

We watched our home being invaded, searched, occupied, and eventually burned to the ground. We saw villagers flee carrying their babies or flee carrying nothing. When my father returned to the fields looking for Faustin and Furaha, who had been working when we ran, I watched him leave and held my breath until he returned.

I longed for my grandmother, who had fled with an uncle toward the border with Rwanda. One afternoon, my mother whispered to my father that my aunt and cousins were approaching our house. "They'll be caught," she said, panicked. I remember seeing their bodies, small and far away, moving slowly toward the house. Then I remember, or I think I remember, their attackers moving faster, bringing fire with them, and that before my mother could scream, my aunt and cousins had been burned to death.

Have you ever heard the noises someone makes when they hunt animals? Screams like bolts of lightning reached us in the cave. I would sit beside my mother, a three-year-old only beginning to make sense of the world, and think to myself, *Wow, so many people in the villages are crying.*

When it was hot, we boiled in the cave, and when it was cold it felt like a refrigerator. No one washed or changed their clothes and soon the cave filled with the rancid smell of our own bodies. Men left as often as they could to try to find food, sometimes killing an animal and sometimes stealing from a farm or a banana plantation, and we shared everything among us. Still, we were always a few days from starving. Many people became sick, but without a doctor to diagnose them, no one knew what exactly was wrong. By some miracle, no one in the cave became seriously ill with disease or infection. Some children, though, died of hunger, which was easy to diagnose and almost impossible to cure. Mothers breastfed their babies constantly, even after their milk dried up, to keep them quiet.

There was nothing to do to pass the time. I sat and worked at being silent, trying not to ask my parents and siblings questions. I slept when my parents told me to sleep and tried to ask to go to the bathroom as little as possible. I willed myself to grow up. I offered to watch over the few items we had taken with us when we left home—a can for water, a pot for cooking, my father's Bible—and when my mother left the cave, I tried to keep Patience from crying by distracting her with games and smiles.

Once a week, on the Sabbath, we all left the cave to pray in a small clearing, hidden, we hoped, by trees covered with dark green leaves as thick and big as an elephant's ears. I grew up in the Seventh-day Adventist church, where children studied our religion separately from the adults. It was important that we carry on this tradition no matter where we were, and adults arranged lessons for us where they could see us from the lip of the cave. Still, some people were terrified that the weekly prayers would draw attention to us. Even on a Saturday, while we knelt in front of the cave pleading with God, we could see smoke rise from villages around us as they burned. Praying soothed us, but the moment we were finished, we rushed back into the shadows of the cave.

After a while, the threat of a massacre was overtaken by the threats that come with hiding. We were anxious and hungry. I was bored. I longed for the days sitting with my mother by our front door eating taro, listening to my grandmother tell stories at night. I wanted to talk and run. I wanted to scream.

Congo's forests are known for being dense and difficult to navigate, full of snakes and other animals that could easily kill a grown man, never mind a child. There was a reason my grandmother's stories urged us to stay away. But in the cave, the most brutal attacks didn't come from venomous snakes or fierce cats. What hurt us the most were the tiny ants that swarmed our bodies while we slept at night, tossing and turning on the hard stones that were our beds. Ants blanketed our legs, each bringing a tiny prick of fire and driving us closer to madness.

I laugh when friends in New York ask me about lions, as though I spent my childhood running from Congo's most glorious animals. Lions are dangerous, but they are rare and beautiful. If you see a lion, you're lucky. The ants in the cave, however, existed only to hurt us. Before the hardship of refugee camps, before I experienced actual torture in a Congolese jail, I was a prisoner of those ants.

They attacked indiscriminately. They swarmed because you dared to leave your home. They were impossible to kill; sweep away a nest and ten were built in its place. Slam your palm onto a pile of them, and hundreds more appeared on your leg. Men in my village who bragged about the time they killed a lion with a spear would groan for hours, wiping ants off their thin bodies, moaning and praying for the ants to leave them alone.

In the cave, pain became constant, and fear was relentless. We startled at the smallest sounds; mothers looked stricken while their babies let out reedy, tired whines. We prayed for someone to rescue us and for God to keep us alive until that happened. Just as I will remember the way my father looked when he stumbled through our front door, bleeding, I will remember those ants for the rest of my life. They taught me that even if you are safe, a life of hiding and waiting is a life of unrelenting, unromantic pain.

✦

HUNTERS DISCOVERED US on Christmas Day while we were outside the cave, praying.

"Are those footsteps?" someone lifted their head and asked. Then, suddenly, the strangers were in front of us. I froze. After nine months of hiding we assumed no one would dare come into the forest, but the men who found us were starving, and came searching for food. What were we supposed to do? We had no weapons, nothing to bribe them with. They stood in front of us, frozen themselves. I remember they wore no expression on their faces.

Then they were gone. The forest, which was never quiet, seemed to hold its breath.

We continued praying, and when we were finished, we returned to the cave and waited. Soon, as we knew they would, the killers arrived. Like the other Interahamwe we had seen, they carried heavy weapons, long guns and bludgeons with sharp edges. Some had machetes, which they gripped tightly, ready to fight. It was almost funny. We were a starving, terrified group. They could have killed us with their bare hands.

"See, here they are," one of the hunters said, pointing to us, proud of the treasure he had uncovered. "We came here looking for food and found where all the Bagogwe from the village are hiding."

"Why are you here?" the killers barked at us. "We thought you went to Rwanda. Have you been waiting for us?" They spoke Lingala, a language common in western and northern Congo that I didn't yet speak; at home, we spoke Kinyarwanda. Our language was also spoken in Rwanda, and this—among a long list of ridiculous things meant to demonize us— would be held up as evidence by our killers that we were foreigners pretending to be Congolese. I watched them block the entrance to the cave, shouting things I didn't understand at my parents and my siblings. They separated the men from the women and the children. My father, who was fluent in Lingala, tried to protect us, but no one would listen. He was shouting into empty air when they began killing.

I want to write everything down so people understand how we became refugees. It didn't happen overnight; our expulsion was the result of generations of political disorder and violence, and the journey from home to our permanent camp took nearly two years. So much happened during those years.

But I was a young child when we first left Bikenke, and most of what

I remember or think I remember is fractured and incomplete. In some ways, this is a blessing. Children who become refugees can forget, our brains growing over the trauma like saplings covering the forest floor after a fire. But even though specific memories are incomplete, our experience lives deep inside us like a diseased organ. We were still learning to process the world when the world turned on us.

Sometimes I remember things so clearly that when I close my eyes, I can read each memory like a book. Other times I think I remember things but can't be sure. Was it cold out when my father showed up bleeding? How many of us hid in the cave? Often what I think of as my memories are only stories told to me by my parents or older siblings, absorbed by my hungry brain. For example, I remember the sweet smell of mangoes growing outside my front door in Bikenke, but I only think I remember the torn clothes the hunters wore the day they found us praying outside the cave. Were the killers really Interahamwe? Or were they the Congolese Hutu fighters we then called PARECO, or Mobutu's soldiers? Were they the local Mai-Mai militias, some of them Hunde, who'd long targeted us Bagogwe? And was it really Christmas? I can't say for sure. It could have been the day after. It could have been any Sabbath. It could have been just a cool day when I felt safe and protected by God.

"Today is your last day on earth," one of the killers said. "You have two minutes to beg God to save you."

They began killing. I stood in the middle of the chaos, watching it happen. For a long time, or what felt like a long time, we were trapped. My uncle Gasasira, the oldest son in my mother's family, took my hand, whether to comfort me or himself. His hand was large and familiar, I was grateful to hold it. We lived in a village with more Hutus than Tutsis. The story of the genocide that had reached us before we fled, of Hutus killing Tutsi friends and neighbors, seemed strange to me; the Hutus we knew wouldn't hurt us, I thought. And even though a lot of them did— and even though for so long the story of the genocide was told in black and white—a few helped us, and I try to remember them as well.

My father was taken that day. Although my mother tried to reassure me, saying, "He'll be back very soon, Mondiant, don't worry," I had a feeling that he was dead. I remember that it started to rain, and the killers wouldn't let us take shelter in the cave. We waited while the rain blurred out the forest around us.

Two days later, when my father returned, he was being dragged by Mbanza, a close Hutu friend he had known since they were children. My father's hands were tied behind his back with rope, and he was struggling to breathe. Mbanza and my father had gone to primary school together, and when they grew up, they would often sit and drink beer, talking about their families and life on the farm. Now he was acting as though they had never met.

Seeing my father, I jumped up, wanting to run to him, but my mother stopped me. "Stay, Mondiant," she said. "Be quiet."

Mbanza brought my father to the front of the cave and then punched him hard enough that he fell.

"I thought you couldn't fall," Mbanza shouted. "Someone told me that Bagogwe men drink so much milk and are so strong they can't fall. I guess that's not true, huh?" I remember the other fighters smiled when they heard this.

Mbanza left my father lying beside us, clutching his chest, and began talking to another fighter. They both listened briefly to their radios. We couldn't hear what they were saying, but the more the man talked, the angrier he got, his face reddening and his hands flying around his body like a bird that had just been shot out of the sky.

The fighter came over to us while Mbanza watched. "You have power in Rwanda," he said. He was furious. I didn't know that Tutsis, led by future president Paul Kagame, had formed a post-genocide government, driving refugees in both directions across the border. I hadn't yet heard the names of the politicians like Kagame in Rwanda and Laurent-Désiré Kabila in Congo, men who would shape our lives for decades. Only my mother, who had followed her brothers' progress in Uganda, knew about the change of power in Rwanda. Still, as far as the fighter was concerned, we were as complicit in the overthrow of the Rwandan government as Kagame himself.

"You are mistaken," the fighter told us. "You will never rule again."

Mbanza came over to us. He looked at us with hatred. "It's been a long time since I killed someone," he said to the fighter. "I want to kill someone." I felt that he was a stranger.

He pointed to my father, who tried to stand up. Mbanza spat in his face. "Stay down," he said. "You are dead today." Then he turned to the other killer. "Go to the base," he said. "I'll meet you there." The soldier walked away.

As soon as the other soldier was gone, Mbanza's expression softened. He whispered to my father. "Where's your family?"

His hands still cuffed behind his back, my father nodded toward us. "Come with me," Mbanza told us.

When we were far from the cave, Mbanza uncuffed my father and turned to him. "Sedigi, we used to be friends," he said. "You gave me cows, we shared drinks together. I don't want to kill you."

He pointed east, deeper into the forest. "You better go to our old school," he continued. "I've heard other Bagogwe have gone there." My father and Mbanza had studied in a school a few villages over from the cave. He would know how to get there. My father nodded. Then his friend walked away, back to the cave, still carrying his weapon.

That day the killers came to the cave might have been Christmas. I'll never be certain. I remember following Mbanza. I remember that it rained, and we didn't eat for two days, waiting for my father to return; because of that, my mother stopped producing milk for Patience. I know that my uncle grabbed my hand when the killers came and shouted at us. I know the day was cold and his hand was hot. I think he held it to protect me, but he was probably also very scared. I remember he was approached by a fighter.

"My name is Gasasira," my uncle told the fighter, raising his hands in surrender. "I want to ask if we've done something wrong." He begged to understand.

Years later, my father told me that the soldier had replied in Lingala. "What a stupid question!" he said. "What tribe are you from?"

"I'm from the Bagogwe tribe," my uncle answered.

I remember that the fighter smiled. "I wish you'd never said that," he said. Then, in an instant, a fighter who had been standing behind us lifted his machete and cut my uncle's head from his body.

I remember seeing my uncle's head on the ground. I remember learning for the first time that when someone dies their joints stiffen, and that by the time someone noticed me standing there, his fingers had to be pried from mine. I think I remember the hiss of the machete swinging by my own head, the sudden gush of blood from my uncle's body like water being poured from a bucket. I think I remember, although it can't possibly be true, that while it lay there severed from its body, my uncle's head looked up sadly at the men and asked, *Why did you kill me?*

Three

For a long time, I refused to tell anyone I met in America that I was a refugee. I said I was Congolese and had an undergraduate degree in education from the University of Rwanda, both of which are true. If they assumed that, like many of the other African students at NYU, I came from a wealthy family, that was fine. Why was it my job to deny them that nice idea? I wanted to make friends, I wanted to graduate.

It's not anyone's fault they don't know what happened in my country. There are a lot of things that I don't understand about that history, and my life is the product of those wars and upheavals. I was born in rural Congo, in the Masisi Territory of North Kivu, and like in the farms and pastures of countries everywhere, politics hardly mattered to our daily routine. The papers we had then, showing our rights to our land and our citizenship, are outdated or destroyed now, but we knew who we were and we knew where we came from. Traditionally, in North Kivu, different communities had different roles. Some were hunters and tradesmen. Bagogwe were nomadic and looked after cows. We were assured that we owned the land those cows roamed on. Maybe we thought too much of ourselves because of what we owned. We thought we would never be poor or weak or hungry.

Occupation, revolution, assassinations, war—all the things that characterized Congo since at least the beginning of Belgian rule, in the late

1800s—were less important to our survival than the health of our cows. Even while they became infamous far outside Congo, dictators like Mobutu in Kinshasa felt worlds away, the capital itself an inconceivably long distance from North Kivu, across a massive, varied, and, in places, foreboding DRC. When he redesigned the flag, we shrugged our shoulders. When he said Congo was now called Zaire, we accepted it. When he had someone rewrite the national anthem, we learned the song the way you memorize a new street name; it was practical to do so. It would be years before we understood how ruinous Mobutu's rule was, how he stole from people and divided the country, leading to civil war. As long as we were healthy and able to work to feed ourselves, we were fine.

During the day, we worked. Even the children who went to school took their place on the farm when they were finished. We lived far from hospitals and treated most illnesses with traditional medicine. If someone was bitten by a snake, a healer in the village, usually an older man or woman, would grind up a paste of plants and herbs, rubbing it over small incisions they made over the bite. Women gave birth at home surrounded by other mothers; after an older midwife moved away from Bikenke and a few women experienced dangerous complications in childbirth, we clung even tighter to those rituals. At night families gathered around the fire and told riddles and stories, sharing food and sweet beer. Generation to generation, no matter how much changed, these were the things that made us Bagogwe. We were happy. We didn't know much about what was going on outside our community.

Like the Americans I have met, I had to educate myself about the history of Congo and Rwanda over the past century. I read books—there are so many—about King Leopold of Belgium and his pursuit of a private African colony, rich with natural resources, and the Belgian enslavement of my ancestors. I read about Congolese leaders like Lumumba, who fought for independence and who is a hero to all Bagogwe. I read about the ethnic violence in the early 1990s, Mobutu, and the legacy of division and violence that still exists today. I read about America's role, both hidden and in plain sight. I don't feel ashamed that my family didn't know this history when we lived in Bikenke. Rural people like us lived through those decades exerting as much influence as an old man shouting at a thunderstorm.

I am still reading all the books about the Rwandan genocide—histories and news analyses, manifestos and government reports. The amount of information and the number of voices can be overwhelming. I have read dozens of personal accounts of the genocide, each intimate, and still so familiar. These are the stories of Tutsis who watched their families die and, sometimes, the stories of Hutus who felt caught up in a frenzy they now say was like being drugged. I began to have access to so many written versions of these stories only after I moved to New York, and discovering them was like discovering another family.

It is a complicated history. I am Tutsi, and I was attacked by Hutus who claimed they hated us because of our ethnicity. That much, I am sure of. But I also lived in a village with many Hutus, some of whom helped us. I grew up in Rwanda, where we grew to distrust all the Hutus who had lived among us, to assume that even the friendliest neighbor was a killer in waiting. To leave the limbo of the refugee camp would be to venture into unknown dangers. At the same time, we were encouraged to heal and to move on. What really happened in Congo and Rwanda, the country I was born in and the one that took me in as a refugee? How do neighbors turn on neighbors? The more I read, the more questions I have. I have the authority to explain only what happened to me and to my family.

I know that during those long years when suffering spread through Rwanda and Congo like a disease, it was the ordinary people of all ethnicities—people like us who looked after cows and farms, who lived far from the cities and who saw politics as something that was told to them rather than something they could be a part of—who suffered the most. I know that Bagogwe were almost entirely displaced, moved from camp to camp until some of us were finally left in a refugee camp in north Rwanda called Gihembe and forgotten by every government near and far for close to three decades.

And I know that if we want our culture to survive, we have to tell people that we are still here. There are not very many Bagogwe Tutsis in the world and very little has been written about us, but our identity and our history are as dear to us as identity and history are to any group of people anywhere in the world.

Before the war, I would have told you all about our stories and riddles; the ritual of sending young men into the forest to prove their manhood; the vital connections between new mothers and the older women who became their teachers. After the war, our stories darken. But who we are and the lives we yearn for, the people we love and the country we miss, the rituals and traditions still passed down from family to family, that is who we were before we left Bikenke. And we are the same people years later as refugees, as proud refugees.

✦

IF YOU ASK MY MOTHER, EUGENIE, what her life was like in Congo, she will tell you that it was normal. Her family worked on the land. They had cows and they drank and sold the milk from those cows. She knows that when her neighbors in North Carolina, where she's lived with my father since 2018, ask her about Africa, they think of the worst. Africa, and particularly Congo, are frightening and foreign to my parents' American neighbors. Perhaps they have heard of Mobutu, to them the archetypal African dictator, but not of the ardent struggle for independence and prosperity launched, and still fought for, by so many other Congolese. Maybe they think of war and genocide but never of families like ours.

My mother answers their questions. She wants them to understand that she longs for life in Bikenke, and when she says that it was normal, she means that every day felt wonderful, safe and calm. We were free and with one another, and when we walked on our land, we knew other Bagogwe had walked the same paths before us. "We didn't have electricity," she concedes under the curious American gaze. "But our life was happy."

She never tells them about the horrors we've lived through. She doesn't mention the massacres and refugee camps, losing loved ones and family members and friends. The topic exhausts her. It turns her off like a light switch. She yawns and stretches her arms above her head, rubbing and closing her eyes as though to block out the memories. If you ask her about life before leaving Bikenke, though, she snaps awake.

Her father worked for a Belgian landowner, feeding and taking care of the horses he kept on his farm, and because Eugenie was the oldest, before long, she worked as well. Every day she fetched water and cleaned the milk pitchers, then helped cook for the family. Often, as a reward, her father brought her chocolate cookies from the Belgian. Food in her home was plentiful, but it was routine—milk and sweet potatoes, fruit, occasional meat—and she remembers the cookies like a miracle. Years later, bringing cookies to her own children made her feel as powerful as a god.

When she found out that her aunt had arranged for her to be married, my mother was furious. She felt betrayed. She was only eighteen, energetic and beautiful, and wanted to have some footing in the world, even to make her own money, before she got married. A couple of years earlier she had started selling milk in the market, taking home small profits that she could keep as her own. That small step toward independence, and the intoxicating feeling that came from helping to support her family, made her even more ambitious. Marriage—especially one that began with her favorite aunt handing her to a stranger—would cheat her out of the life she wanted. She didn't have a choice, though, and soon she was a wife, living a day's walk from her home village, in Bikenke with my father.

Luckily, Sedigi was easy to like, friendly and funny with a wide, toothy smile and a skill for making people feel welcome and loved. My mother settled easily into her new life and began to appreciate the routines and challenges of marriage. Every morning she woke up and prepared food, swept the dirt off our floor, shook out and rearranged the sleeping mats, and waited for my father to come home from the farm. She started selling milk again in the local market, and devised other small business, buying staples like palm oil in Goma and selling it to our neighbors in the village, saving them a trip to the city. Soon she had made so much money that she bought two cows of her own, unthinkable for most women in the village. "I didn't want to always have to ask your father for things," she told me. "I wanted to be independent."

When she had time, she sat with other women, gossiping about what was going on in town, who was getting married and who was having a baby, who had given a cow—a gesture of deep friendship—to whom. They talked about their husbands and their plans to have children. They shared food and cooking supplies. Sometimes they sat beside one another in silence, each working on her own task and staring at the bright green hills of Masisi, where their husbands were working.

Those friends were part of my mother's family; without them, married life in Bikenke would have seemed strange and lonely. Still, after we fled, my mother rarely spoke of them. They faded into our old lives until it was as though they had never existed. Even today, my mother hides the fact that those dear friends were Hutu. What hardly mattered when we lived in Bikenke now seems like a curse. Who knows what we did to invite the violence the first time? It was better to be safe. "I'm afraid they will hear I was talking about them and will come to America to kill me," my mother says. Then she yawns and closes her eyes, signaling that that part of the conversation is over.

My mother was happy, living a normal life, married to my father and surrounded by friends. But she felt that her life began to be wonderful, the kind of life immortalized in stories passed down around evening fires, only after she had children. If marriage was a trap, motherhood was the key to another, better world. My older sister, Furaha, was born in 1983, one year after my mother's aunt tricked her into visiting Bikenke, and six years later came my brother Faustin. I was born in February 1992, and two years after that, my sister Patience arrived and took over the house with her smile. My mother stopped spending all her money on cows and started spoiling us with cookies and real, sturdy shoes to replace our plastic sandals.

We were loved and my mother never let us want for anything. But there is only so much a doting mother and father can control. While we grew up, violence began reaching even the most rural parts of Congo, piercing our normal. In the early 1990s, when attacks first started against Tutsis, three of my mother's brothers went to Uganda, where Tutsis from the region gathered and organized, to fight against Hutu extremists in Rwanda. She listened with her friends to Hutu Power radio reports that described Rwandan Tutsis as animals, ripe for extermination. The radio was on so frequently, my mother began to wonder if perhaps it was true that Tutsis outside our village were different from us, as loathsome as the reports said.

One day she noticed that her Hutu friends seemed more distant. She no longer sat with them every day, cooking and talking about business in town. Information about her kids suddenly seemed private, and she held on to stories of our victorious first steps and wall-shaking tantrums like they were government secrets. Then the friends stopped coming to our house altogether. They began repeating what they heard on the radio programs, calling Congolese Tutsis snakes and cockroaches, celebrating the attacks on Tutsi villages. Shortly before our village was attacked, a Hutu friend of my father's, who had been living with us, was accused of betrayal and murdered. By the time Pelagie poured the palm oil over my mother's head, it was too late to reason with her friends. My mother began forbidding us from leaving the house on our own, worried about something she could not yet define.

But my mother was born in the tumult of early independence from Belgium. The war her brothers traveled to Uganda to fight in, in truth, had no borders. For Congolese people like my parents, violence wasn't broken up by periods of peace. There was no deep breath after independence, just as, years later, there would be no real peace between a First and Second Congo War. Conflict was ongoing, eternal. Although for most of her life it felt far away from us, she was used to hearing about the fighting, which hummed for generations throughout Congo like a song stuck in your head. Still, in those early years, my parents had succeeded in shielding us from it—to a tiny child, the attacks in Bikenke seemed to come out of nowhere, as unlikely as being hit by lightning—but they had been scared for a long time.

When my father came home bleeding from the head, they could no longer deny that it was happening. My mother left everything behind—cows, goats, everything. She rolled up the small amount of money she had saved from her business and stuffed it into a hollowed cow horn, then hid that in our house. One day, maybe, she would come back to retrieve it and use it to restart our lives. In that moment, though, the money meant nothing. She only cared about her children.

"Faustin! Furaha!" she shouted in the direction of the farm, desperate for them to follow her and praying they would find their way. She worried less about them. Faustin was already like another father to me. He showed me how to get water out of the well without falling in and how to milk a cow. And Furaha had been determined to prove her independence since she was old enough to walk.

"Eugenie, let's go," my father said. "You heard what Mbashagure said. I'll come back to get them." And he would, days later, risk his life to find my two older siblings, leading them back, terrified and beaten, to the cave on the hill.

That day, the four of us had fled together. My father carried me, resting my whimpering head on his strong shoulder. I clung to his neck, scared of what his fear meant, watching our home shrink into the distance behind us.

My mother went to Patience. She picked up her beautiful baby, her youngest and most vulnerable child, off the floor. She wrapped Patience in a bright kitenge and tied the kitenge over her shoulder, so it crossed diagonally over her front with her baby's new, unknowing face cradled between her shoulder blades. My mother pulled the kitenge around herself and Patience until it was tight enough that her baby's body relaxed against her own. She pulled it and pulled it until she could feel her baby's plump belly moving in and out against her back as she breathed and sighed, and we started running.

Four

On the walk to my father's school we avoided the main roads that were patrolled by soldiers and rebels. Instead, we moved slowly through the thick forest, barefoot and startled by every sound, no matter how familiar. Monkeys shook the trees around us, and when he heard them my father would whisper for us to stop, worried that the sound we heard was a person hunting us. We were all so scared.

Growing up, my father traveled between Bikenke and the school a few times a year to attend classes. That walk, which took them around five days, was full of promise. With other boys his age, my father carried as much food as he could, and whatever school supplies his family was able to provide him. They marched along together, telling stories and talking about class, knowing how lucky they were to go to school at all.

Legends grew out of those walks. "The forest is very dangerous," my father would tell us. "It took us days and days to get there. We saw animals everywhere we turned." There were lions, he said, and wild African buffalo with sharp, curved horns, ready to attack the young students. In his telling, the walk to school was a hero's journey, one part of a Bagogwe's lifelong quest to prove their bravery.

My father wanted to be a leader, the kind of man that people looked up to. For Bagogwe children—like most Congolese—education was not something to be taken for granted. When Congo was under colonial rule, Belgian authorities did not invest in the education of rural Congolese, and when they were able to go to school they were taught in African languages, never in the French that was required in order to truly become a part of the ruling class. Learning anything, though, was power and liberation.

My father's family insisted that he go to school. Older Bagogwe men, those whose lives had rolled out under the firm grip of Belgium, accompanied him and other village boys on the walk. They wanted him to have a chance in a new Congo, soon to be renamed Zaire. They carried machetes and spears to protect my father from animals, hacking through parts of the forest when there weren't roads to walk on, teaching him how to keep their goal in mind and not be afraid. My father would have walked for weeks to get to school, optimistic and full of energy.

Now we made our way slowly, fearfully, at night so that no one could see us. Branches snapped against my face and arms, and to not cry out I had to concentrate on my fear of being discovered. The forest was so thick it was hard to imagine that anyone had walked here before us, and we felt both that the world had grown impossibly large and unnavigable and that we were being watched and would be discovered at any moment.

We walked at night, when it was safer, and slept, when we were able, during the day. My father cut a large stick from a tree and used it to beat back the thick brush, trying to clear a path. With his free hand he held on to me or Faustin, who, even in his fear, was quiet and contemplative. As the oldest girl, Furaha tried to be a second mother. In Bikenke she bribed me with sweet beignets when I didn't want to take a bath, and when I wet my bed, she caned me. If I got tired, she carried me through our village and, now, through the forest.

I remember the sounds of birds and of monkeys. I remember that although there were a lot of snakes, I wasn't scared. In Congo, I knew nearly every variety of snake, from the highly venomous mambas, as thick as my father's forearm; to the iridescent-green bush vipers, with scales like delicate overlaid leaves; to the harmless, pitch-black tree snakes. Even as a young child, I felt confident enough about which snakes were dangerous and which were safe that I would often pick them up out of the grass, letting them slither over my hands and arms like pets before placing them carefully back down. I knew which ones to stay away from.

In Congo, the logic of a child was simple. Snakes were like people; some were scared of us and some were not, some were dangerous and some were harmless. We wouldn't hurt each other on purpose. If I left the ones with sharp teeth and deadly venom alone, I could play with their gentler cousins. Snakes didn't begin to scare me until we were in Rwanda, where everything seemed so different and there was no one to teach me about what was safe. I felt that when you are far from home, even a snake you know to be harmless could bite you and kill you, and I stopped playing with them altogether.

◆

ON THE THIRD DAY, after the sun set and we had just started walking, I heard my mother scream. Faustin, Furaha, and I were walking ahead of our parents. We stopped and turned to look.

"What's wrong?" Furaha dropped my hand and ran back to where my mother and father stood. The day was still darkening around them, and in the shadowy light, hunched close together, they looked more like animals than people.

My mother couldn't speak. Patience lay still in her arms. "Patience is dead," my father told us. He saw no point in being anything but direct. I remember that my little sister's eyes were closed, like she was sleeping.

When you are forced to leave your home, it becomes hard to keep children alive. Food was scarce, and on days when there was little more than boiled bamboo, parents gave it all to their crying children. My mother held Patience up to her dry breast and offered her nipple for comfort. Patience was already old enough to be demanding food she remembered having in Bikenke, like bread and cow's milk and fruit. The feelings of not being able to give her children food when they were hungry—anger and sorrow and frustration and desperation—took root in my mother like a disease that would never be cured.

That any of us had survived the cave felt like a miracle. But Patience's survival seemed like it could be traced directly to God. Each week when my mother prayed, she prayed especially hard for her youngest baby, who'd had so little time in the good and normal life we left behind before being expelled into an uncertain future. But just because one fervent prayer is answered doesn't mean they all will be. Walking through the forest, my parents prayed for sugarcane and fruit but found only bamboo and eucalyptus, and my mother's breasts stayed dry.

It's so simple, I want to scream: if there had been just a little bit to eat, Patience would still be alive. One moment she was whimpering for food, and my mother worried. The next moment she was quiet, and my mother cried out. I think that if any other kids her age had survived the massacre in the cave, they also would have died on the walk.

"Let's keep going," my mother said eventually, gently placing Patience back into the kitenge. My sister's little body, without any life in it, slumped down my mother's back, threatening to fall onto the forest floor.

"Eugenie, we can't take her." My father put his hand on his baby. "You can't walk with a dead person on your back."

Faustin, Furaha, and I sat and waited. There was nothing we could do. At any moment, we were sure, our parents would tell us what came next.

"No, no." My mother refused to accept what she heard. She was crying, which alarmed me. I rarely saw my strong mother cry. "Let's keep walking. We can't leave her here." She gestured to the glut of trees and brush around us, now darkened fully by night. The forest after dark was the kind of place young kids, like me, feared. I was glad that Patience had been still too young to imagine what lay in the shadows between the trees. She might not have been scared.

My mother wanted to bury her in a way that would honor her and leave her with anything she might need. She didn't want to leave her in the middle of an unknown forest, in a grave we might never be able to find again.

"She's dead, Eugenie," my father said. There was no point in pretending otherwise. "We will make a grave for her here," he said, gently but firmly. "We can make a nice spot."

Slowly my mother took Patience's body from the sling and laid her on the forest floor. She was a beautiful baby, with smooth, dark skin and long hair that my mother still talks about. She liked lullabies and songs, berries and bananas. I remember that day she was wearing a dress with small purple flowers on it.

"Mondiant," my father said, "stay with your sister." He started digging a hole while my older siblings left to find sticks and dried grass to pile on top of it. My mother, I think I remember, sat near me, silent. She looked at me. I was tired and hungry, and my parents worried that I would be the next to die.

I remember that I lay down with Patience next to the root of a bamboo tree. Her eyes were closed, and she wasn't warm anymore. I missed her. I suddenly felt guilty, thinking of a game I used to play in Bikenke to get what I wanted.

"Mama!" I would say. "Patience wants some taro," or "Patience is crying for more milk," or, when I was feeling really bold, "Patience asked if you could bring cookies home today." I knew that my mother had a hard time denying her baby anything, and I exploited that, asking for what I wanted through the baby and then claiming it for myself. Now I wish I had never taken anything from her.

I turned my little sister's head from side to side. It moved without resistance, staying in whatever position I put it in, like a toy. I didn't cry. Lying on the forest floor, I felt something change inside me. I felt as though I was no longer human.

I don't know how I would have reacted to my baby sister's death if I hadn't held my uncle's hand while he was killed only three days before, and if her body had been the first dead body I had touched. Maybe if I hadn't seen so many people die in the year before, I would have felt more emotion. But what was the point of crying there in the dark forest? One day you're walking and your sister is breathing into the soft fabric of your mother's dress, and the next moment she is dead. That death lasts so much longer than her life.

A few minutes later my father came and picked up her body. He handed her to my mother, who wrapped her in the kitenge one last time and placed her gently into the small hole, covering her body with leaves from different kinds of trees. A breeze blew some of the leaves off, exposing bits of the bright fabric. We said some prayers and then we kept walking, this time in total silence. My mother forced herself to stop crying, worried that someone would hear and come kill us.

Five

The boarding school of my father's youth was little more than a brick-and-concrete building with a roof made of iron sheeting. Its classrooms had been looted bare and destroyed. When we arrived, we saw desperate people had taken the wooden desks to use as firewood; even the blackboards and the glass from the windows were gone. Under normal circumstances, the compound would be alive with students, but because of the war the only people there were the displaced, like us.

At school, my father had started to become the man he was. He studied harder than he was expected to, and decided he wanted to work with animals. Like my mother, if someone asked him what life was like before the war, he would tell them we didn't have electricity and our home was small, made of mud and straw. "There was no running water," he would say. "We didn't have roads or infrastructure, but we enjoyed ourselves. We were happy with life as it was."

Like my mother, my father can sound defensive when he's talking to people who assume that because our life in Congo was simple, it was full of hardship, and that we must have become refugees because we no longer wanted to live where we were born. It's the opposite: a simple life made it easier to love the things and people around us. My father's fondest memories, probably in his entire life, are of sitting with neighbors in the center of the village on weekends, drinking beer and singing. He wants people to know we never expected to leave home. He wants you to know that being a refugee is a relief in the way that setting a broken bone is a relief. Once your leg is healed, you want to run again.

After my father turned sixteen he finished his formal schooling and started apprenticing on a farm about a thirty-five-minute walk downhill from Bikenke. The farm, which was owned by a Belgian Catholic priest named Carbone, felt like another world, one in which the colonists, after our fight for independence, had simply retreated into quieter lives as religious men and dairy farmers. My father, though, was used to being around the European Catholics, who came to Congo when he was young and led services in Bikenke. Although he was Belgian, and, to some Congolese who lost family members in the fight for independence, he represented oppression, people in our village grew to love Carbone, and he became my father's mentor and friend. The priest spoke Swahili so well and seemed to love the country so much, my father considered him practically Congolese. He was kind to everyone, and once, I remember, he brought me cheese.

Carbone's farm was huge. My father thinks he must have had thousands of cows, a massive fortune that Carbone shared by training Congolese from all over to take care of the animals. My father learned how to inject cows with drugs when they were sick and how to inseminate a cow. Eventually he began assisting with births, sitting beside a groaning animal, whispering to calm her down and then helping to pull a gangly calf, covered with blood and mucus, out onto the soft grass of the farm. Doing that made him feel as powerful as a god.

It broke my father's heart, then, when he heard that Carbone had fled Congo as soon as the war came to Bikenke, bribing anyone he could to help him travel safely to the airport in Goma. Before he was evacuated by the Belgian government, Carbone visited our village. Rather than warning my father, who considered him a friend, he encouraged us to trust the government soldiers. "They are here to protect us, Sedigi," he said. "The war in Rwanda is far away."

My father didn't know this would be the priest's last visit to our village. He smiled and waved when Carbone told him, "I'll come back, Sedigi. I'll see you soon."

If my father had to guess, he would say that Carbone didn't warn us about what was coming, because he could have been punished, or even killed, by the Interahamwe if he'd gotten involved. Priests had been murdered during the genocide in Rwanda. "I don't blame him for saving his own life," my father says, and he means it. It wasn't a betrayal as much as a fact of life. After that, my father understood how different Carbone's life was because he was white and Belgian rather than Black and Tutsi. The African Catholic priests weren't evacuated to Belgium like Carbone was.

A few weeks after Carbone left, Bikenke was attacked. The Congolese priests who had been left behind rushed to protect villagers and were killed for trying. They were heroes, but we still wish they had been given the chance to leave. We would have been happy, thinking of them spending their lives in the safety of Europe, a reward for their devotion to God.

Leaving the country, however, didn't mean you would live forever. The story goes that one evening Carbone was watching the news in Belgium and saw a report about the violence in North Kivu. He learned what had happened in Bikenke and other villages, the number of dead, the occupations and rapes and slaughters, and the mass exodus of desperate people heading to a border where anything was possible, hoping to get into a country they weren't sure would have them. People say the priest was so distraught that he immediately dropped dead of a heart attack.

Years later, when news of his death reached us in the Gihembe refugee camp in northern Rwanda, my father was surprised by how sad he became. He thought of the priest and all he had taught him. He remembered the farm and the animals, the gangly calf dropping to the earth under the guidance of his younger hands. He thought of home and his childhood and was devastated to learn of the death of the priest who had abandoned him.

✦

WE SLEPT on the concrete floor of the school, crowding among the other Tutsis who had managed to escape. The school had become a center for Bagogwe people, and although we had all been through something terrible to get there, we barely spoke about what had happened. Now was the time to dress our wounds and rest, and to try to comfort one another and strategize how best to stay safe, not to confront the reality of what had just happened.

We stayed there for close to three months. As the days went by, the world outside became more and more of a mystery. There were no telephones. To try to reach someone you had to write a letter and then pay a local person, usually Hunde or Hutu, to deliver it. No one had a lot of money, so the letters were infrequent and had to be important. People wrote to neighbors in their home villages, desperate to connect with missing family members. A Bagogwe chief wrote to let any other Bagogwe know to come to the school, where they would be safe, if they could. Replies were rarely delivered, so we were left to imagine the worst about the homes we had fled. How much remained of them? Who was left? We felt cut off, as though the rainforest was growing thicker around us.

Families pooled their money to hire security. Mobutu's government barely paid people to serve in the army, so we easily found some soldiers who would put aside whatever ethnic or political hatred they had to protect the school. They needed money for food more than they needed to fight.

One of the soldiers, René, was very tall and skinny. His body was more of a boy's than a man's. Still, when he walked on the school grounds in his uniform, carrying his weapon, everyone was afraid of him. Everybody knew that René got what he wanted. When he spoke, no matter what he was saying, it sounded like he was giving orders.

René really liked Bagogwe girls. He praised them for their smooth skin. When a girl caught his eye—and they often did—he would visit the family, as though we were back in Bikenke and he was another young farmer, asking a father for permission to marry his daughter. But René, the government soldier in his wrinkled uniform, a long gun slung over his back, didn't need to ask permission. No one could say no to him.

I didn't understand rape, although I had already seen it happen. Still, even as a child, I could tell there was something evil behind his attention. At least two of the women René raped became pregnant and would raise his children alone in a refugee camp. But we tolerated it; we needed the soldier to protect us.

Several weeks after we arrived, as we knew would happen, our money was almost gone. "You've paid me for three days," René said. "I will protect you for three days."

A group of adults got together to discuss what to do. "How much longer can we stay here?" they wondered. "If there's no one protecting us, are we safe?" It was now widely known that the school, like others in the region, had become a haven for fleeing Tutsis. The killers were close, camping at the base of a nearby mountain. They sat outside their tents, watching us and making noises loud enough so we could hear. They threatened us, shouting, "We will kill you soon." I remember the fear. It would have taken them less than an hour to reach us if René and the government soldiers left.

"Maybe if we beg him, he will protect us a little bit longer," someone suggested quietly, knowing it would never happen.

"Maybe we can protect ourselves," someone else said. "Does anyone have any weapons?"

"We don't have enough," another said. Our weapons were nothing compared with the Interahamwe's. "We have to find somewhere else."

"Where will we go?" The thought was almost unbearable.

"Tutsis have taken over the government in Rwanda," someone said. "I think it's safe for us there. They have a place for all of us to go."

The adults handed over to René what money they had left. "Can you take us to the border?" we asked. He said he could, and people started to like him.

◆

THE ONLY WAY TO RWANDA was around four hours by car, and to do it safely we needed protection. René arranged for trucks to carry us and for two trucks full of government soldiers to accompany us along the way. I don't know how much the adults paid him, but they were so anxious, I assumed they had given all they had.

We piled into the trucks, crammed as tightly into the back as possible. My head was pressed against my father's shirt. I could smell him, and it reminded me of when he'd carried me away from Bikenke. My mother, still thinking of Patience, wedged her body into a small spot on the truck bed and stayed quiet, staring at the forest and the school. Years later she would say she was trying to commit to memory where we were, the formation of the trees and the paths leading up to the school, every brick and the patterns of rust on the metal roofs, even the smell of the latrines and the sound of the birds.

The school was the closest landmark to where we had buried Patience, and my mother thought that one day, who knew how far in the future, she might be able to find her way back to the school and the parting in the trees where we had emerged weeks before, still on fire with grief. She could pick her way through the forest back to the unmarked spot where she had left her baby, see a bit of her bright kitenge poking through the leaves, and sit beside the grave and say hello. Or maybe, she couldn't help but think sitting there in the truck, an animal had already gotten to the body. René threw a tarp over us, blocking my mother's view of the school. She put her head in her arms. We started driving.

The mass of us jostled against one another as the truck drove over the bumpy roads. Through a gap in the tarp, I watched the trees and houses pass by in a blur, normal life happening just outside our tragedy. I didn't know where we were going or when I might see my home again. Like my mother, I was trying to memorize Congo.

Near the border was a camp for Hutus who had left Rwanda. When I was a child, I didn't understand why they needed help. Why did Congo let them in? What did they need protection from? We drove past a playground, where kids my age laughed with each other. *It doesn't seem bad to be a Hutu kid*, I thought. I think I remember that even they taunted us. "We will exterminate you," they sang in Kinyarwanda.

The Interahamwe had set up roadblocks and were stopping cars to see if they carried anyone they considered an enemy. They were immediately suspicious of our covered trucks, escorted by government soldiers. Each time the truck slowed down, we stopped breathing. Mothers shushed their children, as they had in the cave. For a small bribe, they let us pass. We hoped we had enough to make it to the border. Rwanda waited for us like the answer to an unspeakable question.

In the early afternoon, we were stopped at a checkpoint. "Do you have any Tutsis in the truck?" one of the men asked René.

"No," he answered in his booming voice.

It was stifling under the tarp and hard to keep quiet. My legs, folded underneath me, had lost all feeling. My father's sweat stained his shirt, he had begun to stink. Someone coughed.

"Did you hear that?" one of the men at the checkpoint said, pulling away the tarp. He scanned us, as though looking for something he had hidden among us. "These three men are Tutsis," he said, pointing to three young fathers. It seemed random.

Pulling the terrified men out of the truck, the other men joked. "We wanted a real lunch!" they said. "Three men is not enough."

"Oh, well," another said. "Tomorrow we will get more than three."

The wives and children of the men were crying, begging René to help them. Instead, he instructed the driver to leave. We drove away as the fighters killed the men on the side of the road, in front of anyone who wanted to look.

The lives of those men had been a toll. Instead of money, the murderers had demanded a human bribe. No one in the truck could talk from fear. By now we had been so tightly wedged together, and had together seen so much, it was as though we were one being with many heartbeats and a coordinated, hushed breathing. We kept quiet in order to survive. But the wives and the children of the three men who were killed couldn't stay silent. As we approached the border, they were screaming for all of us.

Six

E very morning when I was a child in Congo, in the hour that still looks and feels like night, someone stood at our front door. "Faustin, get your spear," a familiar voice said. "Get your club. Let's go to check on the cows." The voice was gentle but firm, and after a moment of sighing my brother would shrug his tired body out of bed, following the voice into the dawn. *Goodbye*, I thought from my sleeping mat, hearing him leave. *Who are you following?* I wanted to ask, but never did.

I was tiny and I went back to sleep, letting the voice fade into my dreamworld until it was as commanding as the breeze whistling through the gaps in our mud walls. Later, eating the sweet things my mother gave me for breakfast, I would again forget to ask whom the voice belonged to.

When the peacocks started singing, I knew it was morning. I was too young to go to the farm, so I sat in front of our home, a cup of milk in one fist, cooked taro in the other, watching people come and go. Most mornings, Mbashagure's wife would bring their young son over, sitting him down next to me on the swept earth to look at the world. I saw the sun collect on the river down the hill and warm the valley where we kept our cows. When it rained, I could barely see past the trees in front of our house, but when it was sunny, I watched over the entire world. Faustin brushed past me, carrying a jug of milk to the men on the farm. As usual, he did his chores quietly, dutifully, without complaining and eager to learn and, later, to teach me. I watched his back as he walked, knowing that in a few more years it would be me delivering the milk. I felt a surge of strength run through my little body, thinking about that.

When our dogs started barking, it meant that my father was coming back from the farm. I washed the milk and taro off my hands and waited at the gate, holding up my small palms, ready to help when they needed me. On good days, there were little things for me to carry. Our life was a mystery, and every day I looked for clues to how I would fit in. But I could never tell whom the voice belonged to.

One morning, I found my sister while she was washing dirt off some taro root. "Furaha," I asked her, "who does Faustin go with to the farm every morning?"

She looked at me as if to remind herself that I was still a child. "Papa," she said. "You don't recognize him? He gets up early every morning to check on the cows." She smiled.

"There are animals out there," she continued, gesturing out to the farms. "Leopards, elephants, pythons, hyenas. He has to make sure they stay away." I looked in the same direction and saw nothing but green fields. I squinted into the sunlight. "He goes to see how the ranchers are doing."

I shrugged, feeling, for a moment, embarrassed. When my father talked to me, his voice was low and gentle. He addressed me sweetly; his words were a song, not yet a command. I didn't recognize the voice he used with Faustin when he stood at the doorway every morning. It hadn't occurred to me until then that my father could be a different person in different situations, and that who he was to us would change as we got older.

Furaha sat up, enjoying her role as my teacher. A small bruise clouded her otherwise perfect face. She had recently been beaten up by Hutu classmates, an incident that my father insisted was because she was one of the few girls in school and not because she was Tutsi.

Furaha never stopped going to school, but the bullying aged my sister quickly. She had stopped crying when she came home and had started storming around the house, angry. She had always been very devout, but after that incident she became even more religious, insisting on washing all of our clothes before church, and when she got older, never touching alcohol or anything that could be considered a sin. Furaha, who had always seemed closer in age to my parents than to me, started to remind me of my strong-willed, ambitious mother. She wanted to cultivate those qualities in me, too. "Our father takes care of every person and animal on the farm," she told me. "When you get older, you will also have to defend your family and friends."

"Why does he go when it is raining?" I asked. The rain in Bikenke could feel like a roof caving in. Walking through it was like swimming. Sometimes my little legs sank so deep in the mud I thought they were being pulled under, maybe by a character from one of my grandmother's scary stories, one meant to warn me about the dangers of walking alone in a storm.

"A good Bagogwe doesn't care if it rains or not," she told me. "He cares about getting done what he needs to get done every day."

We thought of the Hutus we paid to work on our farms as our friends, and it was only after they attacked us that we tried to see how they might have resented us for insisting on these roles, as though we were born to own land and they were born to work on it. Later, after we had been in the refugee camp for a few years, my father conceded that perhaps the bullies targeted Furaha not because she was a girl but because she was a Tutsi.

If we were living amid violence, like my parents later told us we were, I didn't notice. The grown-ups did a good job of hiding their fears. We were happy. We didn't know anything about what was going on outside our community. Maybe we didn't know enough about what was going on inside it, either.

◆

IN APRIL 1996, the land surrounding the Congo-Rwanda border was a whirlpool of lost and forgotten people. Refugees and internally displaced people had walked or been driven to the camps established on both sides, where families eaten through by genocide and war tried to put themselves back together. People around the world thought that the Rwandan genocide was over, but for millions of people living in Rwanda and the surrounding countries, our suffering was just beginning. North Kivu was on the brink of a new kind of war that would last for decades. Hundreds of thousands of newly displaced wandered, looking for places to rest. We lived on top of graveyards.

My own broken and distraught family first arrived in a refugee camp just across the border in Rwanda, only about two miles from Goma, the capital of North Kivu. Almost one year had passed since we left Bikenke and I was still very young, and at first I saw the camp like a child would. I was excited to see that the tents were big enough to share with other families, and I hoped those families would include young kids like me. I barely noticed the UNHCR logo, a laurel and a pair of hands encircling the figure of a person, all in bright blue, stamped on the sides of the tents, salvaged from previous camps. I had no idea how that logo would follow me and my family for decades, becoming at once a sign of hope, a symbol of all we had lost, and a branding of who we had become.

When I was a young boy, I thought those tents were beautiful; after so much time sleeping in the forest, hiding from murderers, I wasn't used to having anything over my head. Sunlight filtered through the plastic and cast my gangly shadow far across the dirt floor. It was like living inside the sun. I played with the shadows of other kids, still strangers, darting back and forth through the tent, chasing the patterns, laughing. The camp grew with hundreds of new, glowing tents. I was a child. I thought, *Wow*.

I felt sorry for my older siblings, who had to act mature. They stood with my parents in line to register with the Red Cross. "Where are you living?" The workers asked impossible questions. "Where did you come from?" The same time we learned the word "refugee," we learned about the massive organizations that would at times seem designed to help us, at others to hold us back. Our first day in a refugee camp, we took comfort in the presence of the Red Cross. We thought of them as our rescuers.

Maybe I would make friends. Were there only Tutsis in the camp? Were there Hutus as well? Hunde? I didn't know. They gave us cookies! Crumbly cookies the color of fresh milk, which they shook out of large cellophane packets directly into our hands. At home cookies were a rare treat, brought to Bikenke by a visitor or bought by my mother, and handed out after dinner like she was a priest blessing our childhood.

We arrived to find tents pitched on hard, black rock. "It's from when Nyiragongo erupted," another kid, a bit older than me, said, pointing to the massive volcano that loomed in the near distance. Mount Nyiragongo, with its massive, active lava lake, was more powerful than anyone living in its path, whether refugees or Interahamwe. The hard ground beneath our camp had been scorched by previous eruptions. Even Congolese living busy city lives miles away in Goma feared that one day their homes would be buried. It had erupted fourteen years before we arrived in the camp, and the ground was still scorched.

At first, there weren't enough tents. We spread mats, also UNHCR branded, on the rock, lying down and staring up at the night sky until sleep came. We were starving, but not sure who was there to help us. Some people had been so ravaged by ants they had to walk delicately on the sides of their feet, wincing and on the brink of tipping over.

I was a child; I watched everything like it was a movie. Fear felt like a cut my mother could heal, her comforting words a bandage. One second I was scared, and the next I was fine, curious, close to happy.

My aunt Agnes, my mother's youngest sister, though, couldn't stop crying. "I don't like sleeping outside," she told me.

Agnes was twenty-three when we fled Bikenke, and recently married. She was very tall and striking. When her new husband was nearby, Agnes looked even more beautiful. "We're going to have a lot of children," she said to my mother, giggling. On the day of the attack, her husband was watching the cows. He never showed up at the cave or the school, although Agnes watched every day for him. After a while, everyone assumed he was dead, but my aunt kept waiting. "It's just the wind, Mondiant, that makes my eyes water," she told me one day. "I'm just crying because of the ants," she insisted, on another day.

In the camp, we began to experience the empty time that comes with being displaced from your home. After months of running and fearing for our lives, we had time to think. We thought about home and the people we had left. We thought about how close we had come to dying. We thought about the volcano that was now always in sight, boiling its lava and waiting for the day it would turn us into rocks.

While we played, we were oblivious, but the refugee camp was a dangerous place for children. We would drown while fetching water from Lake Kivu. We would fall into ditches that were dug for latrines, the walls of mud caving in on us. We would get lost, running over black rock between endless rows of identical tents until it all became one big indistinguishable mass. Even the adults we passed began to look the same, their appearances muted by identical expressions of grief and fear. They had lost weight and were tired. They wore torn and dirty versions of the clothes we recognized. They couldn't protect us as we'd thought they could, and so none of them were really our parents; maybe they weren't even adults.

Seeing us running through the camp and knowing how easy it was for children to injure themselves, Red Cross workers would catch us and try to reunite us with our families. "What is your name?" they asked, and we would tell them, wondering if we were in trouble. But when they asked us the names of our parents, many of us shook our heads. "Mama and Papa," we would say, and wonder if we would be lost forever. Parents cried every day looking for their lost children.

Our thoughts became weapons we used against ourselves. People sank into grief, retreating from the world. Others were angry, picking fights. Some mothers, unable to care for their children, killed themselves in the nearby lake. "I'm going to the market," they would say, and then walk down to the water. After a few days the government started building a fence around the camp.

I often remember those years as only a collective experience. We fled, we thought, we remembered. We collected our tents and our cookies. We listened to stories about the changing world around us—the war, the genocide, the new leader in Rwanda, the volcano that we swore we heard rumble above us, the other borders we might have to cross. Who was protecting us from the killers now? How long would it take to get home, and when would we be able to go? It was as though we had left our individual identities in our towns and villages when we fled. We hoped, we prayed. We laid out UNHCR mats side by side in our UNHCR tents and we tried to stop thinking about what we had all been through, and then one by one the luckiest among us fell asleep.

For me, the camp quickly became unremarkable. When you're that young, suffering becomes routine. Everyone slept outside, so sleeping in the dust was no big deal. Everyone got sick, so I wasn't scared of getting sick. After almost a year in the forest, I thought, *Wow, the world is so dangerous.* I was relieved to be in the camp. I didn't think about serious things anymore. Compared with life in the forest, I was in heaven. But we didn't stay long.

One day a man—a father not much older than my own—was shot while he put up his tent. The bullet seemed to come from so far away that I thought, watching him fall, that he had tripped over something or been pushed over by an invisible force, maybe the wind, maybe the angry spirit of the volcano watching over us. "Did he have a heart attack?" people wondered, forming a circle around him. My father knew. "Faustin, get your mother's kitenge," he said, and they ran to the man's side, where a pool of blood had begun to form.

"He's dead," my father announced, spreading the kitenge over the body. "He's been shot." Hutu rebels were targeting us from a nearby camp. "These are the people who did the genocide," people whispered. I didn't understand why the government would make a camp for Hutus. I thought, again, who did they need protection from?

We began to forget that any of our Hutu neighbors in Bikenke had ever been our friends. A gulf opened between us, so that no amount of evidence of their own suffering could bring us back together. My mother and father and the church had taught me to love everyone. When we'd prayed in Bikenke, it was outside, Hutus and Tutsis together under the open Kivu sky until it rained and we found shelter. I was too young then, and I didn't really understand the difference between a Hutu and a Tutsi. My mother and father had loved their Hutu friends, and had we stayed in Bikenke, their sons and daughters would have grown up to be my friends. But in the tents in that first refugee camp, I started to hate them.

Seven

After the man was shot beside his tent, we became refugees from the refugee camp. No one knew what to do with us. The next morning, we were ordered by camp officials to hide. We crammed ourselves into the long tents and stepped out only when we had to. I felt like I was back in the cave, worrying about every sound. Shortly after we began hiding, we noticed that the workers who had given us food and helped us find our parents had disappeared, and rumors spread through the camp that even the Red Cross had been evacuated because of the fighting.

If it hadn't been for the Rwandan Patriotic Army guarding us, we all would have been killed in our tents. In the week it took to evacuate all of us from the camp, we listened to gunfire from Goma and the surrounding camps and grew more desperate to leave. They moved us as quickly as they could, but waiting was torture. Every day a UN truck would pull up to the camp and people rushed toward it, trying to shove their children or elderly relatives on first, desperate for them to get to safety.

Even my father, who was normally so fearless and levelheaded, yelled at us when he heard a UN truck approaching. "Come on!" He took off, his long legs carrying him toward the truck, gesturing to us to follow. We ran as the crowd gathered like a storm cloud around us, my short legs struggling to keep up. The volcanic rock was hard and rough underneath my bare feet.

My father would leap onto the truck bed, creating a spot for me with his own body, and then try to pull me up after him. I grabbed for his hands, trying to propel my little body off the ground. I felt the terror of thinking he would leave without me, and the terror of feeling like I would be crushed by all the other people. My small hands slipped through his, and I was drawn back into the crowd. The other refugees were the mud on a rainy day in Bikenke, pulling me. They didn't care that I was a child; they wanted to get on the truck, too.

Every day I struggled to join my father, and every day I failed. "Mondiant," he would say from the back of the truck. "Hold my hand." But I couldn't. Day after day the trucks came and went. Day after day my hands slipped through my father's and he leaped out of the truck, running with me back to our tent with the sound of gunfire around us where the sound of birds used to be, and day after day I felt like crying over my own failure. My father never made me feel bad. "We will try again later," he'd say, jumping down to be with me.

In August 1996, we finally started the fitful journey from camp to camp that would lead us to Gihembe. First we were taken to a small, informal camp where authorities held the displaced temporarily while they figured out where they could live. Hundreds of Rwandan Tutsis who had fled the genocide waited there for permission to go to their home villages. Although they had been through so much, I couldn't help envying them. We were so far from Bikenke; we might never go home. I felt self-conscious in this new camp, which was too small to hold all of us. I wondered if the Rwandans had suffered more and if they had more of a right to be there than we did.

Although I was hungry and my body ached, I learned quickly there was no use in asking my parents for things. They had nothing to give us. In Congo we begged for bread and milk, we whined for bananas and mangoes, and those things appeared. I only had to raise my arms for my mother to sweep me up into hers, or for my father to carry me out of the house to look at the land. Childhood was short, and we remembered it for being quiet and happy. After we arrived in the first camp, my mother, still consumed by missing Patience, told me as gently as she could that things had changed. "You see how life is," she said, yawning, patting my shoulder.

In the second camp, children were in pain from hunger, their stomachs bloated with malnourishment. I helped fetch water for porridge, which aid workers stirred in huge pots to feed the lines of refugees. Getting the water made me feel grown-up and helpful, even though my stomach hurt, too, and even though I also lined up to get the thick, flavorless porridge after it had boiled into the consistency of paste. This was a place for waiting. I fetched some water; I ate some porridge. I slept, I waited, I asked for nothing from my parents or camp workers. I got older. I got used to living my life like an object pushed from place to place.

By November 1996, we were moved again, this time to a larger camp, also in western Rwanda. Once again, we were crammed onto the back of a truck, the same truck that was used to deliver food to the camp, and covered with a large tarp that was secured over the top with nylon cords. I crouched down beside my family. *Why do they need to hide us?* I wondered. Every time we arrived at a new camp we were told that we had left the war behind. Yet it was clear that no matter where we went, we were in danger.

The truck sped across the bumpy, dusty roads, jostling us in the back like cargo. Under the tarp the air was stagnant and hot; people complained that they couldn't breathe. From the safe crook of my father's warm arm, I strained to see the countryside pass by through the gaps, held together with the loosely knotted cords. I looked for signs of danger.

An hour into the two-and-a-half-hour drive, a man sitting close to me caught his neck in the twine. "Slow down!" people screamed. "Stop!" But the driver was too scared. "If I stop, more people will die," he said. People scrambled to untangle the man as he choked and coughed.

I was so scared I could barely see. But I remember that, as with my uncle in front of the cave, the man's head was severed from his body. I think I remember that his head tumbled out of the truck onto the road. We kept driving. "His blood is falling on me," someone yelled. But we kept driving. "Please stop so we can bury this man!" someone else begged the driver. But we kept on going. "I can't stop," the driver said again. "More people will die if I stop." The tarp flapped above the truck, I remember, like a flag.

No one should have to die like that man died. Later we learned that a few children suffocated as well. I was lucky. More than twenty years later, as I write this, these deaths have become details in my story, which has a happy ending.

I remember very little about the third refugee camp. There was no joy, even when people were reunited, and even though my most vivid memories are pleasant ones. When the weather got cooler, my father put all the money he had together with that of another family to buy a goat, which he butchered and roasted on a fire in the middle of the tents. The meat was delicious, spitting its fat into the flames, and the fire smelled like home. My mother, in defiance of everything that was happening to us, became pregnant.

Soon we were told we were to be moved again. "There's a camp in western Rwanda called Kiziba," my father told my mother. "They want us to go there," he said, referring to the camp authorities.

But my mother shook her head. "I've heard that Kiziba is very dangerous for children," she said. Without running water, we would have to walk a long way to the lake where many refugee children had already gone missing. "We can't go there," she said, pulling me close to her. The memory of Patience's death, particularly now that she was carrying another child, would be her North Star for the rest of her life. "Where else can we go?"

We didn't know anything about the camp they were sending us to, we only knew the name. "It's called Mudende," my father said. "We'll leave in the morning."

✦

IT TOOK FIVE DAYS to walk to Mudende. We left with some others, a loose crowd of nearly one hundred lost refugees walking in a fraying group on foreign roads. You've seen pictures of similar walks: Iraqis winding through the desert; children searching for their parents on the shores of Greece; families gathered at the southern border with the United States, waiting and hopeful; Rwandans rushing the border together, just months before we fled Bikenke. If you live in one place, you have one community. It's the people you grow up next to, who own the farms next to yours, the people you go to school with and see in the market every week. Once you become a refugee, you are part of an entirely different community, one bound together by war and violence and poverty and the desire to make it to somewhere safe, without knowing where that somewhere might be.

I was determined not to complain, to mimic the quiet, determined march of my siblings and parents. "Let me help." I held out my small hands to Faustin, who sighed and dug into the bag he had slung over his shoulder. "Here," he said, handing me the empty jerry can we used for water. "Hold this."

We carried a few important things my parents had grabbed on our way out of our home. Along with the jerry cans for water, we had clay pots for cooking and two woven sleeping mats. My father also carried his Bible, which he kept in his pants pocket and which in the years to come would become so worn that it was just a stack of thin papers held together with a rubber band.

On the walk to Mudende, I protected that jerry can as though it had been made of gold. I clutched it to my chest like a baby or carried it on my shoulder. Sometimes the can was empty, and I could hold it by the handle with a couple of fingers. Other times, after I filled it at a stream or a pond, it slowed me down and I had to run to keep up with my family. "Mondiant, give it to me," Faustin sighed when he saw me struggle. But I shook my head. "I'm fine," I replied, picking up my feet. I didn't want anyone to have to take care of me.

Now we walked in the open along the roads, moving as fast as we could. We were so eager to get to the camp that instead of running from the people we saw, we stopped to ask them for directions. "Can you guide us?" we asked a woman walking on the road. We didn't care who they were, or if they hated us. We didn't care if they wanted to kill us. We thought only about getting to Mudende, where we would be safe. No one hurt us; when they knew, they pointed us in the right direction, and we thanked God for that.

We were lucky in other ways, too. In early spring, the weather in Rwanda is nice, not too hot, and it rains only a little. With a bit of drinking water, we could keep up a good pace without getting tired. We tried to walk quickly during the night, when we felt safer, and walk more cautiously during the day. Adults who could afford to bought sugarcane to mix with water, which they gave to the children. It was all we had to eat, and the adults went hungry. We barely slept.

I don't think that many children can walk for five days without stopping. We walked so much my legs began to swell, the skin grew tight and shiny around my ankles and the bones underneath disappeared. We walked so long my legs ached and then began to drag behind me as though in protest. When I felt I couldn't take one more step, I sat down quietly on the side of the road. "Go to Mudende," I said to my family, handing the half-full jerry can to Faustin. "I'll meet you there." Nothing would be worse than slowing down my family, I thought. Faustin took the can from me, groaning at my theatrics.

"Mondiant." My mother's voice was gentle. "We can't go on without you." My father distributed the jerry cans and plates he had been carrying among my mother and siblings. I gave up my can without protest. He picked me up and swung me on top of his shoulders, then started walking again. I wrapped my arms around his head and let my throbbing legs hang over his chest.

I was so young. But living through a war makes you older. When you are three or four or five years old and you spend a year living in a war, you become as wise as if you were twenty years old. You learn when to close your eyes and how to keep them open even while you sleep. You stop asking for food no matter how hungry you are. You see people dying wherever you go, and you say, *"Wow, I'm next."*

Eight

I was three years old when I became a refugee, and I'm twenty-eight as I write this book. How can I explain what it feels like to be forced to leave your home and to rely on the charity of others in order to live safely? For two decades, I lived in a refugee camp, certain that I would spend the rest of my life there. Most of the people I know from Congo will live and die in Gihembe refugee camp. Some of them may have been born and may die there.

Tens of thousands of Congolese Tutsis have fled throughout the years to Rwanda for safety, and the UNHCR and Red Cross, with the Rwandan government, have acted quickly to accommodate them in camps spread across the country. The two oldest camps, Kiziba and Mudende, opened in December 1996, just after the spillover of violence from the Rwandan genocide sparked another civil war in Congo. Nyabiheke camp in the east followed in 2005, and several years later, the country nowhere closer to peace, the UN established Kigeme and Mugombwa camps in southern Rwanda.

These camps received thousands of weary, scared, bewildered, angry, tired Congolese. We didn't know what it meant to be a refugee then, but we would soon learn. Being a refugee meant having to reconcile your gratitude to Rwanda and the UNHCR with an increasing feeling of being isolated and forgotten. It meant weighing your options: Do you try to make a life in the camp, as so many do, opening a tailor shop or becoming a midwife, and accepting your status in Rwanda as a noncitizen, who, even though your rights to work and school are guaranteed by the Rwandan government, will never be accepted outside the camp? Or do you try to leave, going back to Congo, probably to fight, or to another camp in Uganda because you heard a rumor there was more opportunity there? Do you plot a long, dangerous route through Ethiopia and north to Libya, where you might buy a spot on a leaky boat and pray you make it across the sea to Europe? Or do you resign yourself to the limbo of life in a refugee camp?

My American classmates at NYU, like my parents' American neighbors, have little idea what it means to be a refugee. They see my parents as immigrants, with documents and a path, however long, to becoming citizens. My parents can work and rent an apartment. I can go to class and live in a dorm. But as long as we have no citizenship and no passports, and as long as we live far from Kivu and the land that has belonged to our families for generations, we will be refugees.

In Rwanda, when the camps were established, we were so relieved and so grateful. How would we have felt if we had been told we would never leave? We were ushered into camps that by their nature were temporary and yet that, by now, have become essentially permanent settlements. The same is true of refugee camps around the world, in Palestine, where concrete apartment blocks tower above where the tents once were; or in northern Iraq, where Iraqis displaced by terrorism have no prospect of returning home. Refugees live in abandoned buildings, or in cars parked alongside roads, or in churches when there is enough space to take them. Some get jobs and rent apartments in the center of town. You don't have to live in a camp to be a refugee, but for many refugees the camp begins as an oasis and becomes like quicksand, impossible to leave.

In the 1990s, though, when we were fleeing Congo, we didn't think about what the camps would be like ten or twenty years later. That was impossible to imagine. Refugees sent to Kiziba sighed in relief; so would refugees heading south years later. In those early days the camps were gifts.

I would spend my years as a forever refugee in Gihembe, a camp built in northern Rwanda just a year after Kiziba opened. Gihembe was unremarkable; like Kiziba, it was established by the UNHCR and made up of UNHCR tents, perched on a hill. But Gihembe was opened in the panicked aftermath of another tragedy, two brutal massacres that took place in what we then thought of as the most unlikely of places, a refugee camp in western Rwanda called Mudende.

✦

AT THE ENTRANCE of Mudende refugee camp, I had to stop myself from collapsing. After moving for so long, my limbs tensed like springs, it was hard to know how to stop. My body felt like it belonged to someone else. "How long will we be here?" I asked my father, who shook his head. What did he know anymore?

My exhaustion quickly turned to curiosity. The camp was full of kids my age, some of whom had been there for a while and were running and playing as though life were normal. Their skinny legs moved happily, racing between tents. I longed to run and play with them. If only I could kick a soccer ball, I could begin to live as I had in Bikenke. I felt relieved to hear stones hitting shallow bowls on the mancala board. When I saw my grandmother, who had taken a different route to Mudende, I thought that the world was becoming normal again.

I was curious about the camp and eager to explore and meet other kids my age, but my legs had swollen to three times their size. They throbbed when I tried to move. "I can't stand up," I complained to my mother. "My legs hurt." She looked at me through half-open eyes. Where I was full of curiosity and my only complaint was that the pain in my legs might prevent me from immediately finding friends to play soccer with, my mother was as listless as a falling leaf. In our moment of safety, with time to think, she couldn't believe that we had ended up so far from home. Where were our neighbors and friends? Where was the Congolese government? My mother, her belly now noticeably swollen with pregnancy, felt forgotten, and she was.

Mudende, like most refugee camps for those displaced by the Rwandan genocide, had been built quickly. There were not enough toilets, and no kitchens. Human waste and cooking oil ran between the tents and pooled in gutters. Violence surrounded the camp, brewing from the genocide and the anger the displaced Interahamwe felt toward the Tutsi government. Although we didn't know it at the time, aid workers had already started to flee.

I could tell my mother thought Mudende was unfit for humans. She was furious that she not only had to stay here with her children, but had to be grateful for the chance. But the spark of life that once might have made her complain, to march up to the UN officials and tell them people deserved better, was gone. She was still buried under the cloud of silence that had materialized after the first massacre in Bikenke. She was in mourning for Patience, whom she had not been able to keep alive no matter how hard she prayed.

"I'll boil water for a bath," she told me, pulling me close. "It will make your legs feel better. But try to walk when you can."

That night, I ate. First the cookies given to us by aid workers, then some beans and corn, the beginning of a lifetime of rations. Children piled into the tents, each vying for a spot near my grandmother, who had already won everyone over with her stories. We would sleep before our parents. I felt safe for the first time in years, grateful that at least we weren't moving anymore through Congo's impossibly dense forest. I lay on the floor of the tent, using my bag as a pillow, and listened to the sounds of adults talking outside. Their voices quivered. They wondered if they were dreaming. Where were we, they wanted to know, and when could we go home? They asked impossible questions. My father came in to lay his spare shirt over my shoulders, and I fell asleep.

◆

THE BRIGHT GREEN HILLS of western Rwanda around Mudende were close in appearance to but opposite in spirit from northeastern Congo. I could never call Rwanda beautiful, even if the colors were as vibrant as in Congo, the plants as bright. To me, it was an ugly country, a poor imitation of my real home.

From beside our tent the next morning we watched the camp come half to life with people like us, the emaciated and dazed inhabitants of a no-man's-land. Tents had popped up one by one against the hot sun, and weary people began emerging from them, looking around at one another and the landscape that was at once totally familiar and completely foreign as if to ask, *Am I alive?*

I made friends immediately. Patrick and Célestin lived in the tent with my family, and ever since Célestin's mother had demanded that he show me where the toilets were, we had been best friends. They had been in Mudende for almost two months and they had explored every inch of the refugee camp. I lived to compete with them. While I rested in our tent, soaking my swollen legs in the hot water my mother dutifully prepared every morning, they ran around the camp, reporting what they found back to me. "Zone five has the best place to play soccer," they told me. "This area is where the grown-ups play mancala." Patrick, who was more interested in marbles than soccer, led us to where the most competitive players gathered each day and where the best and most beautiful marbles were kept like jewels in the tents of certain lucky kids.

I seethed with jealousy, listening to their stories. As far as I was concerned, my two young friends were like explorers returning home after years at sea. The stories they told—of games and cooking and families sitting tightly together around small fires—were as enticing to me as my grandmother's wildest tales. I cursed my swollen legs, asking my mother for more warm water to pour over them. "I want to be with my friends," I complained. "Soon, Mondiant," she said.

Two weeks after I arrived, when my legs felt better, my friends showed me the camp. Mudende was huge, much bigger than Bikenke. I thought it felt like a city, like Goma, but I had never been to a city. Some families had set up UNHCR tents, like us, while others had stretched blankets over four tall wooden poles to create a roof without walls. Narrow alleys formed between the tents, and hordes of people wandered through them, looking for food and for family members they had been separated from. Because I was young and was free and eager to explore, I mistook their desperation for excitement.

Soon Célestin, Patrick, and I were so close we were like our own country. We shared everything our parents gave us—spare cookies, blankets, marbles, and smooth, round stones we found to use as marbles. When we fought, we settled things on our own rather than running to an adult. We didn't want to make another person feel bad. Even when only one of us wanted to go to the bathroom, all three of us would go; it wasn't fun to be apart from one another for too long.

We had the elastic, optimistic minds of children. We understood that the food we received in the camp was worse than what we had eaten in Congo, but because we were so hungry and it was all we had, we quickly got used to it. Thoughts of home began retreating in our minds like a story our parents told us at night. Together, we could write our own. Our stories would be about playing marbles on the dry ground of zone two, not of running away from men with machetes. I felt bad for that little boy who had been forced from his home in Bikenke, when I thought of him. I rarely thought of him.

We couldn't fathom the suffering of the adults around us who had lived their entire lives with the plentiful milk and meat and fruit of Congo. We didn't know the difference between rebels and government soldiers, colonists and dictators, or even Tutsi and Hutu. We didn't know we were refugees or what a refugee was. Any day we could play soccer was a good day.

I settled into a happy routine. Every morning just after dawn, Agizo, a kid in our tent whom we liked but who wasn't a resident of our private country, woke us up. "Hey, guys," Agizo would say, poking his head through the front of the tent. "Get up, the sun has just risen."

"Is it cold out?" we asked him, curling deeper under our clothes or UN blankets. "Do we need a jacket?"

After a groggy moment, the promise of a game of soccer lifted me out of sleep and I put on a long green cotton T-shirt and blue knee-length shorts. I wore these shorts and T-shirt almost every day. When we had a visitor or went to church, our mothers retrieved for us a clean shirt and pair of pants, which they folded and carefully put away when we were done.

None of the other kids changed their clothing, not even Patrick, whose dream of one day becoming a pilot made him seem older and a little more noble than the rest of us, so I wasn't ashamed. In Mudende, we were all the same. Our soccer ball was made of banana leaves and string; it spun apart with every kick. We played barefoot; our parents couldn't afford food in the refugee camp, so we didn't expect them to buy us shoes. We visited the few safe places where our parents would allow us to go, we played in the same soccer games, we didn't notice that there was no school and no work. When it rained, we took off our shirts and played with the rain falling on our backs, our bare feet slapping the ground, the marbles falling into the mud with a soft thud and barely rolling.

We were too young to know what life in a camp meant. Still, those early days in Mudende were preparing us to be refugees. We learned how to set up a tent and patch it when it rained. We learned how to make that tent into a toy when we had to. We learned how to stomach the chewy boiled beans and corn given to us, and how to treasure each of the cookies. We kicked our makeshift ball as though competing for a spot on the Barcelona soccer team and rolled marbles with the furious concentration of champion chess players. At night, we got used to hearing the camp fill with the tired cries of mothers who missed whomever they had lost.

The camp became our home. We accepted that Mudende was a haven for us and we considered the presence of the UNHCR and the Red Cross workers a promise that our long journey was over. By setting up Mudende, the Rwandan government and its allies were telling us that they wanted to protect us. By staying there, we were telling them that we trusted them. Although we didn't want to be in a camp—show me a refugee who doesn't long for home, no matter how dangerous or difficult that home has become—we played our part. For the refugee camp to be safe, we had to feel safe within it. And so we tried.

We pitched our tents. We held out our hands for beans and rice and boiled the dust off them. We lined up hopeful for more cookies. We gave workers our names and nationalities and villages of origin, words that now felt like part of a dream language. We described to them how we arrived at Mudende and why we left, omitting some of the worst details, and admitted that we, almost an entire people, needed help. We fell asleep, truly asleep, within the confines of the camp. We made friends we loved like brothers, like I loved Célestin and Patrick. We said thank you.

I want you to know that in Mudende we tried to be good refugees. We wanted to feel safe and protected, and to trust that the Rwandan government and aid organizations had saved us. We tried to sleep through the night and wake up with some hope. Then, in an instant, it became impossible.

Nine

On summer days in Mudende our tent became unbearably hot as soon as the sun came up. I didn't mind. Three months after arriving, my legs were healed and strong, and I had become used to the ways the camp forced us to constantly adapt. When the beans we were given to eat were particularly chewy, we left them to stew for days, filling our stomachs with cup after cup of water. On days when we were really hungry, close to starving, and our empty stomachs kept us up moaning all night, we ate bits of blanket my mother boiled into mush, hoping to trick our bodies into thinking we were full.

I knew which parts of the camp to avoid in the cold, and where to go for shade when it was hot. I barely noticed when it rained; I had no shoes to lose in the gluey, knee-high mud, and not far to go with my new friends. I had friends, and that was a miracle.

When the sun started baking our tent, our bodies became like logs in a fire and it was important to get up and get dressed and run out into the fresh air as soon as possible. It was vital to find your friends and try to have some fun in the early morning, before the sun became too hot. The days were full of exploration and games. We were pioneers in a new land, charting our lives with one another. "Look! There's a better path to the water tanks," Patrick would say, leading us to get a drink. Or, "Mondiant, Patrick, this is a perfect place for a soccer game," Célestin would tell us, finding a patch of earth someone had leveled for a tent or garden and then abandoned. "Come, follow me," I would say, waving at them, and run to where I had found a pile of rocks we could use to play marbles or made-up games.

In the evening, it was better to wait until the sun was long gone behind the Rwandan hillside before going inside the tent. If you tried to sleep before the night was fully dark, no matter how hungry or tired you were, you would lie awake, sweating. Patrick, Célestin, and I played until the last seconds of light left the camp, and then we sat together and talked until our mothers demanded we go inside and sleep.

Most of the time, as long as I wasn't so hungry that not even a game with Patrick and Célestin could get me out of the tent, following these rules helped. The nights of running through the forest and hiding from murderers started to become a distant memory; my five-year-old brain was happy to cast them aside. But on the night of August 22, 1997, the war found us in the refugee camp.

At first the sound of frightened birds or cats was outside our tent. I woke up thinking, *Wow, what is happening to them?* A moment later, the sound came inside, and I realized it was people who were screaming. I lay just a few sleeping bodies from my mother, who was by now heavily pregnant with my brother John. Something exploded.

"Célestin, are you awake?" Célestin's mother asked in a panic.

"I am," he said, and moved closer to her.

"Go," she said. "Go, leave the tent." But, again, he moved closer to her.

"Mondiant, we are being attacked," my mother said. "Twatewe mubyuke mwambare." I remember her words best in Kinyarwanda. "Wake up," she told me firmly. "Put your clothes on."

Before the attack in Bikenke, I was beginning to understand what bravery was. In Congo, I had been scared of the animals that roamed the forest and the fields. I listened to my grandmother when she told me how hot the fire was and how dangerous it was to wander through the village by myself. When my parents told each other about a chimpanzee sighting in the middle of the market, I thought to myself, *Wow, Mondiant, be careful of animals that look like people.* I was approaching the age when fear stops being something natural—even welcome because it sends you into your mother's arms—and begins to become something unmanly and stunting, something to push away.

Bagogwe men and women were brave. Boys were expected to begin behaving like their fathers and uncles as soon as they could, helping on the farm and protecting the family. When a Bagogwe boy turned fifteen, he was sent into the forest to be trained in the basic life skills we needed in order to become men. Instead of a formal education, we learned about our wars and poetry, our traditional songs and dances. We built fires at night, which we sat around, sharing our impressions of the day. Elders taught us how to run fast, how to shoot arrows and throw spears. We learned the old Bagogwe stories we would one day tell our own children before they started emulating us.

After a Bagogwe boy finished his training, he was given his own weapons. All the dangers of the forest, told to us by grandmothers in order to keep us close to home, were now tests of our bravery. The boys emerged from the forest having seen wild animals, snakes at their feet, darkness unlike anything at home. They emerged as men, ready to protect the village.

I was torn from my home long before I was old enough to receive any of these lessons or given the chance to show my bravery. I was a child, and years away from having to prove myself to anyone. In Bikenke, my own fear existed inside the bubble of home, where my parents and siblings looked out for me and where all the familiar smells and sounds wove a protective blanket around our house. My fears were ideas and characters in my grandmother's stories, far from real life.

Away from home, first in the cave and then in the school and then in refugee camps, real fear began to settle inside me. It became deep and permanent, growing somewhere between my heart and my stomach. Most days I could ignore it. We were in a refugee camp, after all, with aid workers, across the border from the fighting in Congo. When I played with Célestin and Patrick, I forgot about the fear that had woven itself between my organs.

On other days, during a quiet moment when the rain stopped us from playing all day, I remembered what I had seen on the way to Mudende, and the fear beat harder inside me. It ached and throbbed until it was all I could think about. What was that sound? Who was that walking beside our tent? The camp was in an unknown land, full of strangers. And my parents, once my greatest protectors, were transforming in front of me. They were no longer the king and queen of my small world. They were just two human beings like the hundreds who lived with us in Mudende, people who had been frightened and chased from camp to camp and who now sat beaten down like trees blown over in a storm.

I was never given the Bagogwe training; I was never sent into the forest alone. I was a scared kid; I often thought about my uncle, his head falling to our feet, and about Patience's tiny body covered with leaves and fronds. I thought about that moment in Bikenke when my father came to our door, blood streaming down his brave face. I thought about waiting outside the cave for my father to return and then thinking he was going to be killed the moment I saw him again, and that there was nothing I could do to stop any of it from happening.

◆

"MONDIANT, GET DRESSED!" my mother said again, and I must have, because a moment later I was passing through an opening in our tent with Patrick and Célestin beside me. Near us, I thought I heard a parent begging. "Please kill me," the voice said, "but leave my children alone." I don't know who it was or what happened to them or their children. Sometimes, memories like that burn in my head. Sometimes, I have thrown water on those fires, willing myself to forget.

A bright moon hung in the sky above us. Earlier, before we went inside to sleep, Patrick, Célestin, and I had sat and admired that moon, pointing out how the yellowish light made the camp glow. "It's almost like day," Patrick had said. Now the camp was blindingly bright. Rows of tents were ablaze, pushing their occupants outside into the smoke. Around us, people were screaming. "What did I do?" I heard a man's voice yell, and I looked up to see the bright shine of a machete slice open his arm. "Why are you cutting me?"

We ran without knowing where to go. Chaos and fighting scrambled the camp, and our expertise on Mudende's geography—just that morning a source of childish pride—was stamped out by our fear. We struggled to keep up with our older siblings, and soon we were alone.

"Where should we go?" I asked, looking to Patrick, who was the most confident of the three of us, navigating his way through the camp as though he had lived there his whole life.

"This way," Patrick said, and started running through the tents toward one of the camp's few brick-and-concrete buildings, where he thought we might be safe. Célestin and I followed him without speaking. Maybe if we stayed quiet, they wouldn't notice us.

We moved as quickly as we could. Heat from the fires burned my skin as we ran past the makeshift soccer pitch, past the flat patch where we rolled marbles, past the fence to the outside world, past the blur of violence and the loudest noises I had ever heard.

We saw people running beside us, frantic. We saw young men armed with machetes chase after them, and blood on the ground under our feet. Blood ran through the camp like a river in the rainy season.

We saw the bodies of a mother and father lying in the dirt, their baby screaming between them. We lost track of where we were going.

"What if the murderers are near the building?" Patrick asked. We turned and ran in a different direction.

"What if the murderers are this way?" I asked. We turned again and kept running. Then we turned again, and again. They were everywhere.

We lost control. Not even Patrick, the would-be pilot, knew where we were or where it was safe.

"There's our tent," he said, pointing. We had run in a circle.

"Let's go back inside," I said, tugging on Patrick's sleeve. "Maybe we can hide under our bags and clothes." In truth, I just wanted to go home. I thought that my mother might be there.

Outside the tent I saw my grandmother and my aunt Florence lying on the ground, their faces and hands covered with deep, red gashes. For the first time I understood that those gashes came from machetes—sharp, broad blades that could be swung quickly through the air. Many people in Congo used machetes to cut through the thick plants that blocked our paths through the rainforest. During the genocide the familiar tools had taken on a different meaning.

My grandmother's face was almost unrecognizable under the wounds. I touched her shoulder. Her body seemed stuck to the ground. Although I knew enough by now to know that she was dead, I still shook her, saying her name. Beside her, my aunt Florence stirred and looked up at us. Weakly, she tried to wave us away.

"Run, run," Florence whispered to us. "They are inside the tent." We stared at her.

Florence was only twelve years old when we fled Bikenke. I called her aunt because she and my mother were so close it seemed like they were related, although they were not. In the time since we had left home, she had, like the rest of us, become much older than her years. She stopped playing games and adopted a sober, accepting attitude toward the life we were now living, assuming adulthood before she was close to being an adult. When we were hiding at the school, she never complained. When I cried, she comforted me like my mother would. "It's okay, Mondiant," she sang in my ear. "We'll be going home soon."

Florence carried me on part of the walk to Mudende when my legs stopped working, her arms slung like thin ropes around my body. My head bounced against her slender neck. Now she raised her voice slightly, begging us to leave. "Run," she told us. "They will kill you."

Patrick, Célestin, and I did what she said. Not wanting to go far, we hid behind a nearby latrine. The smell made my eyes water. Young men had been crushed by walls of wet, sinking dirt while digging holes for the latrines, I remembered. "Get back," I told my friends, worried they might fall.

From our spot behind the latrine, we could see the front of our tent. Aunt Florence had stopped moving, pretending to be dead. Her head lay at an angle to her body and her hands were gripped into small fists. Blood from my grandmother's wounds seeped into my aunt's clothes. If you looked closely, though, you could see her chest moving quickly up and down as she took small gulps of air. When the men came bounding out of our tent, I could see her fists tighten.

"They are still alive!" One of the men pointed at Aunt Florence and my grandmother. "Who were you talking to?" he asked my aunt, kicking her like she was a sack of beans until she responded.

"No one," she replied. "I was talking to myself."

Throughout Mudende that night people were saving one other. Mothers threw their bodies over their babies. Fathers hid their brothers. My aunt Florence, watching me come over with my two best friends, told us to run. Then she lay there like bait while we hid.

My aunt Florence was not really my aunt, but she was my hero. She was a child when we left Bikenke, and a child when she carried me to Mudende. And she was a child when she saved my life and was discovered by those murderers outside our tent.

The men swung a spiked club high in the air and brought it down on my grandmother's neck. Her body shuddered. "This one is dead now," they said.

"Be honest," they said to Florence. "Who were you talking to? If you tell us, we will let you go. Do you understand?"

Florence was smart. She knew he was lying. "You left me to die before," she said. "It doesn't matter." Angry, they drew their machete across her neck. My hero, my aunt, was dead. I wish I didn't remember, but I do, that before they killed her, four of the men raped her.

I saw it happen from behind the latrine. I wanted to help her, but I couldn't. I was too scared to move. No one had sent me into the forest with a spear to prove myself or asked me to go to the farm by myself to protect the cows from lions. If they had, I would have run home screaming for my mother. I would have been killed immediately by one of the ferocious animals from my grandmother's stories. I was only five years old, skinny and starving, barely a boy. I wasn't brave yet. And so I stayed like a baby, hiding behind the latrine and crying, useless, tiny, scared. I was just a little boy, there was nothing I could have done to help my aunt. I wish I had helped her.

◆

ONE HUNDRED FORTY-EIGHT TUTSIS were killed that night in the first of two massacres in Mudende refugee camp. To the world, it was a sign that the genocide in Rwanda was not yet over. The Hutus who attacked us that night used their machetes to kill us, just as they had during the genocide. Just as they had done then, they attacked everyone they saw, and it didn't matter that we had done nothing wrong or even that we weren't Rwandan; because we were Tutsi, they were determined to kill us. Aid organizations hadn't protected us, nor had any of the international governments that had expressed regret over not acting during the genocide itself. Not even the Rwandan soldiers who had been charged with guarding the camp kept the killers out; later, we heard that a Hutu commander had lured them away, leaving us vulnerable to the Interahamwe to whom he had sworn loyalty. I began to wonder if anyone was capable of keeping us safe, anywhere we went.

That night, after my grandmother and my aunt Florence were killed, Patrick, Célestin, and I started running again. The men who had raped and killed my aunt called us "snakes" and tried to catch us. "Grab them and bring them here," one of them shouted. But soon something else caught their attention. "Maybe they don't care about children as much," Célestin said. "Maybe," Patrick and I said to each other.

If we stayed in the small spaces between the tents, we could cover some distance before being seen, and we began zigzagging through the camp as fast as our legs could move. After a few minutes, we lost the killers, who couldn't squeeze themselves along with their bulky weapons through the narrow alleys. We ran with our shoulders brushing the plastic of tent flaps and our feet catching on vinyl cords, tripping and stumbling in the soft dirt. We ran without looking back until we were far enough away that we could no longer hear screaming, only the sounds of bullets and grenades. At the edge of the forest, we stopped to breathe.

"Where are we?" Patrick asked, looking around. Nothing looked familiar. Mudende had been transformed into a war zone. The killers, anticipating that refugees would try to escape or that government soldiers might try to protect us, had set up roadblocks and were waiting for anyone to pass. The forest was dark and menacing. We were trapped.

The only other refugees we saw were dead. We were surrounded by their bodies, scattered along the road, slashed and left in their own blood like animals. I had never seen so much death. It was families of dead people, villages of dead people, a whole camp of dead people. Dead mothers and fathers and sisters and brothers. Dead friends. Mountains of dead people, I thought, countries of dead people. I had to stop myself from lying down and giving up.

I had an idea. "Let's pretend we are dead," I said. "Then they won't kill us."

Patrick and Célestin nodded. It was our only chance. None of us knew how to act dead, though, and we didn't believe we could stop ourselves from breathing or stirring. We would have to camouflage ourselves somehow.

"We'll have to lie with other bodies," I said. "Let's move some into a group."

"Off the road, though," Patrick said. "Let's move them into the forest. That way we will also be hidden by the trees." He was so smart. Célestin and I nodded.

My friends and I walked over to a nearby body, a large man who would dwarf our tiny bodies. But even with the three of us trying, we couldn't get the body to budge. "It's so heavy!" Célestin said, dropping the man's foot.

"It's like they are stuck to the road," I said. I remembered my father lying on the ground in Bikenke, how without his spirit he had become meat. I remembered my grandmother, just minutes before. "Try dragging him."

We worked together. Patrick, who was stronger, lifted the body by the arms while Célestin and I grabbed the legs, dragging him slowly off the road. Children were easier to move, but my whole body shook as I pulled them, listening to their weight slide across the dirt. I was terrified. I felt that God should punish me for treating people this way. But I wanted to live, so I kept on working. Soon, we had seven bodies piled up just inside the forest, their limbs interlaced like chain-link.

"What now?" Célestin asked, looking at the pile. He turned to me and Patrick. His eyes were red like he had been crying. I assumed that mine looked the same. I wanted to hug him, but there was no time.

"You go first," Patrick said. "I'm stronger so I can get in last and pull the people back on top."

Célestin positioned himself within the pile, and then I followed. Patrick watched to make sure we were hidden, and then he did the same. How do you describe such horrible things? We were like pieces of kindling wedging ourselves into a fire. We rubbed blood on our faces and arms. The metallic smell made my stomach turn. I closed my eyes. If I moved my hand slightly, I could touch Patrick or Célestin. We willed ourselves not to make a sound, not to breathe. We heard footsteps.

One of the bodies started to moan. "Help," he said to the footsteps. "Help."

"Be quiet," I whispered. "Please." But the man continued to moan and stir, moving our small pile.

The men who heard him ask for help were killers. They came over to our small pile and gazed down at us. "Let's see if those people are dead," one said, and I opened my eyes to see boots in front of us. "He's still alive!" the man in the boots shouted, pointing at the moaning man, who never stopped pleading. In one smooth movement, like kicking a soccer ball, the man in the boots pulled his long knife across the groaning man's neck. His blood was like the sudden flow of lava cascading out of a dormant volcano, covering all three of us.

Patrick couldn't help it. He screamed.

Ten

After Patrick was killed, I began to truly grow up. Life's lessons were no longer contained in stories my grandmother told while we lay sleepily by a fire, about to doze. Life carried you the way a river carries a piece of wood after a storm. You have little control.

Stories became dangerous. If you were lucky enough to survive—to become a refugee—your reward was never having to talk about your experience ever again. Life in a refugee camp was a curtain that closed in front of whatever life brought you there. The grown-ups in my life didn't talk about what they had been through. Growing up meant forgetting. All my life, I've mistaken silence for bravery. I learned that in refugee camps.

The morning of the massacre, before the Interahamwe came into the refugee camp aiming to murder as many of us as possible, I was a refugee, but I could say that I was happy. I had friends and my family close by. Both of my parents were still alive. I played all day and was getting stronger and taller. I knew how to kick a soccer ball made out of banana leaves through a goal marked by plastic sandals. When I thought about Bikenke, I wasn't crippled by homesickness like my parents were.

Agizo woke us up that morning like he always did. "Come play!" he begged us. It was as though no game in all of Mudende could begin until Célestin, Patrick, and I were awake. I enjoyed having this power over the other children.

We ran through the camp, away from one another. That morning, the running was a game, can you imagine? We shouted and laughed and teased one another for being slow. That was our favorite thing to do, that morning.

I could never have imagined that hours later I would be hiding among a pile of bodies, heavy like a collapsed building, and listening to my brave, kind friend begging the soldiers not to kill him. "Please forgive me," I heard Patrick say. "I'll give you money and food."

"Stand up," one of the murderers said to him. He knew it was a lie. He knew that Patrick, the skinny refugee boy in a threadbare T-shirt, had no money or food to give him.

"Please don't kill me." Patrick stood up. "God will bless you."

"Do your job," another man said to the killer. I remember thinking from the tone of his voice that he must have been their leader. Patrick shook in front of them. Then, like fruit being harvested from a tree, his head was cut from his body.

Célestin and I waited for hours until the last of the murderers had left the camp, a line of captives trailing behind them, before we felt brave enough to climb out of our hiding place. I placed Patrick's head near his body; we didn't dare pick him up. Patrick was the nicest of the three of us, and the strongest and most ambitious. If other kids in the camp threatened us or made fun of me or Célestin, Patrick instantly came to our defense. He was certain that one day he would do amazing things. He had never been inside an airplane, and yet he dreamed of flying one.

Célestin and I went back to our tent, where we learned that nineteen people we knew had been killed, including two of my uncles, two aunts, and five cousins. Célestin lost his mother and his brother, Pierre. Patrick's father and sister had both been killed. Six of the kids I played soccer with were dead. We told Patrick's mother what had happened to her son and waited until she was calm enough to follow us back to where we had left his body, and then we helped bury him.

We wrapped Patrick in old green sheets before we buried him. We moved him, cleaned him, wrapped him well, and then moved him again, looking for a nice place. I said goodbye over and over, and I told him I was sorry. Afterward, I sat in the grass in front of our tent, my face in my hands and my elbows resting on my knees. I was thinking of my grand-mother, whose stories—of joy, of fear, of home—would be missing from our lives forever. I was thinking about Florence, and how she sacrificed herself to save us. If she hadn't told us that the killers were in the tent, I would be dead.

I felt like something was wrong with my brain. I couldn't get the sound of Patrick screaming out of my head. I had always prayed with my parents, but in Mudende, I started making a lot of promises to God on my own.

My friend Muramira walked up to me. "Hi, Mondiant," he said. "Are you okay?"

He sat next to me on the grass. I wished he would leave, but I didn't want to be mean. "How did you survive?" he asked.

"I can't explain it," I told him. I was tired, and ashamed. I felt that I had betrayed Patrick somehow. If Célestin and I had been stronger, would we have been able to move the bodies and hide faster? Because Patrick was the last one to climb into the pile, did they see him? Had we come to expect so much of our strongest friend that we assumed he would be brave when we couldn't be, and in his eagerness to prove us right, he was dead?

"Where are Célestin and Patrick?" Muramira asked.

"Célestin is in the tent," I said. "Patrick died."

"Mmm." Muramira nodded. He wasn't surprised by anything anymore. "You know what," he said. "Erick and Tuyambaze were killed as well."

I didn't say anything. I put my head back in my hands, willing him to go away. I was struggling to understand everything that had happened.

"Mondiant!" someone shouted from inside our tent. "Where are you?"

"Muramira, I have to go," I said, relieved. I got up and started walking back to the tent. "I'm sorry about your friends," I said.

He shrugged, looking suddenly stricken. "I'm sorry about Patrick," he said, and started to walk away.

Inside the tent, the adults were discussing where to put the rest of the bodies.

"There's not enough space in the camp," one of the men said. "We'll need to bury them all together."

We would have to dig a massive hole, big enough for everyone. No one knew how we would mark the grave, and what would happen to it if we all left Mudende. Authorities were talking about evacuating the camp, and most people were too frightened to stay. Who takes care of a cemetery in an abandoned refugee camp? But we couldn't leave the bodies where they were, strewn around between the tents and along the road. They were ours.

"Mondiant, where were you?" my father asked. In the early morning, as I had carefully approached our tent with Célestin, watching for killers, my father had seen me and lifted me up into his arms. "You're okay," he said, holding me so tightly I felt like he might crush me. I told him Patrick had died and he hugged me again. "Your poor friend," he said. "He will be remembered."

Now, though, hours later, he was focused. He needed me to be older than I was, and stronger than I was, so that I could help give our neighbors the respectful burial they deserved. I promised myself that I would try.

"I was outside on the grass," I told him. "I was talking to Muramira."

"We still have people to bury," he told me. "Go to the neighbors and borrow shovels and hoes."

I did as I was told. All the people, even the children, were helping as much as they could. I was glad that I was too young and too weak to be tasked with moving bodies myself. Doing so would have reminded me too much of Patrick, and how our plan had failed him.

At the first tent I visited, they had no extra tools to lend us, and at the second they promised to let us use them when they had finished.

Everyone was digging a grave. When I finally got the tools, I returned to the tent. "Good," my father said as he took them from me.

When a Bagogwe boy was sent into the forest, he came out able to do anything his elders asked of him. In Bikenke, if I had gone into the forest, I would have been asked to look after the cows, to protect our village from animals or intruders, to be a good example for the handful of younger siblings my parents planned on having. I would have come out of the forest a new person, closer to manhood. Instead, I had gone into the forest in Mudende to hide from killers under a pile of bodies. I was asked to prove my bravery in a different way.

I emerged from the forest in Mudende with my friend's blood on me and told his mother that he was dead. I was five years old. I put Patrick's head next to his body, and when his mother was strong enough, I led her back to his body. I helped carry him out from the trees, and I helped bury him, and then I helped my father and the other adults dig mass graves for the one-hundred forty-eight people who had been killed, many of whom I knew. I've spent my life since his death trying to prove that I am a real Bagogwe man. I cried then, but I can count on one hand the number of times I've cried since.

Eleven

A few months later, on a December morning around five, Célestin, Furaha, Faustin, and I went out with some friends looking for firewood. It was dangerous to wander too far from the camp, and most refugees were too scared to leave. But we were young and eager, and when we thought about ourselves as soccer players—or when Célestin and I remembered zigzagging through the camp with Patrick a few months earlier—we imagined that we were fast and hard to catch.

Nevertheless, we left camp while it was still dark, to decrease the chances of being caught. We didn't know who the killers were, or who sympathized with them. And in any case, no one living outside Mudende liked to see refugees trespassing on their property. They assumed that we were thieves.

We had been walking for less than an hour when we saw a pile of what looked like luggage, abandoned in the middle of the forest. For a moment, we forgot that we were supposed to be looking for wood.

"What is that?" I asked, pointing to the pile, shadowy in the predawn light. "Are there people around here?" I squinted, expecting to see the figure of Patrick's killer emerge from between the trees. *"I found you!"* I heard him say to me. He wanted to finish what he had started by killing my friend.

Faustin walked closer. "It's a bunch of bags," he said. "They look like they might belong to soldiers."

"Faustin!" I whispered. "Be careful." I was afraid of what might be inside the bags, and I was certain that if the owner found us, we would be killed.

To my older brother, instructions from me were a nuisance to be swatted away, like a fly buzzing past his ear. He kicked at the bags until one opened slightly, and then he peered inside.

"Come, look!" he said. We slowly moved closer.

Inside were dozens of guns and grenades, as well as long, glinting machetes. "Wow," I said. We were used to seeing weapons by now—it was only three and a half years after the genocide, and a few months after the massacre in Mudende—but it was rare to see them up close and left alone as though for the taking.

Our friend Toto gasped like a child. He kneeled beside the open bag, and soon he was rummaging through the weapons, palming the grenades as though trying to decide which one to take for a souvenir.

"Toto, stop," Furaha said. She sensed that we should be more careful. "Let's leave," she said. "The grenades could explode."

"Don't worry," Toto said. "They won't explode. See?" He pointed to the pins lodged in the tops of the weapons. "The pins are still in them."

By now the sun was up. In Mudende, people would be emerging from their tents, boiling water for breakfast. In the forest, though, surrounded by enormous cypress and bamboo trees, the winter light was so muffled it might have been early evening. I could barely see Furaha where she stood, arguing with Toto. But I knew that the later it got, the more likely it was that the owners of the weapons would find us. "Let's go," I said. "Let's get some wood and go home."

"Fine," Toto said. To my relief, he closed the bag without taking anything, and soon we were walking again, the bags behind us.

An hour later, as we were tying together some logs and getting ready to return to Mudende, six men approached us. They wore military uniforms that were as tattered as our clothes. Their skinny knees poked through holes in their pants, and their pockets were dangling off their jackets. Still, even as rags, the army green was intimidating. They were smiling; we backed away, terrified.

"What are you doing here?" they asked.

"We are getting firewood," Furaha said. "But we're finished."

"You live in Mudende, right?" they asked.

We didn't know whether to lie. Could they tell we were refugees just by looking at us, as we could tell they were not just by looking at them? "Yes," Furaha said. "We are refugees from Congo."

The men nodded. They seemed curious about who we were and how we had gotten there. We weren't used to being asked questions. "How many of you are there in Mudende?" they asked.

"I'm not sure," Toto said. "There are a lot of us. Hundreds."

The men gestured behind them. "Did you see our bags?" they asked.

"We did," we said. "But we didn't touch them."

"Someone opened them," they said. "Are you sure it wasn't you?"

"It wasn't us," Furaha lied before any of the younger children could speak. "They're not ours. We didn't touch them. We know we're not supposed to touch things that aren't ours." Furaha was already indignant about how she was treated as a refugee. "We don't steal," she said.

I stayed quiet, waiting for some sign of danger. I looked at the men, their army pants sagging into their scuffed black boots, and decided I might pity them. They looked lost. I was staring at the pants one of them wore, stained with mud and as wrinkled as my own shirt, when a few bullets fell from a pocket onto the forest floor. I gasped and took a step back, pointing at the silver cylinders as they rolled into a little pile. "Look," I whispered to Faustin. The soldier turned to me and smiled again.

"Don't be scared," he said, bending down to pick up the bullets. "We're soldiers. President Kagame has sent us here from Kigali to protect you."

He shook the bullets in his hand. They sounded like marbles.

"Go, take your wood back to camp," another of the soldiers said. "But be careful. There are people in the forest who want to kill you." His smile told us we should run.

We picked up the bundles of wood, stunned. We had never seen Rwandan soldiers look so disheveled, so improper. Their faces and clothes had been covered with dirt, and their eyes had been red and swollen as though they hadn't slept a night since they were born. None of us were brave enough to say it aloud, but we all knew that these were not Kagame's soldiers. These men wanted to kill us.

In Mudende, when we told my uncle about our run-in with the soldiers, he laughed at us. "You were afraid for nothing!" he said.

"I've never seen soldiers that looked like them," I said. "I don't think they were real soldiers."

My uncle patted me on the back. "Kagame's soldiers are here, Mondiant," he said. "Don't worry so much. God will protect us." He was hungry and growing impatient.

But my aunt Agnes gasped when I told the story. Like me, she was suspicious. "Why would Kagame send them if we were out of danger?" she asked. "Why would Rwandan soldiers be hiding in the woods?"

My uncle laughed at her as well. "You're scared?" he teased her. "But you are the scariest person I know!"

My aunt shook her head. "I don't know, I just have a feeling," she said. "I don't know why." Aunt Agnes often had dreams that came true. When I was a child in Bikenke, she used to make me squeal by predicting things about my life. "Mondiant, one day you'll be tall and strong and a great help to your father," she would say. "But you'll also go to school. I know, I dreamed about it."

After we fled, her dreams became darker. She dreamed that her husband was a hostage of the Interahamwe. Before we buried Patience, Aunt Agnes dreamed that the youngest among us would die. She often dreamed that we were running, and woke up with a start, breathing heavily. Now she dreamed of another massacre.

"But never mind." She stood up, gesturing for us to follow her back to the tent. "Dinner's ready. We might as well eat."

Célestin and I spent the rest of the day playing hide-and-seek, our new obsession. We played the game every day when it was dry enough, running through the camp begging strangers to help us cheat. When it rained, we built houses out of mud—elaborate structures with separate bedrooms and spaces for playing—and named the cities and towns that made up our growing imaginary world. We gave each other purple bracelets made of woven thread to signify our friendship, and we never took them off.

Everything between us was a competition. Who could build their mud house highest before it collapsed? Who could find the best hiding place? Even eating, which we did every night side by side from the same shared dish, was something to measure. One night, we competed over who could eat faster. The next night, we judged each other's manners.

We shared our dreams with each other. Célestin wanted to be a doctor or a police officer. After Patrick died, he added pilot to the list. I wanted to be a teacher. If you were a teacher, it meant you knew how to read and write, and both of those skills, which not all Bagogwe were able to learn, seemed like keys to unlocking parts of the world I might never see otherwise.

That night, as every night before bed, I sat beside my father as he read his Bible, watching him scribble notes to himself about what he read. It was the only book he owned, and it gave him such satisfaction to sit with it for hours, turning the thin pages, reading it to himself until I begged long enough for him to agree to read aloud. "Here, Mondiant," he would say, "here's a verse for you." And I would sit up straight and pretend to understand. "Read another," I'd say before he'd even finished the first.

◆

THIS TIME THE KILLERS came chanting about God. "Jesus is coming," they shouted in unison, animated and loud as though they were part of a crowd in a stadium cheering on their favorite soccer team. Célestin and I were asleep on mats made of dried eucalyptus leaves, exhausted from a long day that had begun with collecting firewood. "Did you see the bullets fall out of his pocket?" Célestin asked me before we fell asleep. We were already talking about running into the Interahamwe posing as Rwandan soldiers like it was a story that had happened to someone else. "I did," I said. "At first I thought they were marbles." We fell asleep thinking about our bravery.

"Reka dutangire tubice, twageze mu nkambi," the killers chanted. "We are in the camp, let's get started."

This massacre was well planned by the Interahamwe and their supporters, who, furious at Kagame and his government, saw Tutsi refugees as foreigners propping up the Tutsi government, and as easy targets. The killers spread through Mudende before they made their first noise and killed as quickly as they could. Before they took out their guns, they used machetes and spears, hammers and clubs covered in nails. Before throwing real grenades, they threw small smoke bombs into our tents, forcing us out of our homes like scared, blind animals. When our screaming became loud enough to wake up the entire camp, they killed us however they wanted and chanted murderous things in which God had no place.

As she had months earlier, my mother woke me up. "We are being attacked, Mondiant," she said. "Get up, get up." She spoke quickly, in a panic.

This time, we hurried, jumping off our mats as soon as our mothers told us to, as though escaping was a dance we had been rehearsing. Once again, in the chaos, Célestin and I were left behind. We had gone to sleep naked, kept warm by all the other people, and in the dark, we were unable to find our clothes. Even with the killers approaching and the memory of the last massacre fresh in our minds, embarrassment over our naked bodies kept us from following everyone outside.

"Célestin, grab a blanket," I whispered, wrapping a shawl around my waist and tiptoeing to the opening in the tent. Through the opening I saw the massacre unfolding. It was as though our memories of the day Patrick was killed had come to life. "It's too late," I said. "The killers are all around the tent." Célestin and I looked at each other, panicked. We were trapped.

Musenyeri, whose son, Hakiza, was just a little older than us, had also stayed behind in the tent. He had a machete. "Try to run out the back," he said. "I'll meet them out front." He lifted his machete to his side and walked through the front of the tent. We saw him standing there as stiff as a tree, waiting for the killers to find him.

"Between the tents!" I shouted to Célestin, remembering how we had managed to escape the killers during the last massacre. But this time the Interahamwe were already spread out all over Mudende, and there was nowhere for us to run. My friend stood as still as Musenyeri, as though he were in a trance. "Let's hide," I said, changing my mind. I pointed to a garbage can near our tent. "Let's stay here." I grabbed his arm and pulled him behind the can, which barely shielded us from the fighting. "Crouch down, like this," I said. Célestin had become like a baby who had to be shown exactly what to do. "Be quiet," I said.

The trash can was small, and no matter how tightly we crouched, I knew that anyone who looked in its direction would be able to see our gangly legs or our heads as we occasionally peeked around the sides. I hoped that it would hide us for long enough that I could come up with a better plan. We watched Musenyeri, standing like a soldier in front of our tent, and then, a moment later, the killers as they approached him, holding their own weapons.

"He's not running," one said, laughing. "Why aren't you running?" Musenyeri was silent.

Bananas spilled out of their pockets, landing on the dirt outside our tent. They must have stolen them from refugees they had killed, I thought. One of the killers spoke in a muffled voice, his cheeks full of sweet fruit. "Why aren't you running?" he asked again. He held a machete.

"Stay back," Musenyeri said, holding up his own machete. They laughed again. "I'll kill you," Musenyeri said, and swung his machete at a killer as he approached. He was good with the knife, and he caught one of the killer's arms with his first swing. The man screamed, dropping his own knife and falling to the ground. "You cut off my hand!" he shouted at Musenyeri. "You cut off my hand!" He kept screaming.

The killers stopped laughing. They surrounded Musenyeri. I remember that in an instant my friend's father dropped to the ground beside the wounded man. I remember that his blood and the blood of the killer pooled in front of our tent. "They shot him," Célestin whispered. I think I remember that the gun went off without a sound; it was hard to hear anything but the fear in our own heads. The killers began taunting Musenyeri. "You cut off his hand," one said. "You should eat it." He wore short, black pants and his pockets were bulging the most with stolen fruit.

"I was just defending myself," Musenyeri begged. "He was trying to kill me." Then I think I remember, although I hope I am wrong, that before they killed Musenyeri one of the killers cupped some of his blood in his hands and stood over him, drinking it. A moment later, my friend's father was dead.

"Let's run," I said to Célestin. I grabbed on to his shoulder, trying to get him to follow me, but he wouldn't budge. Célestin was normally animated and loud, so ready to run and jump that his legs were like springs. Now he stared at me, silent and unable to move.

"Please, Célestin," I begged. "We have to leave now, or we will be killed."

He pulled his arms tighter around his knees, curling his body into a smaller ball. "Mondiant, go on," he said. "I'm fine here."

"What happened to you?" I whispered harshly. I was angry at my friend. "What's going on? Let's leave here, they'll kill us."

"It's fine," Célestin said. He rubbed his eyes. A second later he looked up at me, confused. "Why do we need to leave?" he asked. "Who is close to us?"

"The people who are going to kill us!" I felt like shaking my friend. He didn't move. He didn't seem to notice that I was shouting. "The people who killed Patrick," I said.

"Mondiant, leave me." He looked up at me. "It's okay, go on. Save your own life. I want to stay here."

"Let's run together," I begged, pulling on his hand.

"I am too tired," he said. "I need to sleep."

The killers, finished with our tent, were coming closer to the garbage can. In a moment they would see us. I pulled at Célestin's hand again. I felt responsible for my friend, who was no longer himself. But nothing I said and nothing I did could get Célestin to move from behind the trash can. I will wonder for the rest of my life if I failed him. What can one five-year-old boy say to another petrified five-year-old boy to persuade him to leap from his hiding spot and run into a storm of violence? Maybe nothing. Maybe something I haven't thought of.

"Mondiant, it's okay," Célestin said again. "Go and tell my mother I'm here."

I started crying. "Okay," I said. "I'll tell her." I leaped out from behind the garbage can and started running toward the trees, which I hoped would cover me. Remembering the first massacre, I squeezed between the tents until I got there, keeping my head down. Around me was a war. I can still hear the sounds people make when they are killing and when they are being killed as well as I remember any song.

At the edge of the forest, I turned around. Célestin had moved from behind the garbage can and was standing in the middle of the killing. "Célestin, run!" I screamed, but I knew he couldn't hear me. That was the last time I saw my friend alive.

✦

I SPENT THE REST of the massacre at the bottom of a latrine pit, where I had fallen in my panic, fracturing both my arms and my right leg on the way. The pit was hell. It was filled with bodies, some of which must have died in the first massacre and were already decaying and thick with a black sludge made from human waste and the charcoal-like rocks used to keep the pits from collapsing. I was lucky that the pit had been drained recently, otherwise I might have drowned. I passed in and out of consciousness from the smell, my fear, and pain. There were so many dead people I had to touch my face and arms to make sure I was also dead.

Above me the massacre continued. Screaming echoed inside the pit. "Where is that young cockroach," a killer said, and I felt sure he was talking about me. When they shined their flashlights down into the pit, I stopped moving and closed my eyes, hoping they would assume that I was dead. I was so tired that in spite of the smell and my fear, I fell asleep.

The men killed until the morning and then suddenly stopped. *They must have become tired*, I thought. Or maybe with the sun now up, the Rwandan soldiers who had promised to protect us would be able to do their job.

Above me, survivors stirred, looking for bodies. Inside the pit it was still as dark as midnight. Sewage and blood dripped down the walls. I couldn't see the sun; I couldn't believe that it had risen over a new day.

"Help!" I screamed from inside the pit. My cry bounced back at me, hurting my ears. "Help!" I cried again, but no one came. The pit was far from the tents and no one could hear me. My own family were close to dead, at that moment also being discovered and saved. They assumed I was dead. I wondered if anyone would find me.

It took a day for anyone to notice me. Authorities came to evacuate the camp, and Mudende began to empty. They searched the tents and the forest, looking for survivors. I shouted and shouted until my throat hurt.

Finally, a man peered over the edge of the pit. "There are people inside!" he yelled.

A long cylinder of a flashlight shone on my face, and I squinted. "I'm alive," I said. "Help me, please. I think my arms are broken."

One man—a hero like Aunt Florence—climbed into the pit and fastened a strong cord around me, which they used to lift me out of the pit and into the day.

Twelve

Nearly two thousand Tutsis were massacred in Mudende before we were evacuated by the UNHCR and the Rwandan government. I lost Célestin and Patrick, my aunt Florence and my grandmother, as well as my friends Ndungutse, Muramira, Erick, and Tuyambaze. Agizo, who woke us up each morning to play, was dead. Musenyeri had stood in front of our tent to protect it and was killed for trying.

My mother had given birth to John between the two massacres, almost without my noticing. One night she lay down on her mat, her belly swollen toward the tent ceiling, and a few hours later we were being rushed outside by a group of women who would be her midwives. I sat with Célestin, talking sleepily until my father told me it was safe to return, and I entered the tent to John's new, frantic cries. He cried again when the killers returned, and my mother, the memory of Patience like a hallucination, ran with him tied to her chest, not able to think about anything but keeping her baby safe.

She and John were both attacked but survived; they have machete scars that lock together like a puzzle, as though they were one body sliced through. Faustin was also seriously wounded by machetes, and my father and Furaha were injured in explosions. Aid groups and the Rwandan government used helicopters to take refugees to nearby clinics in Gisenyi, the border district where Mudende had been established. My family and

I were driven separately to a nearby clinic, but it was chaos there. I didn't know for sure that they were alive. Hospital authorities even separated my mother from John; by the time we were all reunited, weeks later, she was no longer producing breast milk.

Of all the lessons I've learned during my life as a refugee, those from Mudende were the hardest. At five years old, I was already certain of a lot that no child should ever know. I saw how cruel the world can be for no reason. I understood how quickly the pleasant circumstances of existence can change, and how suddenly a life can end. Just as I was becoming old enough that the riddle of the world should have started to make sense, inexplicable and unpredictable violence tore my world apart. That is a hard lesson for a child to learn, but I have always been a good student.

Mudende taught me that even the places you go to for safety can fail you. Being in a refugee camp didn't mean you were protected from violence. Although the first massacre set off a siren letting the world know that people in Rwanda were still in danger, we became victims of a second massacre. When the Rwandan government sent forces to protect us, although they were so few, I thought we were safe. The UNHCR and even the American government had condemned the first massacre, but the killers had found simple ways to continue their spree. They set up roadblocks to stop the Rwandan forces from reaching the camp, and they had planned their attack. Célestin was dead.

Refugee camps are meant to collect people who are weary and in danger. After a war, what could be more important than that? But we were as vulnerable in Mudende as we had been in Bikenke, perhaps we were even more at risk; the killers, many of whom were refugees themselves, fleeing violence they had perpetrated or were accused of perpetrating, surrounded us. We were easy prey, trapped by the camps that were built to protect us. At least in Bikenke, we knew where to flee to. We weren't strangers without maps or compasses. At least at home, we weren't stripped of the senses that let us know when there was danger and when to run.

We arrived at Mudende with nothing; many of us had left our weapons, or tools that could be used as weapons, at home. We had eaten very little and moved slowly, in pain. We were mourning the people we had lost, and, when we allowed ourselves, we thought about our lives back in our home villages, and those thoughts depressed and sedated us. We were too tired to fight. Some of the measures the aid workers took to protect us made us more vulnerable. They drew a border around us, but that border ended up holding us in for the killers.

Refugee camps in Congo and Rwanda became battlegrounds. After the massacre in Mudende, the world could no longer pretend that the Rwandan genocide was over. When I think about how safe I felt when I first arrived at the camp, I feel naive, even stupid. What did I think the blue UNHCR logo meant? It was a well-meaning talisman that did nothing to protect us. The killers in Mudende came across the border from Congo. They had infiltrated the Rwandan armed forces, and some had been sent to Mudende to protect us before they helped orchestrate our slaughter. Others, we later heard, were local Hutus, so angered by the existence of a camp for outsiders in their home that they wanted us dead.

Mudende taught me that refugee camps are often dangerous places. Refugees have endured violence in camps in Niger and Syria and Sierra Leone; racist attacks in Germany; destruction of their homes in France. I think I understand how they feel. I hope that, unlike us, they learn how to talk about it before the silence becomes another wound.

◆

THE NIGHT AFTER I was rescued from the latrine pit and taken to a clinic for my fractured bones, the camp most survivors were moved to was also attacked. Now, though, Rwandan forces were able to protect the survivors of Mudende. Still, when I heard about the third attack, I lost all hope that I would stay alive. I thought about Célestin, paralyzed, unable even to try to save himself when the killers raged through Mudende for a second time. I felt that this was an apocalypse for Bagogwe Tutsis.

My fractured arms and leg were treated by doctors, and I was given a cane to walk with while I healed. My young bones were shocked by what they had just been through. I had no idea where my parents were. But I had survived.

Now I waited and wondered, alone. Where would we be safe? It felt as though the entire world wanted us dead. First, the Rwandan authorities took us in buses to a small transit camp, where we were told to wait until they could move us again. We sat on the ground or on plastic chairs, staring at nothing. We asked questions that no one knew the answers to. Thousands of refugees waited in the transit camp, weeping for their families. I remember the sound of the crying and screaming, so loud and panicked it was as though we had never left Mudende. At the transit camp, the killers tried to attack us again. No matter where we went, it seemed that we would always be running. "When will we be safe?" people moaned.

Eventually, the authorities decided to move most of us to where it was safer, far from the border, to a camp called Gihembe that was filling with survivors of Mudende. Pregnant women and children who were not seriously injured were put into buses, while everyone else had to scramble to get into a UN truck, the kind usually used to deliver food to the camps. People leaped and shoved to get onto the truck. Even the most kind-hearted man would have stepped over his own grandchild to get on that truck. Everyone was terrified to spend one second longer in the transit camp. That kind of terror can turn you into an animal.

I didn't care where I went. I couldn't see how it mattered. I was an orphan; my entire body hurt. In that way, I was also like an animal. By the time I was five years old, killers had already taken away so much of what I loved. They took away people I was with all the time, people I thought I would be with for the rest of my life. They took away people I loved, like Aunt Florence and Patrick, because they had saved my life.

I'm sorry to say that even today I'm surprised when I see people crying when they watch a sad movie or listen to a sad song. To me, it's simple. If someone cuts your arm, you might cry. Otherwise, why bother? I don't understand it, and I haven't understood it since I was five years old.

The world is bad, I thought as I waited in the transit camp, that much is a fact. The world took love from me and gave nothing in return. That feeling grew inside me as I waited to die in the latrine pit, and it was still growing even after I had been rescued and brought up into the sunlight by other refugees. It grew as I waited to be evacuated from Mudende, and it grew on the journey across Rwanda. The feeling that the world was waiting to take the things I loved grew into a fact. It became stuck inside me. It was still there when I arrived at Gihembe. Maybe it's still there today.

PART TWO

We are thousands of youth on this mountain

We play soccer, we praise God daily

We cross borders against our bright future

We are conquerors, we quell earthquakes

Those we throw away are diamonds

Thirteen

In a refugee camp, everything becomes a number. How many women live here, and how many of them are pregnant? How many boys have disappeared, and have they gone to fight with the rebels in Congo? How many children this month have leaned over deep wells looking for water, and how many have made it back to the refugee camp alive? Are any of them in school? How many of those pregnant women were raped during the conflicts?

Sometimes, the math can be difficult to understand. If, by some stroke of luck, I have one bar of soap left over after I distribute rations to the camp, and I sell that soap to buy some counterfeit Converse at the local market, does that make me a thief? If the United Nations World Food Programme sends seven pounds of corn, six pounds of beans, four cups of cooking oil, and nine ounces of salt per family per week, but half the beans are full of maggots, does the family starve? After all, according to WFP records, six pounds of beans were delivered to the family on time. It's up to us whether we eat them. If the next week, because of the organization's funding, there are slightly fewer beans—five and a half pounds, say—how many people will fall asleep grabbing their stomachs? Will any die? And if the delivery the following week is eight pounds—eight miraculous, abundant pounds of beans—do we get those starved loved ones back?

How much money per month does a refugee teacher make compared with a Rwandan teacher? How much does the Rwandan government spend so that Gihembe camp can exist, and how much money does it receive from the UNHCR to keep the camp open but at arm's length? How many refugee camps—from the settlements in Rwanda, to the border camps in Turkey, to the squalor in France—are there in the world today, and how many will there be twenty years from now? How many people will die in those camps? How many children will be born in them?

As soon as I arrived in Gihembe, my forever refugee camp, I started counting everything. Gihembe consisted of a few lettered villages and a dozen "zones," clusters of a couple hundred tents blocked off for easy tracking by camp authorities. From the kitchen, where at first I slept with other children who had been separated from their families, to the latrine there were fifty regular steps and, as you got closer to the smell, fifty hesitant, smaller ones. The tent I shared with my parents and siblings, when I discovered they were alive, was mercifully farther than that. Teenagers walked five or six or ten or twelve hours to look for firewood, and even more to get to school, where refugee students sat at the back of the classroom like leftovers.

Refugees had a difficult time finding work outside the camp—the UN and the Rwandan government put programs in place to hire refugees, and discriminating against refugees was made illegal, but in practice few managed to infiltrate local economies—so we devised our own businesses, sewing clothes or lugging groceries for small amounts of money.

As I got older, each year some of my friends went to Congo to fight with rebels. Their absence upset the balance in the camp. When I found out one of them had been killed—minus one from my small world—I could hardly walk, the ground felt so unstable.

Days in the camp were long with little to do. The click of stones on mancala boards counted down the seconds. Many people drank alcohol to speed up the minutes. For as long as I can remember, we had only enough food to cook one proper meal to eat every two or three days: one scoop of chewy corn and one of flavorless beans. We received the food toward the end of each month; eventually, we began receiving money instead, less than ten dollars per person per month, which my mother carefully budgeted so that we wouldn't starve. I thought rice and meat were only for rich people. Everyone—whether you were a young baby or a dying old person—was used to one meal every two to three days. It never added up to enough. In the refugee camp, we were always hungry.

♦

I ARRIVED IN GIHEMBE confused and alone. My parents and siblings were in a hospital, and for a few weeks before my father appeared to reassure me that we would be a family again, I lived like an orphan. My belly was distended with malnutrition, and I lined up twice a day with other children, once for breakfast and once for dinner, holding out my plastic bowl stamped with the UNHCR logo for a porridge specifically meant to treat protein deficiency.

Our suffering was both invisible and visible, and for those first few weeks the UNHCR focused on treating what it could see. Days revolved around eating. In the mornings and evenings my throat burned with porridge. I ate everything they gave me because I wanted to get stronger. After the last of the porridge had been scraped from the plastic bowl, I joined the other children left wondering if they were orphans.

We watched shadows from the trees sway across the kitchen walls and wondered aloud about where we were. "When do you think our parents will get here?" we asked each other. "Do you think they'll have us sleeping in the kitchen forever?" The whole country was in chaos, and there didn't seem to be any organized effort to reunite families. All day a Red Cross worker stood in the middle of the tents with a megaphone, calling off names. "Is this your son?" the worker shouted. "Are you looking for this person?" His announcements were earsplitting but useless. Unless your family was in the camp already, you had no hope of being reunited.

Once or twice before my father miraculously showed up in the camp, stepping off a bus filled with refugees who had been injured in Mudende, I felt so sad that I slept outside by myself under a tree. If I couldn't talk to my parents, I didn't want to talk to anyone.

"They are probably dead," the other children said. "Do you remember what happened in Mudende? It was like hell."

"We survived," I would say, lying on my stomach on the sleeping mat, my head resting on my folded arms. "If we survived, then why wouldn't they?"

"If they survived, then where are they?" they replied. "We're here, so where are they?"

I couldn't answer, so I went outside. The wind in Gihembe was so strong it sometimes felt like it could knock you down the hill the camp was built on. I lay on the grass, imagining rolling down the hill into a river and drowning.

Two weeks later I was eating by myself when I saw my father and Furaha waiting in a food line. They were overjoyed to see me. "How did you get here?" my father asked, holding my shoulder. As much as I wanted to mirror his excitement, I admit that my heart sank when I saw him. "Where's Mama?" I asked, but he didn't know.

We soon found out she was in the hospital, and two months later, she came to Gihembe, along with Faustin and John. That first night back together, I couldn't sleep. I had longed for my mother, but she and my brothers arrived covered with bandages, blood still staining the white gauze, and I was too scared to hug them. Still, I knew I was lucky. The same week I was reunited with my mother, the other two children who had kept me company in the kitchen found out their parents had in fact been killed. "We will see you around the camp," they said to me when I left the public kitchen to join my family in our assigned zone, where we would live in a tent together.

"I'll see you," I said. I didn't know what else to say. Many orphans lived in Gihembe. Every day a new one was found and counted.

Fourteen

Although Gihembe felt isolated from the rest of the world, an imitation of a town, Rwanda is densely populated, and our host community, a town called Kageyo, was only a short walk from the camp's front gate. You could throw a stone from a tent in Gihembe and have it land in someone's house in Kageyo, it was that close. On a very still night, I could sometimes hear people shouting in their homes in Kageyo, and I wondered what it would be like to sleep there, in a real house under a real roof. When I thought about things like that, Gihembe felt like the worst kind of prison; I was so grateful to be there, and so desperate to leave.

Kageyo was a small, poor village, but it was close to the paved road and had a busy weekly market, a few small bars and cafés, and stores where people sold out-of-reach luxuries like toys and candy. People in town lived in houses made of concrete and bricks, and, most amazing to me, they had running water and electricity. At night the houses glowed with fluorescent bulbs. Moths thumped against the glowing, gauzy white curtains. I never cared about having electricity until we were so close to it in Gihembe.

Refugees visited Kageyo mostly to go to the market or, on very special occasions, to buy beer or treats at the small stores. Some of the villagers didn't like us, but the presence of the refugee camp opened up new opportunities. Villagers sold candy and beer to refugees. Bars projected soccer games and American action movies on their walls, charging us a small amount to sit and watch without having to order anything to drink. Before refugees began opening their own shops in Gihembe, everything we wanted had to be bought at the Kageyo market.

In Kageyo, if you were lucky, you could forget for a moment that you lived in Gihembe. I made friends, one of whom, Kayezu, was the best goalie in the area, and he visited Gihembe just to play soccer. Kayezu didn't care that because he was older, nearly nineteen, he was stopped at the gate and asked to show ID, or that we didn't have food or drinks to offer him. He didn't judge us for living in tents or playing barefoot. It was harder for a young person, who was far from rich himself, to identify differences between a Rwandan and a refugee. Kayezu and I only cared about soccer.

If you had a little bit of money you could take it to Oswaldie's bar, where the kindly Rwandan had set up extra tables and charged around one dollar per five people to watch a movie or a soccer game on his television. Oswaldie was missing a leg and walked using crutches. He was nice to refugees, even young boys like me, and a few times I came close to asking him what had happened to his leg. But he was Rwandan and I was a refugee. It wasn't appropriate for me to ask him about his personal life.

Oswaldie's bar was one simple room with some plastic tables and a good roof that protected us when it rained. He sold beer and kebabs made out of beef or goat, and although we couldn't afford to buy anything off the menu, it was a thrill just to sit in the room among the Rwandans and watch a game or a movie. The barman befriended us. He knew our names and waved to us when we passed through on our way to look for firewood or water. Even if his kindness was in part a scheme to create more business for himself, I still liked Oswaldie. Sometimes if you showed up before a big game empty-handed, he would let you watch anyway. "Try to bring money next time," he would say, smiling at us.

Unless they had something to sell us, most of the people in town didn't want to interact with refugees. They repeated vicious rumors, saying that we were all HIV positive, or that we were all displaced murderers, running from the crimes we had committed. Most of them were Hutus who had stayed in Rwanda through the genocide and in the immediate aftermath, or who had fled to refugee camps in Congo and returned. To them, we were a reminder, sometimes of the horror they had witnessed and sometimes of the violence they had perpetrated. "Why did they come here?" they would grumble. "As though we have enough ourselves."

Even after the Rwandan government and the UN established programs to help refugees start businesses and get jobs outside the camps, it was nearly impossible to find work. Rwandans were poor themselves. Why would they want to give up pay or opportunity to a refugee?

Growing up in Gihembe, I felt that most people in Kageyo looked down on refugees. When we first arrived, President Kagame had not yet passed a law making it illegal for people to discriminate on the basis of ethnicity, and the local courts that would help communities come to terms with the genocide had yet to begin. But people understood the power of hatred. They had seen violence grow out of words, and rumors harden into machetes. They whispered.

"Where are you going, Tutsi? What are you doing, Tutsi?" they muttered when we passed by their homes on our way to look for firewood and water. Villagers distrusted boys in particular. They assumed we were fighters in children's clothing, or thieves waiting for the right moment. We were so poor that they didn't trust us to walk on their streets. When they saw us coming to town, they would take their laundry inside.

A few of the villagers couldn't keep their hatred limited to words. One of them, an enormous man named Mahidi, used to attack refugees during the night after he was drunk on banana beer. Mahidi worked as a bouncer and was always out late. If you went to watch a game at night at Oswaldie's bar, you had to be careful that Mahidi didn't track you down and beat you, his breath sweet with beer.

When I was growing up, I felt ashamed of how the villagers viewed us. Seeing a mother hurriedly unpin her laundry from the line when she spotted us coming made me want to cry. But sometimes I thought it was fair to be angry that Kagame's government demanded they treat refugees kindly or offer us work. They were poor, too. They had also been through a terrible war. Maybe they were right to fear us. We were hungry, and hunger can make you crazy. Who knew what we were capable of?

I admit that our hunger did sometimes drive us to steal—fruit from a private vine or cellophane-wrapped cookies from the weekly market. Sometimes we gathered in a whispering group around a living room window to watch the World Cup on a stranger's television until he chased us away, cursing. Who could blame the villagers for protecting themselves? Maybe, if given the chance, we would have ripped their clean laundry down off their lines. Maybe we would have gathered by the hundreds near the open window, laughing at the old man as he hobbled toward us waving his walking stick and demanding that we leave. Maybe one of us would have hit him if he had come close.

Stealing is shameful in the Bagogwe culture. We were taught at a young age not to disgrace ourselves and our families by taking what didn't belong to us. And in Bikenke, this lesson was easy to follow. What was there to steal? Fruit cost nothing when it hung ripe on the fruit tree. Our cows gave us all the milk we could drink. We were never hungry.

Being a refugee changes you. I stole twice in my life, once a bit of money from my mother so I could watch a Champions League match in Oswaldie's bar, and the second time some passion fruit from a farm when I was starving.

Maybe that is truly who I am. Maybe our neighbors in Kageyo were right to hide their laundry and lock their doors when the refugee children walked through town. If given the opportunity, what were we capable of? When I think of it like that, I am grateful that the villagers didn't trust us. They prevented us from becoming the thieves we were destined to be. They stopped us from betraying our culture more than we already were. Without their suspicious, judgmental eyes, I might have forgotten about who I really was.

Fifteen

In 1999, almost a year after we arrived in Gihembe, my friend Kazungu had an epiphany. Kazungu and I lived near each other in the camp, and we met the way I met most of my friends, drawn together by a shared love of games and stories, anything to distract us from the feeling of dread we sensed from adults. I quickly realized that Kazungu, who was an orphan, was particularly bright and daring, often getting into the kind of trouble that made grown-ups smile before they started yelling. We had been trudging through knee-deep mud for a half an hour, our pants so heavy they felt like they were made out of concrete, when he stopped and smiled. "Let's just take them off," he said. "We can walk faster if we carry them."

"Genius!" I laughed and pulled mine off. Kazungu was good at turning life in Gihembe into a game.

"Hurry, hurry," he said. "Before anyone sees us."

We turned a corner and found ourselves at the back of a line. "What are they waiting for?" Kazungu wondered. I shrugged. We were far from the gates where our food was delivered to us. Adults and children were in line together.

"Hey, kids!" A man started walking toward us. He wore a uniform we had never seen before and carried a piece of paper. He didn't look happy. "Why are your legs bare?" he asked. "That's not very sanitary, don't you think?" He shook his head at us.

"We were sliding in all the mud," I said. "Our pants were really heavy. It took us so long to walk anywhere in camp. Kazungu"—I gestured to my friend—"thought it would be better to take off our clothes so we could walk faster. We didn't know there would be so many people here." I suspected I should feel ashamed of our exposed legs, but I was proud of our innovation. The man's anger seemed to fade.

"How old are you?" he asked.

"Eight," I answered. "We are both eight."

"Eight years old," he said, and made a mark on the paper he was carrying.

"Okay, now, could you do one thing for me?" he asked. He was smiling. "Just a little trick to test your age." Without birth certificates or ID cards, it was hard for refugees in Gihembe to prove how old they were. Some people had already forgotten. "Can you lift your right hand over your head and touch your left ear?" He demonstrated, making us giggle.

"Sure," we said, eager to please. Kazungu and I reached our right hands over our heads and touched our left ears, laughing. The man was now smiling widely at us. "That's great," he told us. "You can start with the other eight-year-olds." And just like that, I was enrolled in school.

At home, my mother waved her arms in delight. "Mondiant, that's so wonderful!" she said. In Bikenke, most children went to school long enough to learn how to read and write, and my mother hadn't been sure if we would get the same chance as refugees. "This is good news, Mondiant," she said. "You'll need to learn for when we leave here, so you're not behind when we get back to Congo."

I started first grade the following Monday. The school was in a tent in the middle of the camp, at that point operated entirely by refugees. As a project, it was both practical and nostalgic. Refugees who had spent some time in school in Congo stepped in as teachers, donating whatever they had brought with them—a third-grade geography book, a fourth-grade study guide of Swahili vocabulary—leading students through lessons in hopes of building a smarter and more capable generation of displaced people. "We want there to be no barriers for you if you want to go to high school," they said. "Or find a job." Before aid organizations came to Gihembe and established a school, we were taught in Swahili, not Kinyarwanda, and used Congolese, not Rwandan, curriculums at a school the refugees named after Patrice Lumumba, our revolutionary hero. "You'll know how to read and write by the time you get home," the refugee teachers said, echoing my mother.

Even after aid organizations began to help, changing the name of the school and providing Rwandan textbooks, resources for learning were scarce. Without formal classrooms or supplies, we learned however we could. Before every lesson, a teacher chose two students to each hold up one side of a long strip of paper, which the teacher used as a blackboard. When those students started complaining, their arms wilting toward the floor, they were replaced with two others, and so on, until the lesson was finished and the paper was rolled up and stored for studying later.

Instead of chairs, we sat on stones, trying to arrange ourselves with the shorter people in front so that everyone had a clear view of the long paper. We had no desks or pens or books. I was so determined to do well that I used a broom bristle to scratch notes into my thighs, taking down so much of the teacher's words that some afternoons when I returned home I had to spin in circles in front of my laughing family and beg them to help me decipher the scratches.

Unless their parents could afford to buy them a notebook, all the kids in Gihembe studied this way. I didn't get my own small notebook to write in until fourth grade, when my father could afford one, and we continued studying in the tent until the teachers had pooled enough money—skimmed carefully from the fifteen-dollar-a-month stipend paid by an aid organization—to build us a one-room brick schoolhouse.

At once, I was deadly serious about my schooling. Nothing—not hunger, not exhaustion, not the dread that still simmered throughout the camp—could have stopped me from going to class. We started at eight in the morning and ended at four thirty in the afternoon, studying science and math, reading and writing. Life in Gihembe was like being strangled. Going to school taught you how to breathe.

At midday, even though none of us brought food or went home, we had a lunch break. Accustomed to our stomachs growling, we used it to play. The school was near a graveyard that, because it was already cleared of rocks and trees, made the perfect soccer pitch. We played soccer until the teachers shouted for us to come back.

After class, now desperately hungry, I would race home, certain that if I were late to dinner one of my siblings would eat my portion of beans and corn. But every evening when I showed up at our door with sweat running down my face, my brain whirring from what I had learned, my mother would smile at me and hold out some food she had been hiding from my siblings. She was proud of the fact that I was the best in the class, and would never let me go hungry. "Here, Mondiant," my mother would say, gesturing for me to sit beside her. "We saved this for you."

◆

AS THE MONTHS AND YEARS PASSED, Gihembe started to look less like a refugee camp and more like a settlement. Tents bloomed outward in two large sections from a spine of mud-and-tin buildings so that, if viewed from above, it began to resemble a pair of lungs, surrounded by neat rows of farmland and patches of forest. Paths, some wide and well used and others narrow and just for curious kids, grew in circles through the camp, all eventually connecting at the exit, where an official road led south to Kageyo or toward the churches and filling stations in Gicumbi, a larger and more distant town, where I rarely went as a child. Kigali was only an hour-and-a-half drive south along a highway, but it would be over a decade before I ever saw the city.

Just as the school moved from a tent into a brick room, people began replacing their own tents with mud-and-wood buildings that were much better suited to the extremes of Rwandan weather. We chopped down trees to make doors and built separate structures for kitchens and private bathrooms. Walkways from zone to zone were flattened by foot traffic and, eventually, lined with small gardens and grassy lawns.

The blue-and-white UNHCR tents were demoted to a hanging door or a curtain in front of the kitchen, stretched across the top of the walls until it could be replaced by a metal roof, or used to collect rainwater. Even after Gihembe came to resemble a town in its own right—with shops and a school and real homes—those scraps of UNHCR tents remained, forever tangled within the machinery of the refugee camp.

Everywhere, refugees tried to go on. Without clear answers about when we might be able to go home to Congo, we did our best to make life bearable. We went to school, marveled at our new homes, celebrated marriages. Once a year, on a day commemorating those lost in the Mudende massacres, women dressed in their most beautiful traditional Bagogwe clothes, some brought with them and some masterfully tailored in the camp, and danced, and when the UN began celebrating World Refugee Day at the camp, they took out those clothes a second time.

Life went on in more literal ways. Two years after we arrived, my mother became pregnant with my sister Asifwe. We were stunned when we found out. She and my father were so battered and at times so hollow that it seemed impossible that they could create a life. But they had. Refugees throughout the camp were trying to replace the love they had lost on the way to Gihembe.

On the night she told us, Faustin, Furaha, and I had spent hours complaining about our empty stomachs, which felt twisted inside us as though they were trying to eat themselves. I was so hungry I thought I might not be able to sleep, and I worried about being tired at school the next morning. "We are learning about the rain tomorrow," I groaned to my mother, who was busy boiling the last of our corn. Environmental studies were important in the Congolese curriculum. I imagined that meant learning about my home, about what the rain felt like and how plants grew on our ancestral land. I could replace the memories I had lost of Congo with new information. But if I didn't eat, I couldn't sleep, and when I was tired, I had a hard time learning. "Can we eat now?" I complained.

"In a moment," my mother said. "First, I have some news that might make you happy." She waved the three of us over and we sat down, waiting. "I'm going to have another baby," she said. "A sister or brother for you. A blessing from God."

My mother smiled, telling us her news. She had longed for more children since the moment Patience died, but not even John, as much as she loved him, could replace the baby she had lost. Many nights, she fell asleep thinking about Patience's small, still body pressed against her back in those final moments before anyone noticed that she had died. My mother thought so much about those moments that she practically lived inside them. She wanted to be a mother again and again.

Older refugees, like my parents, were stubborn, even stupidly so, when considering our future. "This isn't where we live, really," my mother would sometimes say. "Our home is in Congo." If she lost that optimism, she thought, she might as well be dead.

At the same time, my mother never clung to fantasies. She was aware, perhaps more than the rest of us, of how difficult life was in the refugee camp, and she blamed herself for many of those difficulties. When we asked for something, or when we groaned about our empty bellies, she despaired. She felt like she was no longer a mother. A mother is able to give her children food. In Gihembe, she thought, God was our only parent. How could she have another baby?

In Congo, married couples needed big families to work on the farms and ranches. Refugees didn't have farms or ranches, or money or food, but we also didn't have easy access to birth control or education about family planning. Even people who swore they would never bring a child into the refugee camp ended up having babies. If there had been more privacy, they probably would have had even more.

The births were identical to how they had been in Bikenke. Women, moaning in pain, banished their husbands from their tents and were surrounded by other mothers. We listened to them scream through the night. Unlike in Congo, women in Gihembe could be taken to a hospital if there was a serious complication. But because women did not have the food they needed during pregnancy, and were weaker—and, the older Congolese refugees said, because we didn't have access to our traditional medicine—more women died in labor in Gihembe than in Bikenke.

But she had become pregnant as a refugee for a second time, so she forced herself to imagine the best future possible for her children. She imagined walking the eleven or twelve hours from Gihembe to Kigali and getting a job, making money, and eventually moving us to the city, where we could all go to school. She imagined making food for us every day, rather than every second or third day. She imagined swaddling her new baby on her back and returning to a peaceful Bikenke, where she would raise her children—those born in Congo, those born in Rwanda, and those born on the run—in the home where Patience once lived, wrapped in the sweet memory of her lost baby and close to the warmth of her new ones.

When we were fleeing, we had barely noticed her pregnancy with John, but in the stillness of Gihembe, news of a new sibling made us furious. "This is terrible," we said. "We are hungry, and you are having another baby?" We didn't want anyone to live the life that we were living.

My mother sighed. "You aren't happy?" she asked. "It's a blessing."

"How can a baby want to be born in a refugee camp?" Faustin asked. He was the angriest, his fists balled up in his lap. At least I had school, I had friends to play soccer with. I had a new notebook to write in and the excitement of learning every day. I had my mother's praise when I returned home from school. Faustin, who was older, had much less than me.

"That's fine." My mother stood up to get our dinner. "You'll be happy when you meet the baby. And we won't be here forever." She poured the corn onto our communal plate. "It's a blessing," she said again. We nodded as we ate, feeling guilty for making her so sad. "You're right," we said. "It's a blessing."

Eight months later, my sister Asifwe arrived, one of a generation of refugees born into the limbo of Gihembe refugee camp. Those children seemed so different from us. Those of us who were born in Congo had survived so much, and our trauma tied us together. We remembered running from our homes, crossing the border, and losing so many people we loved. As hard as we tried to forget it, we still remembered Mudende.

But we had also experienced a life outside the refugee camp. Congo, to us, wasn't an imaginary place. We could picture ourselves living there again.

If you are born in a refugee camp, you only know poverty. You only know hunger. You feel disconnected from the world, and struggle to imagine your place in it. Because they didn't eat enough, many women in Gihembe couldn't nurse their babies, which most Congolese women were expected to do for as many months or years as their children demanded, and the refugee generation grew up deprived of the nutrition of breast milk. They knew their parents only as depressed and disconnected. They were spared the horror of Mudende, but they carried trauma of a different shape.

Still, I'll be honest. I one hundred percent wish I had been born in the refugee camp instead of in Congo. For as long as I have been alive, people have told me that the first three years of my life—waiting for my brother and father by the entrance to our house in Bikenke, smashing taro into my mouth—were the best of my life. People told me nothing would ever be better than when I was a little baby. But I can hardly remember those years. I would trade all the sunsets in front of our house in Congo, all the creamy bites of mango, all the stories from my grandmother, not to have suffered through the Mudende massacres.

We shouldn't have said those things to our mother, though, even if they were true. I wish we had always been kind to one another. We loved our sister Asifwe the second she was born, just as we loved our youngest brother, Baraka, when he arrived two years later and as we loved John, a blessing born between massacres.

Sixteen

I n 2001, a war was raging in Congo between the Congolese army and various rebel factions, and Joseph Kabila—who had taken over as president after his father, Laurent-Désiré Kabila, was assassinated—was trying to build support for bringing peace to the country. Because of that war, and the wars that had preceded it, North Kivu was in turmoil. Rebels fought each other and the government; people had lost their land and were displaced; poverty was rampant. We knew of all of this when some local leaders, mostly low-level but at one point a representative of the governor of North Kivu, showed up in Gihembe, telling us to come home. We knew how bad things were in North Kivu, and yet we sat up straight and listened to them tell us otherwise.

"There's no reason for you to be here anymore," they told us, appealing to our patriotism. "President Kabila has made the country safe! Come home, help keep him in office."

When patriotism failed, they made us feel nostalgic for our old lives. "Remember your land and your livestock?" they asked. "Remember the green pastures and beautiful forests?"

Other times, they described our return as though it would be so easy and so natural, there was no reason to resist. "Everything is waiting for you at home," they said. "We have buses to take you there, and the border is open. Why not?"

When none of that worked—when we remembered the violence that had pushed us out in the first place—they scared us. "Things are safe in Congo, so there is no reason for Kagame to keep the camps open," they said. "Soon they will stop delivering food to you. They will come take your tents away. You have to come home or you will starve."

When one week our rations didn't arrive at camp, people in Gihembe started to wonder if the representatives from Kivu were right. Was the World Food Programme no longer going to feed us if we stayed in Rwanda? Was it time for us to leave?

We were told our homes were waiting for us. In Congo, they said, we could reclaim our land and our cows. Our lives would go back to the way they were before we were attacked and made refugees. They said that after so much unrest, and after years that Bagogwe people were told to go back to Rwanda or Ethiopia, there were people in Congo willing to accept us and fight for us. These men had traveled all the way from North Kivu to Gihembe to find us. "Bagogwe belong in Congo," they said. "Come home."

"We can get our farm back," my father whispered to my mother, when he thought Faustin and I were asleep. "We can see if it's safe, Eugenie," he said. "Then you can come and join us.

"Life could go back to the way it was," my father continued. He imagined that if he crossed the border, the years of violence and death would disappear like a sun setting over a mountain after a long day. "I need to go home and see."

My mother looked at her hands. She was sure that if we went back to Congo, she would never see us again. But my father had spent years in Gihembe just waiting. He had no work, he owned nothing. He was the chief of nowhere. Every day his body grew thinner and thinner, his arms became bones. When we asked for something that he couldn't give us—at the beginning, we did this all the time—he seemed to shrink even more. My mother knew this; she was also shrinking, and she couldn't deny her husband the chance to reclaim part of what he had lost.

So she let us go. "Take Faustin and Mondiant," she said. "We will wait here for you."

The next day we boarded a long bus, one of fifteen headed for the border. It was packed with people, mostly men and boys, as well as some orphans and mothers who had lost their families. We only took a few things with us, some cooking pots, the same ones we had carried from Bikenke, and my father's Bible. "Don't worry, everything else will be waiting for you at home," the representatives from Congo told us.

My mother cried saying goodbye to us, and looking at her face, I felt a pang of fear. How long would it be before I saw her again? But my father's eagerness was infectious, and Faustin and I took our places on the bus with the excitement of boys being taken on our first real adventure.

Because I was still a child, I sat on the floor. My father gave up his seat for a pregnant woman, who smiled at him as she sat heavily on the bench, shoulder to shoulder with the person beside her. There was joy in our discomfort. We thought our time as refugees was over. As the bus pulled away from Gihembe, we sang gospel songs.

I tried to picture Congo, but all I could recall was the fighting that had made us refugees, and the fear that had taken over my life before we arrived in Gihembe. I thought of my father showing up at our door, bleeding from the head, and his friend holding a machete and telling us to run.

Luckily, I could rely on memories that were not my own. In Gihembe, when there was nothing to do—and there was rarely much to do—people sat around, talking about Congo. They closed their eyes, trying to transport themselves home. "It's so green, Mondiant," my mother would tell me, stroking my head before it was time to sleep. "Especially after it rains. It's easy to find food there." By the time we boarded the bus heading back to Congo, I had listened to adults in Gihembe sing about our home for years. They called it a "lost paradise." They never talked about the violence that had pushed them out.

Sitting in the crowded bus, I imagined Congo as they described it: lush and beautiful and peaceful, where Hutus and Tutsis lived and worked happily together, even married each other. There were hundreds of tribes, all living in a country that, had there been no Belgian colonialism or long dictatorship, would have been rich from its own abundant resources. One day, they were sure, it would be rich again.

In their Congo, the violence that had displaced us was an accident. Why on earth did Hutus decide to hate Tutsis? It made no sense to them, and no one in Gihembe tried to explain the politics, the inequalities, or the mass displacement that had led to genocide. They didn't learn about colonialism and the rotten leaders that followed. Nor did anyone explain that sometimes people wanted to kill you simply because of who you were.

Because the war was crazy, they thought, one day it would end as quickly as it had started, and we would all be able to go home. Maybe we would fall asleep one night after our dinner of chewy beans and corn and be awakened by an announcement that it was time to leave. Thanks for waiting so patiently, the UN representatives would say. Your home is safe for you again. You are no longer refugees.

When that day came, we would be ready. It would take us only moments to pack. I had the clothes I wore and my special occasion spare set. I had some school supplies, which I would try to take against my mother's gentle chastisements. "Mondiant," she would say, "there's no need for you to have those in Bikenke. You'll learn to work on the farm and, if you want, we will send you to the same school your father went to with new things." Perhaps, I thought, our small classroom would be the one thing I missed about Gihembe.

How would we say goodbye to the camp? Would we fold up our tent and return it to the UNHCR so that it could be redistributed to other countries? Around the world, more and more people were fleeing human rights catastrophes and wars. They were leaving home in search of food when climate change made it impossible to grow the crops they had relied on for centuries. They were being expelled by intolerant governments, leaving in the middle of the night for anywhere but where they were. I would have been happy to give them my tent, my sleeping mat, even my school supplies. Maybe all those refugees, children like me, would end up being as lucky as I had been. I survived the attacks in Bikenke. I survived running and starvation. I survived two massacres in Mudende. And now I was going home.

In these fantasies, the Congo we return to—the one described by my neighbors in Gihembe—has abundant animals for milk and meat, and fruit dripping from trees. Branches heavy with mangoes hang low enough to the ground that even a ten-year-old boy like me can pick them easily, stuff my pockets with fruit, eat until I feel sick, and still take home enough to feed all my siblings. In Congo there is money for cookies and gifts of cheese; there is beef on Christmas. In Congo, there is Christmas.

By the time we left Gihembe, I hadn't eaten in two days. I was so hungry that despite the excitement and the happy noises that filled the bus, I quickly fell asleep.

◆

IT TOOK FIFTEEN HOURS with no stops to drive from Gihembe to the border, passing through Kigali along the better roads. Crossing was easy; Kagame kept the border open, and government soldiers, seeing the buses, waved us through. Ten thousand Congolese refugees were returning from Gihembe and Kiziba camps. We were giddy, hopeful for the first time in years. We were welcomed as if they had been expecting us.

As soon as we crossed into Congo, it began to rain. Sheets of water fell on top of the bus, blinding the driver. A curtain of fog grew so thick around the bus that soon it felt like we were driving through the rain clouds themselves. We lurched and dipped through puddles that filled the deep potholes along the main road. I was transfixed by everything I saw. I craned my neck for a view of the world outside. This was a Congolese rainstorm. I thought, *Wow*.

We turned onto a dirt road taking us up the mountain. The rain was even heavier now. As the bus struggled uphill in the thick, slippery mud, the rain blocked out the sun until it was as dark as night. Our driver pushed on the gas pedal and cursed. For every ten feet forward, we slid five backward. Fog swallowed the green cliffs around us.

The mood in the bus changed. People were awake and screaming, terrified that we might fall off the side of the mountain, and that our dreams of Congo would end before we had even reached our home villages. "Stop!" they yelled to the driver. "Please, let's wait until the rain has stopped." But the driver was determined to keep going. "I know what I'm doing," he insisted. "It's fine, sit down."

He pushed and pushed, and the bus grunted. Smoke and the smell of gasoline drifted through the cracks in the windows. Passengers continued to beg him. "There are children on here," they said. They offered to drive the bus themselves, although few knew how to drive. "You could kill us!" they shouted. Finally, the wheels caught in the thick mud, and the bus came to a stop. The driver, defeated, turned off the engine. "Thank God," my father whispered to himself.

It rained for hours while we sat in the middle of the road, waiting. Inside the bus we were calm and tired. I fell asleep again with my head against my father's leg and dreamed of nothing, and when I woke up we were moving again. The rain had stopped, and the fog had cleared. Through the bus window I could see the green fields and hills of Congo. It was as beautiful as the refugees had said it would be, and I was relieved, seeing that we were in the right place and thinking that we had been correct to come. There was no violence outside the bus window. There were no roving militias or killers with machetes, waiting to overtake a bus full of returning refugees. I thought I had never seen anything so beautiful in my entire life. I thought, *How lucky I am to be from here, a paradise.*

Soon we were on the other side of the mountain, driving along a narrow road through the forest. Dark green plants and tall, wet trees grew tightly around the road, as though moments from overtaking it. My father tapped me on the shoulder. "Your mother is from this place!" he said, pointing happily into the forest. The density of it scared me; I remembered how difficult it had been to run through the plants when we had been fleeing. But the forest had also saved us. Without it, we would have been found immediately by the killers who had come to our door in Bikenke. Because of that, I tried to love it. I told myself, This is where my family is from.

I looked through the window, desperate to see my mother's village. But all I could see were the thick plants and the dark, shadowy places for animals to hide. "Where is it?" I asked my father. "I only see trees."

"There, Mondiant." My father pointed through the window. "There's a house right there. Do you see it?"

I looked where he pointed. Just beyond the trees were the ruins of structures, small packed-mud-and-straw houses like the one I had grown up in, reduced to shadows. The roofs had caved in and the walls had crumbled under their weight. Grass grew out of the floors and thin trees stabbed their way through holes in the bricks. Animals wandered inside the wreckage. There were no humans there to shoo them away. There was no one there to rebuild the houses.

I couldn't see my mother's village. All I could see was the wreckage left behind by the same killers who had come to destroy Bikenke. I could imagine exactly what they had done. First, they had torn through my mother's village, killing people with machetes and guns. Those they hadn't killed ran for their lives, like we had. Like us, they hid in the forest, and the lucky ones made their way to the border and, eventually, to Rwanda. For days, the killers stalked the village, making sure everyone was gone or dead.

Then the killers occupied my mother's village. They took everything they could from the villagers. They stole all there was to eat, as well as the firewood and pots to cook in; the mats and blankets my mother and her neighbors had slept on; the bright kitenges they wore and tucked newborn babies into; the small handmade games they had played. They went through each house in the village, taking everything my mother and her family and neighbors loved and gave to one another.

After they had stolen everything, the killers destroyed my mother's village. They burned the houses that still stood with anything left inside. They tore up plants and toppled fences. Then they left, assuming the rain and animals would destroy the rest. By the time my father and I passed by, my mother's village wasn't a village. It was a museum of the war.

I turned away from the window in fear. "What's wrong, Mondiant?" my father asked. His eyes glowed with happiness, as though in looking through the bus window he was looking at the past. "We're almost home."

I shook my head. I didn't want to say anything to ruin his good mood. "I'm just tired," I said.

"Mondiant, I know it's not going to be exactly the same as before," my father said. He put his hand on my shoulder. "But it's Congo. Don't you remember the mango trees? Do you remember how delicious and sweet the mangoes were?"

I nodded. Mangoes so ripe your mouth filled with juice with every bite.

"We can eat mangoes like that again," he said. "Every day, as many as you want." He was so hopeful that I couldn't help but smile.

I cast memories of the killings in Bikenke from my mind and looked out the bus window again, trying to see the country anew. The region where my mother was from was even more beautiful than Bikenke, which was mostly farmland, tamed and cultivated. My mother's village was wild. Monkeys jumped through the ruins, hopping from branch to branch over the fallen roofs as though exploring a future without humans. I liked that the forest was so powerful it grew quickly over the footprints left by people, reclaiming its land.

Congo was alive. Occasionally, the driver had to stop the bus to let monkeys and antelope cross the road. Horses galloped by the bus; I had never seen animals like that up close. "Those belonged to a woman we called Madame," my father explained to me and my brother. "She was a white woman from Belgium. When she left, she couldn't take her horses with her."

My country was beautiful. It was ten times more beautiful than Rwanda, even though the towns in Rwanda were cleaner and more famil-iar. Rwanda is hilly and green, but, to me, less lush; farmers, I have heard, have to use more technology just to get the food to grow. But in Congo, I thought, things grow easily, nourished only by the earth. I still think that Congo is the most alive place in the world—more than Rwanda, more than the United States.

This place outside the bus window wasn't exactly like the refugees had described it. It was more. The Congo I was coming home to was ravaged and tragic. It was struggling, and the refugees watching it through the bus window were tragic and struggling as well. We had come home to recover, and after we crossed the border, we found that Congo needed us as much as we needed Congo. That purpose breathed life back into every-one on the bus. Everything was going to be wonderful.

We moved quickly now over the roads. People started singing again. This time the older people led everyone in the Congolese national anthem. We were refugees when Mobutu Sese Seko was ousted and "La Zaïroise" once again became "Debout Congolais." We started learning the new lyrics across the border from our homeland, singing them at the beginning of school or during holidays. We didn't know why they had changed, but it didn't matter. When the music began playing in the camp, everyone stopped what they were doing and started singing, frozen in place until the last word was sung, a protest of our expulsion from home. In the bus the words were familiar and sweet in my mouth. "Arise, Congolese," we sang. "Let us hold up our heads, so long bowed. And now, for good, let us keep moving boldly ahead, in peace." We sang, "Oh, ardent people, by hard work we shall build, in peace, a country more beautiful than before."

Seventeen

A few hours later, in the early evening, the bus stopped in Kitchanga, a town about one hundred miles northwest of Goma. We looked at one another in confusion. "Why have we stopped here?" we asked. "They told us they were taking us to our villages."

"Get out." The driver threw open the door and stepped outside, stretching his arms over his head. It had been a long trip. "Come on," he said, not unkindly. "Rest."

Slowly, we unstuck ourselves from our seats, uncurled our legs from where we slept on the floor, and gathered the small things we had brought with us. The driver was already throwing larger belongings onto the ground beside the bus. "Are we staying here?" a man asked him, but the driver shrugged. Kitchanga was home to an informal refugee camp, a mass of tents and ad hoc structures woven into the town and the surrounding hills, and many of the people on the bus had transited through the camp on their way to Rwanda. It was a place they never wanted to return to, and it was far from their home villages.

"You're staying here just for a bit, I think," the driver said. "We've been traveling for a long time. Aren't you happy to be back in Congo?"

"Yes," we said, looking around in a daze. "Of course we're happy."

Kitchanga, like my mother's village, was unrecognizable compared with what it had been before 1993, when the area filled with displaced people and refugees. Congolese and Rwandans of all different ethnic backgrounds were taken to Kitchanga, where they were told they would be safe. Tents sprang up by the hundreds, giving shelter to terrified Hunde, Tutsi, and Hutu people. Almost immediately the town, which was normally majority Hunde, was overtaken by the displaced.

Authorities hoped that giving survivors food, shelter, and some peace could help them rebuild their lives. But it was impossible for them to live among one another while conflict burned their countries to the ground. Hunde, who considered most Congolese Tutsis to be foreigners brought to Congo by Belgian colonists, allied with Congolese and Rwandan Hutus in Kitchanga. Just as they had in Mudende, killers overtook the encampment. Surviving Tutsis fled the country.

In our absence, Kitchanga became a center of fierce battles and political maneuvering. Just like Gihembe, it grew from a tent camp into a semipermanent town of mud-and-wood houses. UNHCR tarps were repurposed as roofs and then eventually replaced by corrugated tin, perched like hats on the mud walls. A new primary school opened, and buildings sprang up in place of the holes first used for toilets. People set up stalls selling candy and fruit, and planted gardens. Unlike Gihembe, where at least we were safe, Kitchanga remained tense, ready to explode, and the people who lived there were prepared at any moment for more violence.

Throughout Congo, conflicts erupted out of economic, ethnic, and political grievances, with Kitchanga and all of North Kivu province at its heart. People lost faith in the central government to protect them or anything they owned, and armed groups, many of them supported by wealthy Congolese in Goma or politicians in Kinshasa, formed, offering their help in exchange for loyalty. Like the Congolese army they took part in ravaging North Kivu.

The fights they took on were both big and small. Some fights spanned borders and lands belonging to millions, while others erupted over petty neighborly disagreements. Some fights were evidence that the ethnic divisions that had fueled the Rwandan genocide would continue long after the genocide was officially over, while others were simply a reaction to enduring poverty. Some battles seemed to be for the soul of Congo, while others were about the pride of one man. To resolve every one of these disputes, the armed groups—including the majority Hunde Mai-Mai; local Hutu combatants; the Interahamwe; and a newly forming pro-Tutsi group—along with the Congolese army, used as their preferred method brutal violence.

When our bus stopped in the camp and we wearily disembarked, asking questions no one could answer, Kivu was in the middle of what would become known as the Second Congo War. The First Congo War had ended in 1997, and another conflict, known as the Kivu conflict, would begin just after the end of the second Congo war, and persists today. These names and timelines are good for teaching the history of Congo, I suppose, to a classroom of people removed from the country. But in reality, as it had been when my mother was young, the conflicts have no break, no period of peace between them. They are ongoing, a wall preventing us from going home and living peacefully.

As North Kivu became more embattled, certain rebel groups, particularly those claiming to defend the rights of the minority Tutsi population, felt outnumbered. President Kabila, meanwhile, wanted to construct a narrative of peace to help him maintain leadership, one that depended on the return of Congolese refugees. They came up with the same plan, to opposite ends. Representatives from North Kivu traveled from Congo to refugee camps in Rwanda with a message they knew the refugees were desperate to hear. "It's safe," they told us in Gihembe. "You can go back to your village and everything will be normal again."

They came from Kivu to sell us a story, and it was easy for them because we had written that story ourselves each night in our tents in Gihembe. We believed them readily; we finished their sentences. We said goodbye to our families and packed our things. We boarded the buses and sang gospel songs all the way. And now we stood beside that bus wondering what we were doing in a refugee camp, and if we had been fools.

◆

THE RAIN SHOWED no sign of stopping. It left a gloss on the black volcanic rock and threatened to glue our feet to where we stood beside the bus. I stayed close to Faustin and my father, checking every few minutes to make sure they hadn't disappeared into the unfamiliar new world.

"Where are our houses?" someone asked. "Where are we going to sleep?"

"You'll get UN tents," the driver replied. "Go over there." He pointed to a line of people.

"It looks just like Gihembe," Faustin muttered, soft enough that our father couldn't hear. We joined the line where local administrators were handing out packages. People stood patiently—we were used to waiting in lines—but confusion rippled through us. "Is this where we are staying?" we asked, when we got to the front. "When do we go to our villages?"

The authorities waiting for us were Congolese. They welcomed us home in Swahili, which was sweet to hear, but they had no answers. "We don't know how long you'll stay," they said. "It's okay here. But don't try to go to your village alone. Wait until you know whether it is safe."

"Safe?" a man wondered, shouting from behind us in line. "What do they mean? The governor of Kivu himself told us it was safe to come back." The man looked around. "Is there anyone protecting us?" he asked, and, again, the Congolese administrators gave him apologetic looks. "Just be careful," they said.

Faustin, my father, and I collected our things from the authorities. Many of us were given white-and-blue UNHCR tarps identical to the ones we had been given so many times over the years, blankets, and some corn to eat. It was raining too hard to begin cutting trees into poles to hold up the tarp, and so we walked through the town looking for somewhere dry to rest. "We'll have to spend the night here," my father said. "Come on." Faustin and I walked behind him, struggling to keep up, staring at the camp as we passed through, so familiar and so strange at once.

"There." My father stopped outside a school, where some people I recognized from the bus were already sleeping underneath the awning. "That will keep us dry."

There wasn't enough room under the awning for the three of us, so Faustin and I slept first while my father stood beside the school, talking to other men. My brother and I watched them for a while, blurred behind the curtain of rain that fell off the awning. My father lifted his arms and waved his hands the way he did when he was impassioned about something, but he spoke softly, I assumed so he wouldn't scare us or keep us awake. Drops of water splattered on our feet and legs, and we shivered together, but soon we were dry enough to fall asleep. I slept full of hope that the next day, we would go to Bikenke. I was still very young.

In the morning, we awoke to a rainbow. It stretched from mountain to mountain, taking up the whole sky. I had seen many rainbows in Rwanda, but none as brilliant as this one, and I felt certain that everything was going to be okay. "Faustin, do you see it?" I poked my big brother awake.

"What, Mondiant?" he groaned. "I was sleeping."

"The rainbow," I said, pointing to the sky in front of us. "It's huge!"

Faustin sat up and looked into the distance. His expression didn't change. He was older, and he remembered more about our time fleeing Bikenke and hiding in the cave. Although he was still a child, he remembered the massacres in Mudende the way an adult would. To my brother, they weren't stories or fragments of memories. It would take more than a rainbow to reassure him that we were safe.

But he loved me and didn't want to upset me. He turned to me and smiled. "It is enormous," he said. "A rainbow as big as Congo."

"I think it's a good sign," I said.

"I'm sure you're right," he said.

My father came up to us. He was bouncing with energy, but it was clear from his red eyes that he had barely slept the night before. "Let's go," he said. "They are taking us away from this place."

"To Bikenke?" Faustin asked.

"I don't know," my father said. "I don't think so. Somewhere nearby where we can set up our tarp, I think."

"Did you see the rainbow?" I asked my father.

He nodded and touched my shoulder. "Let's go, Mondiant," he said. "Maybe the new place is closer to the rainbow."

I have to admit that sometimes when I write about these things, I feel embarrassed about how childish I was, how naive and how hopeful.

◆

WE PITCHED OUR TENT on the side of a mountain about twenty minutes away from the town. Faustin and my father used machetes to cut down skinny trees to use as poles, which they buried deep in the hard ground before stretching the UNHCR tarp over them. The ground was uneven with black volcanic rock, which cut our bare feet and dug into our shoulders and backs when we tried to lie down. We leveled it the best we could with hoes we borrowed from other refugees before laying out a carpet of leaves and sticks to sleep on.

We had normal conversations. "How was your night?" my father asked us.

"Fine," Faustin replied, evening out a layer of leaves for his mat. "I slept well. Did you, Mondiant?" I nodded.

"Are you hungry?" my father asked, as though he didn't know we were desperately hungry. We nodded and he poured some dried beans and corn into a pot. "Let's boil this now for dinner," he said.

As the beans boiled, my father lay down on the mat of leaves. "Will you two be okay?" he asked. "I need rest." We nodded. He stretched his arms underneath his head and a moment later was asleep.

That day, Faustin and I sat in front of the tent, looking down at the valley. Below the black volcanic rocks, the hills of Congo were a glowing green, surrounded by swamps covered in neon flowers and full of animals we had only heard about in stories. Even Faustin, who was still wary of our return, admitted that it was beautiful. "It looks nothing like Rwanda," he said. "How is that possible?"

We sat in silence, overwhelmed. We were sure we would be back in Bikenke soon. We had already come so far! All refugee camps feel temporary at first, a place to wait for the next place. But that informal camp on a hill in the same province as our home village felt like a mirage. We thought that in an instant it would blow away, revealing Bikenke. We just had to wait for our father to make that happen.

The next day I met some people from Kiziba, one of Rwanda's oldest refugee camps. Like us, they had been told that if they didn't return to Congo, they would lose their land and their home forever. One of them, Kabayiza, was around my age and liked many of the same things that I did. We immediately made plans to play soccer and marbles, although we both acknowledged that we probably wouldn't be friends for long. "Soon we'll be back in our village," Kabayiza said to me. "And you'll be back in yours." We would play while we waited.

On the third day, a man who identified himself as a local leader visited our camp. He was scruffy and barefoot like we were and, like us, looked confused.

"Who are you?" he asked some men who had gathered around him. He spoke Swahili.

"We're Congolese who left during the war," the men answered. "We were living in refugee camps in Rwanda, and then people from Kivu told us it was safe to come home." They were agitated. "Who are you? Where is the governor?" We had been told in Gihembe that North Kivu's highest-ranking officials were waiting to help us reestablish ourselves in Congo.

"I don't know the governor," he answered. "I'm in charge here. No one told me you were coming." He spoke cautiously, as though afraid. But soon he seemed to relax. "Are you thirsty?" he asked the men, and then sent his companion to get some beer.

After a few hours, he left. He had no answers for us. "I saw some buses," he said. "I'll ask if they are there to take you to your villages. I'll come back soon." Men, buzzing with beer, smiled and thanked him.

The fourth day, we were given larger rations of beans and corn. Stashing the bags beneath our tarp, my father noticed Faustin and me staring at him. "It's just in case," he said. "We can take what we don't eat here to Bikenke with us." He joined some men who were sitting on the hillside, waiting for signs of the local leader.

By the fifth day, the leader still hadn't returned, and the men began to get impatient. They stood on the hillside watching the valley, willing his thin body to appear on the path to the camp. "He said he would be back, but he didn't say when," they reminded each other. "It's only been a couple of days, I'm sure we will get answers soon."

Days passed, then weeks and months, and he still didn't return. We ate the beans my father was saving and stopped talking about when we would return to Bikenke. The camp continued filling with refugees returning from Rwanda, and we watched as they carried their tarps up the hill, looking for a patch of soft earth amid the rocks. We offered to help them dig holes in the hard ground to anchor their wooden poles.

When they asked questions, we tried to remain hopeful. "A leader visited us recently," we would say. "He was so kind, he welcomed us home and brought us beer. He said just wait a few more days and they would take us to our villages."

"A few more days," they repeated. "That's fine, we'll wait." Like us, they arrived singing. They slept on mats of leaves and sat on the hillside waiting. We sat with them as the days passed without answers and without movement. We nodded at their familiar, mounting dismay and joined them in their disappointment when their smiles faded.

Eighteen

After a few months the UN High Commissioner in Geneva heard about the camp filling with returned Congolese and issued what he referred to as a statement of "grave concern" addressed to the Rwandan government. The UNHCR, he wrote, would not be associated with such a movement, which he called "forced repatriation" that "appears to be neither voluntary nor sustainable." Aid workers abandoned our camp in protest, leaving us behind, alone and exposed, with nowhere safe to go, about a two days' walk from Bikenke.

"When will everyone else come?" I asked my father. "We can't ask them to come here until we know it is safe," he told me. I worried I would never see my mother again. Some nights in order to fall asleep I had to pretend that my mother was lying nearby, even if that meant I dreamed I was in Gihembe.

Because of our arrival, violence around our camp was intensifying. The influx of Tutsis into Kitchanga had made local Hunde and Hutus angry. To them, it was a repeat of our original sin; just as we had followed Belgian commands to take over the newly cultivated lands in North Kivu, we had followed the orders of Rwanda and local Tutsi-sympathizing militias to retake that land. It didn't matter that we were also starved and weary, looking only for home. To these Congolese we were foreigners, there to once again assert our dominance over them and Rwanda's dominance over

Congo. They had endured nearly a decade of fierce war. I had no idea how angry they were.

After a few months, most of the people we came with had returned to Rwanda or gone to a new refugee camp in Uganda. Others, mostly young men, had joined a newly forming rebel group made up of Tutsis and their allies. Some were in jail. Without steady rations of food, those of us who had stayed behind grew desperate to make some money. A group went out looking for work on a farm and, hours later, came back grinning. "We met some nice people," they said. "They own a farm, and they said they will pay us to help."

We celebrated the possibility of work, as well as the discovery of kind neighbors. It was a relief to know that not everyone in North Kivu hated us. Being a refugee is lonely no matter where you are. Being a refugee in your own country can make you crazy.

The next day dozens of people left the camp for the farm, following the promise of work, walking through the forest toward the farm. I saw them go and was sad that I was too young to help. "This is a good thing," my father said. "Once people get used to us being back, maybe they'll let us begin to go home."

While we waited for them to return, we distracted ourselves with thoughts of what they were doing, what life might be like in Congo away from the camp. "I wonder if there are cows on the farm," I said to Faustin. "I wonder if it's like home."

Faustin was more interested in what the work was like. He was ready to join the adults. "I'm definitely strong enough to work on the farm," he said. "I was already doing that at home. I'm sure I can learn to take care of the animals." He wanted to be like our father, educated and accomplished.

That night, Faustin and I sat in front of our tent watching the edge of the forest where the people had disappeared earlier that day, but no one came out. Finally, it got so late we went to bed. We were disappointed, but we didn't think anything of it. "They are staying overnight on the farm," we figured. "There must be a lot of work."

A few days later, when they still hadn't returned, their relatives began to worry. "They should be home by now," they said. "Should we go look for them?" But the forest, which was always dangerous and unpredictable, seemed even more menacing since it had seemed to swallow up the refugees. They remembered that the authorities in Kitchanga had warned them about leaving the encampment. "Better to wait," we thought. "There must be a lot for them to do on the farm."

After a week, people began to lose hope. "Something must have happened to them on the walk," we reasoned. We weren't from Kitchanga, but we knew enough about the Congolese forest to know how easily it swallowed people up. "They must be hurt or have gotten turned around," we said sadly. It was easy to lose your way or be bitten by a snake, or to die because of an infected wound. Perhaps they had met a dangerous animal and, without the weapons usually carried by Bagogwe men and only their emaciated bodies to defend themselves, they were killed. Sobs echoed from the tents where their family members lived, but only for a night. We were all used to life as it was, taken away in a moment. The forest is the forest, we thought.

A few days later, we learned the truth. A refugee had been walking through the forest, looking for food and firewood, and had come across a jumble of bodies near an Interahamwe base. "There were at least ten of them," he told us. "They were scattered." When we asked if they had been killed by an animal, he shook his head. "Machetes," he answered.

"It's the Interahamwe," he said. "The same people who did the genocide in Rwanda. They want to overthrow the Rwandan government, and they live here in Congo. There was a fight."

"There's always fighting," we sighed.

There was no time to mourn. "We have to get their bodies," someone reminded us. No one wanted to think about their loved one lying dead in the forest. "Bring whatever you can to defend yourself."

We didn't understand yet the dangers that lived around Kitchanga, how much fighting we had missed while we were in Rwanda and how dangerous things had become. The same unrest that had made us targets in Mudende, where displaced and angry Hutus and their supporters attacked the refugees they saw as connected to Kagame and his government, threatened us in Kitchanga. Poverty and Congo's endless conflicts added fuel to the violence. We were caught in a war we were only beginning to understand when the hundreds of us—men, women, and children—gathered whatever we could find and went into the forest looking for the bodies.

I wasn't scared, even as a child; everyone was going, and I felt like I was a part of something important. I liked that I had been asked to help. The adults had machetes, while the children picked up rocks and sticks. "We can't let them stay in the forest," my father told us. "It's important to give them a proper burial." He still thought about Patience, covered by my mother's kitenge and some leaves.

The refugees hadn't made it very far. We found their bodies near the edge of the forest, just a short walk from our camp. I recognized the gashes that covered them as machete wounds. I smelled the by-then-familiar smell of blood and rot.

Now a little frightened, we ran to them and tried to lift them as quickly as we could. The strongest among us heaved bodies across their shoulders and started walking, others had to push the bodies in carts. No one asked me to help move them, and I didn't offer. My excitement over being part of a grown-up mission was replaced by dread. I could only think of hiding during the first Mudende massacre with Célestin and Patrick. I remembered holding my breath while the killers walked closer to us, and I wanted to run from those thoughts. It might sound ridiculous now, but back then the memory of Mudende was scarier than anything we were living through.

It was dark by the time we made it back to the camp, dirty and tired, talking about how lucky we were that the killers hadn't found us. Faustin had lost two friends. Seeing their bodies back in the camp, arranged with the others to be cleaned, wrapped, and buried, I felt sad for the first time. We slept that night but not well.

After that, there was no denying that we had moved back to the middle of a war. Sometimes the Interahamwe attacked our camp during the day, when we could defend ourselves. Men gathered together on watch at the edges of the camp, beating drums when they saw the killers coming toward our camp. The loud, frantic drumbeats were our cue to gather anything we could find—sticks, spears, precious machetes—to defend ourselves. The killers had their own array of weapons: their own spears and well-used machetes, as well as sticks picked up from the ground on their march to our camp, and clubs fashioned from other sticks. They didn't shoot us with guns. We were weak and hungry, stuck in one place without anyone to defend us. They said they didn't want to waste bullets or grenades on us when it was easy enough to kill us with a stick.

Elders organized young people to throw stones. On the mountain, it was easy to collect enough for an arsenal, and soon we had our favorites—small stones that buzzed like bullets past the killers' ears; medium stones that left bruises on their heads; stones like boulders that were nearly impossible to throw but could cause serious injuries. We started to become like the killers themselves. If we'd had guns instead of stones, we would have murdered them.

Most of the time, though, the killers attacked us at night, when we were asleep. When they did that, we had no time to gather our weapons and position ourselves along the periphery of the camp. We began leaving the camp at night to sleep in the forest or on the banks of the swamp near Kitchanga, where we felt safer, returning to the camp after sunrise, tired but alive. We were always ready to run. Whenever a rumor spread through camp about the killers coming, or someone heard a noise that sounded like an attack, or someone had a bad feeling, we fled as quickly as we could into the forest.

It quickly became apparent that no one was coming to help us. The local aid workers who had greeted us in Swahili and handed us our tents were gone. The situation in Kivu was too dangerous for most to stay. We realized that no one from any Western countries—where leaders cried over the genocide and denounced the violence, celebrating Kagame and, later, the fall of Mobutu—would send us help in North Kivu. The Congolese leaders who had traveled to Rwanda to tell us to come home, reclaim our land, and live in peace also disappeared.

That day, we lugged the bodies of refugees who had walked into the forest so hopeful and never returned, and we buried them as well as we could in the rocky ground of the camp. We prayed over them and we cried. After they had all been buried, we dispersed through the camp back to our tents and shook out mats to lie on. Faustin, my father, and I talked a little bit but never about what we had seen. We made small talk to distract ourselves from what was happening. That's when we knew for sure that we had been betrayed.

✦

MY FATHER COULDN'T ACCEPT being a refugee in our own country, running from the killers as we had when I was a child. It was too much of an indignity for him to bear. He insisted that Faustin and I enroll in the town's school, and every day, no matter the danger from the Interahamwe, we walked down the mountain to the town and studied.

Determined to save us from dying in the camp or joining the rebel groups fighting the Interahamwe and the Congolese army, as so many of the boys who had come with us from Rwanda had done, my father found work. In the morning when Faustin and I left the camp for school, he traveled to nearby farms to help with the cows. Even while violence swirled around us, his work was valuable, and he was able to buy food for us long after the aid organizations had abandoned Kitchanga. My father would have worked all day and night, he would have joined the rebels himself, if it had spared his sons from having to become fighters.

One day my father came back to our tent and instructed us to pack. "Quickly," he said. "I want to get to town before it gets dark."

"Why?" Faustin asked as he put his meager belongings—some clothes, a few school items—into a plastic bag. "Where are we going?"

"Are we going to Bikenke?" I couldn't help asking.

My father shook his head. "Not yet," he said. "But a man I work for has an empty house and he said we can stay there. It will be a lot safer."

My father's employer was Hunde. Although many Hunde had sided with the Hutus against us, this man was one of the many who didn't want to fight. My father said he was one of the kindest people he had met in all of Congo. "For people like him, it doesn't matter that we are Tutsi and he is Hunde," my father explained. "All of those distinctions, they are artificial. They didn't mean anything until the war, and, after the war, they won't mean anything again."

For the first time in our lives, we lived in a house made of concrete, with a roof that didn't leak and a real kitchen. Protected from the wind and rain, Faustin and I slept better than we had since leaving Bikenke. My father's employer told the neighbors to look out for us. "My friend Sedigi will be living here with his sons," he said. "Protect them." People who might have been suspicious of us helped us. "They are Tutsi, but we know them," they reasoned.

My father, who made friends easily, bought some beer to take to the neighbors. "I know how to take care of animals," he would tell them. "If you like, I can take care of yours for free." Soon those neighbors were like a fence around us, looking out for us when we left to buy things at the market or collect firewood or go to school. I studied Swahili day and night, determined to learn the language well enough that if anyone stopped us, they would never guess that I had spent any time outside Congo.

Faustin and I were more content than we had been in a long time, certainly more than we had been since arriving in Kitchanga. We were in school, and we had a little money because my father was working. I fell in love with Nyiramariza, a beautiful Tutsi girl at school who was so smart that when she spoke, I swear, even the teachers took notes. When the teacher instructed us to find rocks to sit on, I found the biggest and flattest for Nyiramariza and carried it for her. I sat next to her every day, even though it meant that I spent more time trying to make her laugh than listening to the lesson. Refugees were bullied at school, called the same names used by the Interahamwe or mocked for being barefoot or unable to speak Lingala, but I went in part to please my father and in part to see Nyiramariza.

A few months after we moved to the village, my father came home from the farm with some news. "You boys are fine now, I think," he said. He was eating beans as he spoke to us; he always came home from work hungry. "We are," Faustin said. "We feel safe." I shrugged. "Sure," I said.

"Mondiant, how is school?" my father asked.

"Good," I said. "Some of the students are mean, but I love the teacher."

"I'm glad to hear it," my father said. He drank some water. His face became serious. "You boys know we can't stay here forever," he said. We nodded, although I wasn't sure what he meant. The house? Kitchanga? I had long ago given up the fantasy of returning to Bikenke. "I have a plan," my father continued. "But I need you both to promise me you will be okay by yourselves before I carry it out."

Faustin nodded, trying to act like an adult. "Of course," he said. "We are fine."

"It's still too dangerous to go to Bikenke," my father said. "It's at least a day's drive away, and I can't take a car or truck. I've decided to go to Kinyana instead. It's much closer and people will know me there. I can get money and send it to you, and then you can come join me."

Kinyana was my father's ancestral village. His father and grandfather had been born there, and before the war, his family had owned a lot of land in Kinyana. If my father's mother had lived, he would have been raised there as well. I only knew the village through the stories my father told me, stories of our great family and our connection to Congo. "I can sell the land, and we can use the money to leave here," he said. "Or I can get work taking care of animals. But there is no future for us here."

We nodded, pretending not to be scared. Even after our disastrous return to Congo, we still believed that our father knew what was best for us. "We will be fine," we told him. "We'll wait here for you." Faustin and I were both still so young, but we knew how to take care of ourselves. We knew how to boil beans and how to avoid running into rebels and government soldiers, and what to say to the rebels if we couldn't avoid them.

"When will you be back?" I asked. I couldn't help it, I was scared.

"Soon, Mondiant," my father said. "Don't worry. I know my village well. I won't get lost." In spite of all we had been through since crossing the border, my father still had hope that his homeland would protect him. "Things will be better," he told us as he cleaned up his dinner and went to bed.

Early the next morning my father packed his Bible, clothes, and a small amount of food into a bag. He gave Faustin some money, around thirty dollars, that he had been saving. "This will be enough for you both to eat while I'm gone," he said. Then he smiled at us, told us not to worry, told us to be good and go to school and not talk to people we didn't know. We watched him walk out the door of the concrete house and disappear.

My father had been gone for some months—long after most of the money he left us was gone, and life, which was isolated beyond anything we had experienced, had become even worse than it had been, living in the tent—when a stranger showed up at our door with a letter. "I've walked all the way from Kinyana," he said. "Are you Faustin and Mondiant?" We opened the door for him.

"Hello, my sons," the letter read. "It's been so long. I miss you so much. I am very sorry for not coming back to you when I promised I would. Soon after I arrived here, Mai-Mai rebels arrested me. There is no chance for me to get out of prison.

"Find your way back to Gihembe. Find your mother and your siblings," he wrote. "When you do, give them my greetings." A pile of Congolese francs, the equivalent of one hundred dollars, fell from the letter. It was by far the most money that Faustin and I had ever seen.

Nineteen

Through everything, school was the center of my life. I think this must be true for a lot of refugee children. It doesn't matter what the classroom looks like or who the teachers are, or even what is taught. It doesn't matter if we are threatened by violence. We will risk everything to study. If parents can send their children to school, all hope is not lost. An educated child—one who reads, writes, can speak up and feel empowered—doesn't have to accept a life as a refugee, like their parents might. And that child can grow up to become a messenger for their whole community.

Since leaving Bikenke I had felt herded through life, moved like cargo from one camp to another. In Kitchanga, fate drove most boys to one place, a rebel camp. But I wasn't ready to accept my place as a fighter. After my father left, I tried to think of my future as something unwritten by fate. I decided to take some control by going to school.

Every morning our friend Kabayiza met Faustin and me in front of our home and we walked the rest of the way to school together. It was better to be in a group. We walked in silence, looking around for any sign of danger. Villagers, watching us descend the hill, yelled insults at us as we passed by. "There are the Tutsis," they would say. "There are the cockroaches."

They didn't care that we were young and just wanted to study and learn. To them, we were nothing. Because of the risks, only two dozen refugee children dared to go to school, but Kabayiza and I had been good students in Rwanda and we were desperate not to fall too far behind. I thought about Nyiramariza. Knowing that I would see her every day made it easier to make the walk.

The school in Kitchanga was made of wood and metal. It looked new, but it was cheap and temporary. Like the villagers, our classmates bullied us. They watched us from the doorway as we approached in the morning, shouting cruel things, and then ran to the window to continue to taunt us. "Why don't you speak Swahili?" they asked, overhearing us talking to one another in Kinyarwanda. "You're not really from Congo."

We liked the headmaster and the teacher, who didn't care who we were or where we had lived. They respected us because we showed up to class and studied. When they were around, the bullying stopped. Still, they didn't punish the other students when we told them about how we were treated. "That's too bad," they said, as though this kind of hatred was a fact of life.

The teachers also asked questions that made me feel like an outsider. "Mondiant," Mokasa, one of my favorite teachers, asked. "Are you Rwandan or are you Congolese?"

"I'm Congolese," I said in Swahili. "I was born in North Kivu, not far from here."

"Hmmm." My teacher seemed genuinely confused. "Then why are you living in the refugee camp?"

Now I laugh, thinking about that question. *Where do you want me to begin?* I think. But in the moment, I felt ashamed and unwanted. "I will tell you later," I said.

We felt abandoned and alone, scared and embarrassed about how naive we had been in our eagerness to return. We were used to being refugees in Rwanda, which we never thought of as home. Being a refugee in your home country is like drowning in an inch of water. Even school began to break its promise of safety and acceptance.

Throughout my life, I have been cushioned by luck. I survived the violence in Bikenke, young enough that when I look back, those days feel like stories I heard rather than a life I lived. I was carried when I couldn't walk. Patience died and I did not.

I lived through both Mudende massacres, and all the long journeys on foot and by truck and bus. Even in our makeshift refugee camp in Kitchanga, where Hutu and Mai-Mai rebels attacked us every day and every night, the area where I lived was spared. I don't know why. Faustin, my father, and I were never hurt. We moved to the concrete house. I did well in school and thought I could change my future by studying. The rebels stayed away from me. I don't know how I got so lucky. I prayed no harder than anyone else.

But after my father left us in Kitchanga, my luck began to run out. I knew what routes to take to school to avoid the fighting, and I diligently walked them every day. Faustin and I closed the door to our concrete house and avoided strangers. I studied and tried to blend in with the other students at school. Soon I spoke Swahili as well as my classmates. None of it mattered. The rebels caught me another way.

◆

AFTER WE RECEIVED THE LETTER from our father, Faustin and I tried to go on living normal lives in our house. I used some of the money to buy a new school uniform, feeling the stiffness leave the material as I walked around our house, showing it off to myself.

But the war started to close in around us, demanding our attention. Most boys had left to join the rebels, and we felt watched wherever we went. It seemed that fighters, both rebels and government soldiers, memorized the routes we took from home to school, so that no matter how inventive we tried to be, they always found us. In Kitchanga, it was impossible to avoid government soldiers or rebels, who wanted either to kill you or to recruit you. Staying home to avoid them would have been like staying home for fear of the sun.

One day I was walking with a handful of other refugee students when we came across some government soldiers. They also mocked us, calling us the same names as the villagers. "Cockroaches!" they shouted. "You're not really from Congo." We tried to ignore them.

That morning, they stopped us. "Where are you going?" they asked, blocking our paths. Light shone through worn patches in their old uniforms, but they stood confidently in front of us and carried weapons.

"We are going to school," I said. "You'll make us late." It was 7:45 and school started at 8:00. The headmaster and teachers punished students who arrived after the first bell, and if refugee students came in after the morning bell, our classmates made us feel even more like we didn't belong.

Some of those classmates walked by, looking at us curiously. They were also scared. The soldiers stopped them. "Where are you from?" they asked in Swahili.

"Here, in Kitchanga," they answered. "We live here."

"Okay, go." The soldiers waved them through. We watched as they continued on to school, walking so quickly they were almost running.

"You." The soldier turned to me. He pointed to bags at their feet, filled with potatoes, bananas, and plantains. "Carry these." He pointed to an empty truck nearby. "Load them onto the truck," he said.

"We need to get to school," I said again. "Those other kids, they are in class with us."

"It doesn't matter," they said. They raised batons over their heads, threatening to beat us. We knew that if we said no, or if we were older, we probably would be killed.

Immediately, we each picked up a bag and heaved it onto our thin shoulders. The bags swelled with bananas and plantains. The sweet smell that seeped out made my mouth water. How long had it been since Faustin and I had eaten until we were full? We were so worried about running out of the money our father had sent us that we ate as though we were still in Gihembe, sharing one spare meal every other day. Now I felt my stomach tighten as I struggled to lift the bags, pulp from the fruit spilling onto my new school uniform, staining it.

We carried their cargo for hours until, finally, all the bags were loaded onto the truck. "Go," they said, scowling at us, and we started running toward the school. "Where have you been, and what happened to your clothes?" the headmaster asked when we finally showed up at school. We shook our heads, too scared to tell him the truth. "We're sorry," we said.

Another day, Faustin and I were walking through a small village between the camp and the school when we heard a man yell, "A young Tutsi!" I covered my face as the soldier walked toward us, and when he was close, I started running toward a thick patch of bamboo. He fired his gun at me but missed. I fell on the ground in a patch of bamboo and curled myself into a ball, watching him come closer.

"Get up," he shouted at me.

"I can't," I said. I held my knees to my chest.

"We will shoot you," they said.

"Go ahead and shoot me," I replied. A piece of bamboo stabbed into my foot and my whole leg felt like it was on fire.

The soldier kneeled down close to me. "We are not doctors," he threatened. "We are not going to inject you with anesthesia first."

He and his friend pulled me onto the road and beat me. People passed by in cars without stopping. I woke up in a hospital, where a doctor and nurse took pity on me. "Are you alone?" they asked kindly. "Where is your family?"

"They are in Rwanda," I said.

The next day I went to school, my new uniform stained with blood and my face covered in bandages. When he saw me, the headmaster ordered me to go home. "Other students will be scared when they see you, Mondiant," he said. "Come back after you heal."

✦

IT WAS DURING SCHOOL that I moved my first dead body since Mudende. We were in the middle of class, each of us furiously studying for the upcoming exam, when we heard gunshots nearby. We did our best to ignore the fighting, which was constant. If our interest turned away from our studies, teachers would shake their heads at us. "Pay attention!" they chastised. The fighting was just a distraction, like a loud truck passing by or a sudden heavy rainstorm.

That day, though, the noises came closer and closer to the school, growing louder until they echoed in our classroom, shaking the blackboard. Even the teacher seemed scared. Some of the students started moving toward the window, trying to see what was going on. "Don't go outside," the teacher shouted. "Get down on the floor, like this." He lay on his stomach with his arms over his head. "Now," he said, his voice muffled, "get down."

With the teacher on the floor, we saw our chance. "Let's go," I whispered to Kabayiza. We tiptoed toward the door. Our teacher, with his face turned toward the ground, didn't notice.

The school overlooked a smaller hill, where we could see the end of what must have been a ferocious battle. From the doorway, we felt the cracks of guns and watched people fall to the ground after they had been shot. We saw small bombs land near people's feet, the flames climbing up their pants legs and engulfing their shirts. We heard screams of fear and excitement. We gasped, also in fear and excitement.

The school bell woke us from our trance. "Why is the bell ringing?" Kabayiza asked no one in particular. It normally rang once in the morning to signal the beginning of school, and once in the afternoon to send us home. "Who is ringing it?" he asked, confused. We looked at each other and shrugged.

Rebel soldiers—the same pro-Tutsi men who often tried to recruit refugees like me—stood in front of the school. They were flying with energy, having just defeated a group of Congolese soldiers. Their eyes were bright with triumph.

People at the school and in the town supported the rebels over the government soldiers. But there were a dizzying number of rebel groups in North Kivu at the time, each claiming to represent a certain interest or ethnic group—some, more than one—and each capable of what seemed like indiscriminate violence.

We all thought that the government, though, was worse. The Congolese government exploited our fears and left us poor and hungry and alone. It had been incapable of protecting us from the Interahamwe in the 1990s, and now it had stopped trying. Every day we spent in Kitchanga, it became easier to justify joining the rebels.

"We need to get the bodies," one of the rebels said to us. "Come help us." He made it sound like a request—"If you want to, come"—but we knew it was an order. Even the teachers followed the rebels.

In the valley, bodies lay like pieces of chopped wood. "Mondiant, you take the legs and I'll take the arms," my friend Mark said, moving to the end of the body of a young man, his face torn through with a bullet. I nodded and grabbed on to his ankles. Just as I had been in Mudende, I was surprised by how heavy the body was. I remembered my father lying in the middle of the road while we were escaping Bikenke, barely alive, and how it looked as though he was made only of meat.

It's not easy to touch the bodies of people you don't know. They are heavy and hard to carry, and while you are moving them, you wonder: Who are they? Do they have family? Mark and I carried the young man toward the rebel base in silence. I wondered how he had been killed and why he had been fighting. Did he believe in a cause, or had he been caught in the valley with no other options, no money, no school? That fighter, I thought, was a refugee, too.

We worked in the valley for four hours. The rebels watched us so closely that, at times, it felt like an audition. After we had moved the bodies that lay close together in the middle of the field, we started to hunt for them in the taller grass and bushes where they were hidden. We walked slowly, looking for a shoe or a hand, and later the remnants of a uniform or a spent grenade, or the spot of blood that might mean there was a body nearby.

Walking in the thick brush on the edge of the forest, I saw a body. "Mark, can you help me?" I shouted. He ran over. We were already used to seeing the dead.

The man lay completely still. Blood seeped out of large machete wounds on his arms and neck. One of his legs was nearly severed at the knee. But when we were near him, Mark and I both screamed. "His eyes are open," I said, pointing. "He's alive."

The man lay staring beyond us. His eyes were brown like mine. "What do we do?" Mark asked, terrified.

I walked out to the edge of the forest. "Hey, come help us!" I shouted to the other students. "Is he dead?" I asked them when they joined us. But they ran away, also too scared to touch him.

A rebel came up behind us, annoyed that we had stopped working. "What's going on here?" he asked.

"What should we do with this one?" Mark asked. "He's still alive."

"Hmmm." The rebel walked over to the man. He kicked him hard in the ribs, near one of his wounds. "He's not alive," he said. "Pick him up."

Mark took the man's legs, and I took his hands. I was sure that at any moment he would wake up and attack us, but he didn't. Instead, he just stared at us as we carried him. I learned that some people die with their eyes open.

Living like that changes who you are. It changes what you are capable of doing. You might go to fetch water or buy some food one day and step over a body. Life was like that everywhere; not a day passed without death entering into it. Let me say one thing again. People can be like animals.

Now I'm twenty-eight years old, and I couldn't touch a dead body. I can't look at a car crash when I see one on the highway. It's hard for me to see dead and injured people, and I feel sick at the sight of blood and mournful even for strangers. I am afraid of being killed. I look at some-one with an injury to their legs and I think about my own legs.

Back then, when I was younger, I could see someone on the battlefield with their legs blown off and pick up what was left of their body to be buried without caring. I was capable of doing anything that was de-manded of me. If you told me to walk from the camp to a village that was days away through the forest while being hunted by people, I did it. If you told me to pick up a corpse, close its eyes with my own fingers, heave it onto a truck, and then go back to the valley and do it again, I would. If you told me that in the future I might see and do worse things, I believed you. Even the mind becomes dysfunctional.

Twenty

A few months after the Second Congo War ended, hundreds of homes belonging to refugees in Kitchanga were destroyed. Faustin and I were still living in the concrete house and going to school every day. We wanted to follow our father's instructions, but we had no idea how to get back to Gihembe. Plus, exams were approaching, and we were determined to pass. Somehow the exams still mattered to us.

Normally there were about ten Tutsis in our class, but one Monday we arrived at class to find that everyone was absent but us. Even Charmante, who was very active in class, always raising her hand and asking questions, was missing. I looked around, hoping to see Nyiramariza, but she never arrived. "She's returned to Rwanda," a classmate told me.

My heart was broken, but I still went to school with my brother. On Tuesday and Wednesday, there were still no other Tutsi students. We stopped asking why and kept our mouths shut. Our classmates looked at us like we were crazy. "Why are you coming?" they asked. "Aren't you scared?"

"Let's study at home until the exams," I suggested to Faustin.

"You're right," he said. "But first, let's go back to the camp. We should find out what happened to our friends."

We studied at home that week, our windows closed, leaving the house as little as possible. On Saturday, as soon as the streets had filled with people going shopping at the market or visiting friends, Faustin and I made our way up the hill to the refugee camp. "Be quiet, Mondiant," Faustin said, as if it mattered. People stared at us the whole way.

As we approached our old tent, it was clear something was wrong. The camp was quiet, and the alleyways between homes were nearly empty of people. We smelled the metallic smell of blood and the acrid smell of burned plastic, which made us cough. There was no conversation, no music, no clink of the mancala stones. No one sat outside their homes drinking beer and talking. Everyone we saw walked quickly, as though running from something.

Interahamwe often set fires, as they had in Mudende, forcing people to run out of their homes and through the camp into the forest. Now the camp was almost completely burned. Homes lay in charred fragments beside destroyed vegetable gardens. It was as though Congo's volcano had erupted, erasing all life in the refugee camp.

"Thomas lives close to the gate," Faustin said, pointing to our right. "Let's see if he's there." I followed him until we came upon an empty and smoldering brick home. "It had a straw roof," Faustin said, standing in front of it. "It must have burned easily."

"Let's find Gasana," Faustin said. Gasana, one of his closest friends, had been missing from school. "I think his tent is this way," he said, pointing north. He walked faster and I followed him.

Gasana's tent was still intact. When Faustin saw the unblemished white and blue, he started running. "That's his mother in front," he said, pointing at a woman sitting in front of the tent in a wooden chair, feeding kernels of corn to some ducks.

"Hi, Aunt," Faustin said, using a respectful greeting. "Where is Gasana?"

Mama Gasana stopped what she was doing and looked up at us. The ducks started to quack and stomp in angry protest. "Faustin," she said. "It's good to see you."

"I haven't seen Gasana at school," he said. "Do you know where he is? I'm worried about him."

Mama Gasana shook her head sadly. "He's gone," she told him. "He was recruited with all his friends. The rebels came and took him away.

"It's dangerous for you to be here," she said, throwing the rest of the corn to the ducks and gesturing to the front of her tent. "Go inside," Gasana's mother told us. "Otherwise, they will find you, too."

Rebels had been plucking young men out of the camp for months, she explained. Some of them went willingly with the pro-Tutsi rebels, angered by the attacks from opposing groups. Others, starving and hopeless, followed the same rebels' promises of food and better shelter. Still others were coerced or threatened into joining Hutu or Mai-Mai rebels; they lived and fought in fear. We didn't ask why Gasana had left. It didn't matter.

We heard voices. "Those are PARECO," Gasana's mother said. "Hide." She pushed us through an opening in the back of the tent.

Gasana's mother kept pigs and goats behind her tent, and Faustin and I found a hiding place behind piles of manure. The smell made me gag, but it was safe. Four rebels dressed head to toe in green camouflage and carrying automatic weapons entered her tent. From our hiding spot, we strained to hear what they were saying. I felt ashamed that we were hiding instead of protecting her.

"Where are your children?" they asked.

"I don't have any," Gasana's mother said.

"Are you barren?" they asked.

"I had some children," she replied.

"Where are they?" one rebel asked, his voice rising in anger.

"Five were killed in Mudende," Gasana's mother said patiently. It was a story she was used to telling. "Two were killed here six months ago. My last son went to fight."

The rebels continued to interrogate her. "Who recruited your son?" they wanted to know.

"I don't know," Gasana's mother answered.

"You're lying." The rebels sounded angry now. Faustin and I walked slowly away from the manure, crouching beside the tent to peek through gaps in the fabric. Gasana's mother stood with her back to us. Two or three—I can't remember how many—rebels stood in front of her. I remember their heavy black boots tracking dirt into her tent. Now they were shouting.

"We saw two boys sitting with you just now," they shouted. "Where are they?"

Gasana's mother refused to tell them. "I don't know," she said. "I've never met them before. They left." The rebels hit her, an old woman, on the head and threatened to kill her. "If we ever meet your son, we will kill him, too," they said, and hit her again.

If the rebels had found us, they would have killed her immediately. But she didn't tell them where we were, even when she was lying on the ground bleeding. I don't know why she risked her life to save ours. Until that day, she hadn't even met me. Maybe she saved us because my brother was friends with Gasana. Maybe she loved him because he knew her son, or because we were all refugees.

We waited until they left and then went back into the tent. Gasana's mother sat in a chair, pressing a wet cloth to her bruised face. She had been crying. "Go out the way you came," she said. "Be careful."

It was twilight by the time we left what remained of the camp. We hoped that in the dark, no one would be able to tell that we were Bagogwe. We had been told our entire lives that we looked different from other Congolese people—taller, thinner, with longer hands and fingers—and although this crude distinction was a myth, designed to make us feel foreign, hiding our bodies from Hutus had become as instinctual as covering our mouths when we coughed. Faustin held on to my arm to keep me from falling. Close to town, we came across more PARECO, the Congolese rebels, identifiable because they were speaking Lingala, on patrol.

"Stop there," they said. "Who are you?"

"My name is Waluamba," I replied in careful Swahili. I worried that if I gave them my real name, they would know that I was Tutsi and they would kill me. "I was buying cigarettes for my father."

That time, for some reason, the rebels let us go. Maybe it was too dark to see who we were. Maybe they were tired and had someplace to be. Faustin and I returned to the concrete house, knowing how lucky we were. We cooked some food for dinner and ate in silence, the yellow light in the kitchen buzzing with insects. We didn't know how long our luck would last.

"Mondiant, one of us has to try to go back to Gihembe," Faustin said. "There's no way we can stay here."

I nodded. The longer we stayed in Kitchanga, the more likely it was we would be recruited or killed.

"It's too dangerous for you to go," Faustin said. "There's not enough money for a car. I'll walk with Thomas."

At first, I didn't know what to say. I was only eleven years old, and I was terrified by the idea of being alone in Congo. But I knew that Faustin was right. "You should go," I agreed. "You're faster."

"When I get there, I'll send money for you to join me," Faustin said. "Just stay here. Don't talk to anyone. Be careful."

"I'll be fine," I said.

I'll be honest, I am not a very brave person. Giving fake names to rebels in order to avoid being taken was a sign of cleverness, not bravery. Going to school even when there was fighting was a necessity, and therefore not very brave. If I gave up on school, I would be giving up on life.

I haven't had many moments of real bravery in my life. I didn't want to be sent into the forest to survive on my own. I didn't care if that meant I would never be a real, grown Bagogwe man. But I was brave when I let Faustin go back to Gihembe. I don't want to be boastful, but it was brave to live in Congo alone.

◆

AT ONE THE NEXT NIGHT, Thomas knocked on our door. I hugged Faustin goodbye, but I didn't say much. I worried that if I said goodbye too many times, I would start to feel truly lonely. For the first time in my life, I was completely alone. In search of company, I left the concrete house and returned to the camp, where I moved into an abandoned tent near Gasana's mother, the only person I knew there. We started helping each other. I fetched water and she would cook for us both. She rarely talked about the seven other children she had lost, but maybe because he was Faustin's friend or maybe because she hoped he was still alive, she talked a lot about Gasana.

"He is a very scared kid," she told me, stirring a pot of beans. "I worry about him trying to fight.

"When he was born, I was relieved that he would be my last," she said, laying out some laundry. "Seven children is a lot for one woman. Now I wish I were young and could have more.

"Maybe Gasana has become a brave boy," she told me, feeding the ducks. "I think he will be fine."

"He will be," I always told her. "When I go back to Rwanda, I will take him and you with me."

I had no idea if Faustin had made it to Gihembe or if my father was alive or dead. No one had a phone, and I didn't know how to send a letter. Refugees who were only two years older than me, barely teenagers, were being recruited by the rebels, and I thought it was only a matter of time before I was forced to join as well.

It became clear to me that my only option was to leave Kitchanga. I decided to walk to my mother's village, where I would look for a woman my mother affectionately called Mama Zawadi. They had been friends before my mother married my father and moved to Bikenke, and although she was a Hutu, I felt sure that if I found her, she would help me.

One afternoon I said goodbye to Mama Gasana. She waved from

where she sat in front of her tent, watching, as always, for Gasana to come home. "If you see him, tell him I said to come home," she said.

"I will," I replied, as I always did.

My mother's village was a seven-hour walk from Kitchanga. Instead of going through the forest, where I knew rebels often robbed and killed people, I followed the road, praying that I wouldn't meet anyone. I had nothing that could be stolen, and I was too young to fight. But in North Kivu, it was best to avoid everyone.

It was the hottest time of year, and even though I left early in the morning, sweat began to run down my forehead and into my eyes as soon as I left the camp. I could smell my shirt as it began to stick to my body. My feet stung on the hot ground. A few hours after I left the camp, I heard voices around me. "Where are you coming from and where are you going?" a voice boomed. Two men came out from between the trees carrying guns and RPGs, the characteristic diamond-shaped heads balanced on their shoulders. They were rebels from a group I couldn't name; in North Kivu, men were always taking up arms together.

"I am from Kitchanga," I said. "I am going to Burungu."

"Are you a rebel?" they asked.

"No," I said. "I'm a student. I'm in primary school." By now I was so used to encountering the rebels that I could answer them before the question had even left their mouth. There was no point in running away. If they wanted to kill you, they would kill you. If they wanted to recruit you, they would take you away.

"Which tribe are you?" they asked. "Where are your parents?"

"I don't know my tribe," I lied. "And I don't know where my parents are." That, at least, was half true.

I waited for them to yell or to strike me. Instead, they turned away and looked down the road, where a large van was driving into view. The van excited the rebels. "Whatever's inside, let's take it," they said. It was as though God, given the task of rescuing me once again, had sent something to distract the rebels, in this case a van carrying green plantains, rice, and a driver terrified and ready to surrender everything he had. "You, stay there," they instructed me. The rebels stepped into the road to stop the van from passing.

"I have no money," the driver claimed, shaking by his van.

"We don't believe you," the rebels said. They beat him and threatened him until he admitted he was lying. They pulled some money from his glove compartment and then unloaded everything he carried onto the road. Huge sacks of plantains and rice surrounded our small group by the time he tearfully drove away. Then the rebels turned to me.

"Give us money or we will kill you," they said.

"I have nothing," I insisted. "I am going to Burungu to find food. I didn't eat today or yesterday. The day before, I only had a little." Unlike the driver, I had nothing to pacify them. I assumed that when they discovered that, I would be dead.

Instead, they told me they would let me go. "You're Tutsi, right?" they asked. I said nothing and eventually they gave up. "Let's just release him," one of them said, annoyed, and the other nodded in agreement.

I remember this rebel well. He carried a long spear and wore yellow pants. He was scruffy but authoritative. He stood in front of the others, and although he was talking to them, he was looking at me. They did everything he said.

"But first, will you help us carry these things to our base?" he asked.

It took five trips between the road and the base to carry everything the rebels had stolen from the driver. The bags were heavy. Lifting one, I felt like I might sink into the dirt. But I was so scared I could have carried the van itself if the rebels had demanded it. I worked until it began to get dark, hardly noticing when it started raining.

For the first time, I saw a rebel base up close. I was surprised that it was more like a refugee camp than my home village. Rebels slept in tents, although they were sturdier and bigger than the UNHCR ones, and some had homes made of bricks or wooden planks. They had similar food, but much more of it. They now had fruit, and I swore that I could smell roasting meat somewhere on the base. After I had carried the last bag, they turned to me. "Go," they said. "Never come this way again."

I felt so grateful that they were letting me go that I thanked them over and over. "I will never come back this way again," I promised. "Thank you," I repeated. "Thank you."

Twenty-One

In Burungu, everyone assumed I was a child soldier. They closed their doors and windows when I walked by. I sat by myself in the shuttered market underneath a bright umbrella, watching the rain fall on the tin roofs and hoping it would stop soon so I could find Mama Zawadi. Villagers stared at me from cracks in their windows. They could see I carried nothing. I had no weapons or bags that could be concealing weapons. I was barefoot, wearing ripped black shorts and a shirt with a Detroit Pistons logo in the middle, so big and stretched out it fell off my shoulders. Still, they hated me.

That night, rather than scare people by staying in the market, I slept in a marsh near the village. The tree canopy protected me from the rain, and I was so tired that I slept deeply. But the marshland was wet and dirty, and when I returned the next morning to find my mother's friends, I was even more disheveled than I had been the day before. My shorts were caked in mud and the T-shirt was so heavy with water it had stretched down almost to my knees.

I hadn't eaten in days. In my hunger I stopped caring what people thought of me and started asking for directions, desperate to find my mother's friend. Finally, a man stopped to listen. He wore battered pants and his shirt was stained with mud; he looked like my father when he came home from watching the cows. "Do you know this family?" I asked him, describing Mama Zawadi.

"I do," he answered. He was a cowherd and knew everyone within a fifty-mile radius of the town. "I even know what street they live on," he said. "They don't live in this village, though." He pointed to a mountain. "They live on the other side of that." I thanked him and started walking again.

I was so tired and so lonely that I climbed without thinking once about my hunger. I stumbled over gray rocks that threatened to collapse beneath me, holding on to plants and skinny tree trunks for support. The mountain seemed unending, but somehow I made it. I still think it's amazing what people can do when they are desperate.

Mama Zawadi's village, although close to Burungu, was majority Hutu and mostly intact. She lived in a modest but welcoming mud-brick home with a tidy thatched roof and a small garden in front. A woman sat by the door, measuring cassava into the enormous mortar where it would be pounded before cooking. Seeing this everyday Congolese chore made my mouth water and my heart ache for my family, and almost immediately I recognized the pretty face my mother had described.

"Good morning," I said, smiling as wide as I could to let her see I was friendly. She put down her pestle as I approached. "Do you know Nyira-kavange Eugenie?" I asked.

"I do." Mama Zawadi smiled at the mention of my mother's name. "How do you know her?"

"She is my mother," I said.

At once, Mama Zawadi stood up and came to me. She embraced me, not caring that I was filthy or that she had never met me before. I felt her warm arms around me and was happier than I had been in years.

"Come inside," she said, and I followed her into the warmth of her home. She gave me a glass of thick, sweet banana juice. I drank it and instantly felt better.

Once I was settled in, Mama Zawadi began asking me questions. "I know that Bikenke was attacked," she said. "How did you get here?"

I told her the story of our escape from Congo. "We were attacked as well," she said. "But because we are Hutu, they let us stay here."

I told her about my mother. "She had two new babies in Gihembe and one before we got there," I said. "Patience died when we were walking."

"That beautiful baby," she sighed. "Eugenie is still in Rwanda?" she asked.

I nodded. "My entire family is in the refugee camp," I told her. I didn't want to talk about my father. "My brother went back there as well, and I need help to get back, too."

After I had finished talking, my belly full of banana juice, Mama Zawadi stood up. "There's not much that I can do for you," she said. "The war makes most things impossible. But I want to help Eugenie's son, if I can." She went to a bag in the corner of the house and took out a pair of pants and a shirt. "Here," she said. "I should have given these to you as soon as you came in. You must be so cold."

I stayed at her house all weekend by the fire, eating and talking to her family. It was the safest I had felt since Bikenke. On Saturday I went hunting with one of her sons, and on Sunday Mama Zawadi returned from her farm, her arms full of taro and sweet potatoes for me to take back to the camp. When I left, she hugged me again.

"When you see your mother, tell her we are thinking about her," she said. "Tell her we wish she could come home. I want to meet her new babies." I nodded and said I would tell her.

I left the town happy. My stomach was full, and I carried enough food for a month, balanced firmly atop my head. I walked quickly up and down the mountain, and no one stopped me when I stumbled my way over the roads.

But by the time I made it back to Kitchanga, my good mood had faded. The camp was the same barren, burned, desperate place. There was no banana juice, no family to talk to by a fire. Mama Gasana only blinked when she saw me. "Did you see my son?" she asked. I shook my head.

I climbed into my tent, alone. I had food now, but what was the point of cooking it? Instead, I slept for days, barely moving. I was so lonely.

✦

SOON THERE WAS no avoiding the fighting. There were no safe roads or paths through the forest. War surrounded us like weather.

One day I was walking home from school with two of my Hunde friends, Kasaleka and Muhindi. It was blindingly hot, and we decided we would go swimming in a river we passed by on our way home. We chatted as we walked—about school, about sports. We tried never to talk about the war or about our families, even though both of my friends still lived at home while I was alone in the refugee camp.

The river was murky and huge, gripped by a strong current that made it nearly impossible to swim against the waves. Muhindi and I ran in gleefully, but Kasaleka hung back onshore. He wasn't a very strong swimmer. "I'll stay here," he said. "It's enough to splash some water on my arms and legs."

Muhindi and I were playing in the water, grabbing sticks and rocks to keep from being swept away by the current, when we heard Kasaleka shout. "Run! Come out of the water!"

"What did he say?" Muhindi asked me. It was impossible to hear him clearly from the river.

"Let's go back," I said.

Kasaleka stood on the bank, waving at us wildly. "Katanyama are coming!" he shouted. "Katanyama" meant "flesh cutters." Everyone, from young students to old refugees, used this nickname for the Congolese soldiers, who seemed to kill without thinking, as though they were slaughtering an animal. We began swimming faster, desperate to reach our friend, but before we could get to the shore, we heard gunshots and saw Kasaleka collapse to the ground. From the river we saw dark blood pooling around his head.

"Katanyama!" Muhindi said. "Let's go to the other side." But the farther we swam from shore, the harder it became to fight against the current. We sputtered, trying to keep our heads above the water. If we had tried to cross, we would surely have drowned. "Where do you think you are going?" we heard the soldiers shout. "Come out of there or we'll shoot you!" With nowhere to go, we did as we were told.

Three government soldiers stood on the bank, holding their guns and waiting for us. Kasaleka lay dead beside them. I tried not to look at my friend.

"Are you going to call us katanyama, too?" They scowled at us. It was an insulting term, which Kasaleka had used without thinking. The soldiers hated the nickname, though, which they knew was used to mock them. Kasaleka had been unlucky. He was Hunde, and if he hadn't said the word, he would probably still be alive.

We climbed out of the water. "We're sorry," Muhindi said in Lingala. "We're sorry."

"Do you know who we are?" they asked.

"Of course," Muhindi said. "You are soldiers."

"You don't think we are katanyama like your friend?" they asked angrily. We were shaking now. We were so scared.

I said nothing. Lingala still sounded foreign to me. I worried that if I tried to speak it, they would know that I was a Tutsi refugee. And if they found that out, I was sure they would kill me. "Is he dumb?" the soldiers asked Muhindi. "Why isn't he talking?"

"I'm not," I said in Swahili. "I can speak."

They stared at me. "Are you Tutsi?" they asked. I shook my head.

"Show us your hands," they said. Slowly, I extended my right hand forward, hoping it wasn't shaking. They turned my palm upward, examining it silently, tracing the lines. They looked at my face like I was an animal being examined in the market. "You are Tutsi," they said. "We can tell."

"I'm not," I insisted. "I'm Hutu, from Bikenke," I lied. "That's why I speak Swahili so well and don't speak Lingala."

They started examining my palm again. I didn't know exactly what they were looking for. I was always hiding my face, my body, my voice, worried they would reveal who I was. But if you asked me to identify a Congolese Hutu or a Hunde, or even another Tutsi, just by sight, I couldn't.

"No, you're Tutsi," they said. "Your hand is long, and your face is thin and narrow." Because I was starving; they were right. My face, now full, back then was only bone, ready to shatter at any moment. "Come with us," they said. They turned to Muhindi. "You can leave." With an apologetic look in my direction, my friend sprinted away from the water.

As soon as they ordered me to follow them, my body began feeling as heavy as lead. I lost control over my arms and legs and I fell to the ground, my forehead and stomach pressed into the wet dirt. The sound of the river drowned out all other noise, and I had to close my eyes to stop from fainting. "Come on!" the soldiers screamed at me. "Get up, let's go." They kicked me in the ribs. I tried to move, but I could only stand for a second before falling again.

They pulled me up. "You are lucky we don't kill you here," they told me. My vision was blurry and blood poured out of my chin and mouth, where it felt like I had lost all of my teeth. I watched as they threw Kasaleka's body into the river, and then I did my best to follow them out of the forest. "Walk quickly," they said. I picked up a piece of bamboo to use as a cane and followed them.

We walked away from the river toward a nearby village. It was evening, and as we walked, we passed crowds of people standing outside, talking to one another. Seeing them, I felt relieved. Surely, I thought, someone in the crowd of people would rescue me. The villagers watched, but no one helped me. No one said, "Forgive that child." When they saw us coming, they ran inside their homes, terrified.

Near the market, I fell into a pile of sugarcane. The stalks spilled out in front of the stall, clattering onto the packed-dirt road. The soldiers hit my ribs with their guns. "Stand up," they shouted. The vendor didn't yell. He barely looked at us. He rearranged his sugarcane, and then he also went inside.

The sun set and it got chilly. Wind blew into my wounds, making me groan in pain. My limbs tightened and I fell over and over, feeling like I was turning into wood. Finally, I passed out.

✦

I STILL HAVE A SCAR on my chin and a damaged tooth from that walk with the soldiers. But I don't tell anyone what really happened to me. If they ask, I say that someone elbowed me during a soccer game.

I spent three weeks in the Congolese jail. It was the most secure building in the area, built of concrete blocks so that no one could see inside. All the other captives I saw were women and children. Most of the men were gone, either dead or fighting. Their wives and daughters had been caught on their way to the market or church. They were brought alone and prayed for their families. They had no idea what had happened to their husbands, or why they were being held captive.

We were given no mats to sleep on, and the soldiers flooded our cells with stinking water that came up to our knees to prevent us from resting on the floor. Our room stank of mildew and human waste, and after a few days my legs turned pale and the skin began peeling off in chunks. At mealtime, the soldiers tossed food through the windows and we would have to search for it in the water if we wanted to avoid starving.

Every day the soldiers killed someone, a child or a woman, within view of the jail. Although they had guns, they chose to use an ax, swinging it into their heads or chests and then leaving their bodies chained to the chairs where they had been executed. It seemed they did it at random; at least, I had no idea why someone was taken one moment, and another the next. I assumed that any day it could be me.

Many days we heard the sounds of women crying while the soldiers raped them. I came to see that rape was as bad as, or worse than, other weapons. A gun was painful. A gun was swift. Rape, on the other hand, was meant to be degrading as well as deadly. The rapist hoped to shame a woman and her family, killing their souls before killing her.

One woman, Mama Cecile, was always praying. Her daughter, Cecile, had been raped on the veranda with everyone watching through the gaps in the bricks. Cecile fought them, so the soldiers held her arms and legs as they raped her. Afterward, to punish her for resisting, they put her in the execution chair and cut off her limbs, so she bled to death.

Every morning I was caned ten times. The cane left long, oozing wounds on my legs and back that made it hard to walk. Still, it was better than being killed, I thought. It was better than being raped.

While I waited for them to kill me, the soldiers made me a spy. Almost every day I was sent to a nearby village with Jacques, another young spy, who became my friend. The village markets were big and open; with the war going on, people were scared of going there, but they had to in order to buy necessities. Jacques and I would stand in the middle of the market, watching people walk quickly by us, frightened by the sight of two unfamiliar boys, waiting for our chance.

Our job was to steal food and supplies for the soldiers, and report to them if we saw any Tutsi rebels. The soldiers also wanted us to find girls for them, beautiful ones they could pretend to date. When we found a girl, a soldier made a show of visiting her home and talking to her parents about marriage. "I would like for your daughter to visit us on the base," he said, and the parents nodded their agreement. They couldn't say no, of course. In this way, the soldiers made me complicit in their campaign of rape.

"What if we just ran away?" Jacques asked as we sat in the market, careful not to let the open wounds on our legs touch the ground.

"Where would we go?" I asked. It seemed unlikely that we would make it very far. No one in the village would help us. And where was safe? The soldiers were in the streets and in the forest; they were in Kitchanga and all the villages around Kitchanga. Even the refugee camp was almost completely destroyed, abandoned by everyone who had vowed to protect us, with the surviving refugees cowering in their homes, yearning for the tedium of Gihembe but aware that of those who had left, surely only a few had made it to the border alive.

"Besides, if they catch us . . ." I didn't have to say it. Jacques knew what would happen. A few days earlier another boy had tried to escape. He had been spying with us in a village, sitting and watching the people, when he stood up suddenly. "I'm not going back to jail," he announced casually, as though he was telling us it was time to stop playing soccer and go home for dinner. "I'm leaving," he said, walking off toward the forest.

That day the soldiers killed two people. They killed one person in the morning, which was their ritual. And in the afternoon, they killed the boy who had tried to escape. I heard his screams from my cell and I felt more hopeless than I ever had in my entire life. I wondered if my father was in a jail like this. If I ever tried to run away, I thought, it would be only if I decided I wanted to die.

But three weeks after I was caught by the soldiers, I escaped. Early one morning pro-Tutsi rebels attacked the compound, scattering soldiers and opening the jail doors. In the chaos, I ran out of the cell, the sores on my legs oozing and infected. I ran through the streets and the forest; I ran until I saw the remnants of the refugee camp scattered up the hill near Kitchanga. I felt like I was returning from war. I climbed into the tent I had left and curled up on the floor.

For the first time since arriving in Congo, I could see the rest of my life clearly. Anyone could kill me whenever they wanted to, I was sure of that. If I were killed by rebels, at least people outside Congo would recognize it as murder. My death would anger other refugees. Maybe it would anger the UN or a government official.

If I was killed by Congolese soldiers, people might assume they had the authority to kill me. They might think that I had done something to deserve my own death. Nobody would ask them, "Why did you kill

Mondiant?" and no one would scream that my death had been unjust. Maybe they would even think that because the Congolese soldiers did it, I deserved to die.

The rebels were violent, and I was terrified of each group, even the one that claimed to support my rights as a Tutsi. But the Congolese soldiers scared me even more. They were part of a system that thrived on killing. The world they offered me was worse than the one offered by the rebels. If you wanted to be alive in the world where the Congolese army was in charge, you had to leave Congo and become a refugee. I sat in my tent and thought about what I had been through in jail, and I waited for the rebels to find me.

Twenty-Two

I became a child soldier. What else do I need to say? I've read enough in English about Congo to know what people think when they hear that term. For me, some of those things are true. Some are not. It is enough just to carry or clean a gun, or to remove bodies from a battlefield and cook food for the rebels, to be a part of them. You don't have to fire a gun to be a child soldier. And, in the end, it wasn't fear or hunger or loneliness, or even gratitude or anger, that drew me to the rebels. It was a bird.

Bagogwe men were not known for being good hunters. We raised livestock and tended to farms; those were our jobs. When we became refugees, though, we lost our cows and our land, and we had to let go of cultural norms in order to survive. In Gihembe, we would have hunted every day if we could, but no one had the weapons or access to land or knew the layout of that land well enough to learn how to hunt. If we strayed too far from the refugee camp, we could be arrested for trespassing.

In the early days in Gihembe, before refugees devised ways to gain some independence, we were like children. We relied on aid organizations or the Rwandan government for food and, eventually, money, and if those supplies were too small or too slow to arrive, we accepted that there was no alternative to hunger. We forgot how to take care of ourselves, and the skills we used to take so much pride in became, like so much of Bagogwe culture, a distant memory.

In Kitchanga, though, the aid organizations hadn't been distributing anything for many months. I had long ago eaten all the food I carried home from Mama Zawadi's and spent the rest of the money my father sent. I was starving, and I needed to learn how to take care of myself.

I ate sweet berries and chewed on roots and chicory, dipped my fingers into beehives to scoop out some honey, just to survive. I forgot what cooked food tasted like. From dawn until sunset, I foraged for anything I could find, walking through the forest with my eyes turned downward for so long that I forgot what the sky looked like during the day.

Step by step, I was becoming acquainted with my homeland. If I walked too long on the dry grass of a pasture, I craved the soft carpet of leaves and moss of the forest under my feet. I recognized the calls of parrots and pigeons and could spend hours watching an antelope bound from hill to hill. The Congolian rainforest, which in its entirety across western and central Africa is larger than the state of Alaska, astonished me. Thousands of species of animals—elephants, hippos, lions, chimpanzees—live in the forest, making their homes among the thousands of species of plants that refuse to grow anywhere but Congo.

Colonists enslaved us. European explorers like Henry Stanley and David Livingstone, and novelists like Joseph Conrad, tried to define Congo as a brutal land, a land of plagues and massacres. They called it "dark," and warned other Europeans against visiting. Still today, Congo has a reputation as a forbidding place. When I would tell classmates in New York where I was from, I could see them imagining a place that, as far as they were concerned, was unlivable.

I am not naive about my homeland. I know firsthand the violence you can encounter on a walk through the forest. But it is up to me as an educated Bagogwe to tell the whole truth, and I reject this racist characterization of my home. Congo has been victimized by perpetual war, but it is not all war. Congolese people want to live in peace at home. The forest can be hostile, but it is rich; it kept me alive. When I was starving and scared and alone, the land sustained me. Other Congolese people also sustained me. We took care of one another the best we could.

After my escape from jail, I lived among the homes of three Hunde friends, Binta, Munihire, and Leneo. They were skilled hunters, and they offered to teach me. "We'll show you how to shoot animals," they told me. "Then you'll never be hungry again."

Every morning I followed my friends into the trees and across the wide, hilly fields in pursuit of anything we could find. We left early, while the birds were still sleeping in their nests and the larger animals were out looking for prey. We carried bags for the animals and wore shorts and T-shirts that we took off if it started to rain, preferring to hunt naked rather than in sopping clothing. "You start with those birds," Munihire said, pointing at an African green pigeon. The birds were plentiful, but difficult to shoot, camouflaged by their fern-green feathers. I would have to train my hunter's eye to spot a telltale red stripe around its beak. "The birds are good practice," he said.

Every morning for two months we went looking for animals. I watched my friends to see how they handled their weapons, and I imitated their whispers. They had spears that they threw in graceful arcs at antelopes and monkeys. I made a slingshot from a forked stick and an elastic band, which I wore around my neck and used to clumsily lob rocks at the pigeons.

My friends took pity on me and gave me a portion of each animal they caught—monkeys, African jacanas, sometimes an antelope—each a beautiful part of my beautiful country. "It's a shame for you to spend all day running through the mountains and the forest and go home without anything," Munihire said, teasing me.

"He's still learning," Leneo said. "The time will come when he'll do it well." Leneo was encouraging and supportive.

When I got frustrated, Leneo helped me find birds sitting high above our heads. "Mondiant, I've found something for you that will be easy to shoot," he would say, pointing at a bright bird sitting close enough that I could see its rainbow of feathers. "Take your time," he would say, as I pulled a rock back in my slingshot. "That's okay, next time," he would comfort me when that rock invariably sailed past the bird into the trees.

"What happened, man?" Munihire wouldn't let me forget that I had missed a bright bird. He was the most impatient among us. "Did you miss it? It was too close to miss."

"I did my best, man," I would say. "I was close."

"You weren't close," he would say, teasing me the entire walk home. "You're getting worse and worse, you couldn't hit a tree."

One day we were crossing a river on our walk home when I noticed that my shin was bleeding.

"Wait," I said to my friends as I sat down on a rock. "I hurt my leg."

"How?" Munihire asked. He sighed and looked at his bag, which was full of meat. "I'm hungry, do you need to look at it now?"

"I don't know," I told him. "Maybe I cut myself when Leneo and I were chasing after that antelope. Let me wipe some of the blood away." I poured river water over my shin, watching my blood dye it a light pink. I didn't want to draw attention to myself by returning to Kitchanga with a bloody leg, carrying a bag full of antelope meat. It wasn't appropriate for Bagogwe to hunt, and even though I was desperate to eat, I felt ashamed to be straying from my culture.

Blood continued to rush out of the small wound. I felt light-headed and leaned back against the rock, closing my eyes. "Here." Leneo handed me a cup of water mixed with sugarcane. "Drink this."

"What a life of luxury I live," I joked, leaning back against the rock and drinking the water, my eyes closed in delight.

When I got up, I felt like a new person. I walked with energy, thinking about how good the antelope would taste and excited about sharing the meat with Mama Gasana. Along the way, I noticed something bright on the forest floor. I slowed down to get a better look.

"Why are you stopping?" Binta asked me. "Does your leg hurt?"

"Look," I said, pointing at a passion fruit vine just below which a peacock was happily eating, unaware that it was being watched. "It's a huge bird. And it's barely moving."

"Are you serious?" My friends came back running, pulling rocks out of their bags to load into their own slingshots. "Where is it?" they asked, ready to shoot.

I wanted to prove to my friends that I had learned something over the past two months, and that I could contribute. "It's mine," I said. "I will shoot it myself."

I aimed a rock at the peacock, squinting my eyes and pulling back my slingshot. My first shot sailed past the bird into the woods, its pearly feathers barely moving. The second rock did the same, and so did the third. My friends watched me. Even Leneo was beginning to get anxious. "It's going to fly away," he said.

"I'll get it," I said. "Don't worry." My hands were shaking now. The peacock hadn't moved. Its bright feathers remained stuck to its back. I loaded another rock and focused again, shooting it toward the bird. When I missed, I shot another and then another.

Finally, Munihire lost his patience. "I can get that bird in my sleep," he said. "Watch this." He lay down in the grass and hoisted his slingshot in the air, loaded with one large black rock. "Stand back," he said, and let the rubber band go. An instant later, the bird fell over into a pile of passion fruit, squealing in pain.

"I told you one stone was enough for me." Munihire laughed, getting up and dusting off his shorts.

I ran to where the bird lay, wounded and crying. It was so beautiful, and so frantic in its pain that I couldn't touch it. Leneo came up behind me and picked up the bird by the neck, its tail feathers tightening protectively around itself as my friend shoved it into his bag. "Let's go," he said. I followed him, ashamed.

My friends were delighted with our hunting excursion. "A peacock and an antelope!" they said, racing back to Kitchanga. "We've never brought home a peacock."

I walked slowly behind them. The bird's screams echoed in my head, reminding me of Mudende, or the Congolese jail, or when we fled our home in Bikenke. I felt suddenly that I had to save the innocent bird from death. *If the peacock were a person*, I thought, *it would ask for mercy.*

I caught up to my friends and tapped Leneo on the shoulder. "That is my bird," I said. "Give it to me."

They looked at me like I was crazy. "You saw it first," Munihire said. "But I shot it."

I stood in front of them on the path, crossing my arms and blocking their way, trying to look intimidating. "It's still alive," I said. "You didn't kill it. You failed. Give it to me."

My friends had never seen me angry before. It seemed to shake them. "We have the antelope," Leneo reasoned. "I doubt the peacock will be as delicious."

"Let's just give it to him," Binta said. "I want to go home and eat."

Leneo grabbed the bag from Munihire and threw it at me. "Take it," he said angrily. And then the three of them pushed me off the path and walked away.

The peacock writhed inside the bag. I spoke to it softly all the way home. "Don't worry," I said. "I'm not going to eat you. I couldn't kill you anyway, I don't know how!"

Munihire, Binta, and Leneo never spoke to me again. I returned to my old tent, the same one my father had pitched so long ago, with the peacock, which I named Mubarikiwa, meaning "blessed" in Swahili. Mubarikiwa roamed freely outside my tent but never left the camp, and soon people came from around the camp and the town, curious about the beautiful wild bird that I had adopted as my pet. Among the visitors curious about the young refugee and his pet bird were rebels.

✦

BEFORE HE BECAME one of the most feared rebel leaders in North Kivu, the commander had been a schoolteacher. When I heard that, I couldn't help liking him, even though I was scared of the beret-wearing fighters who followed him, blocking the roads, demanding taxes and allegiance from villagers, driving their trucks through towns like a conquering army. The commander was from North Kivu, and his group, which had grown out of the genocide and the second war against Kabila's government, with the stated purpose of defending Congolese Tutsis, was a menacing presence on the hills beside the camp. Until they freed me from jail, I had never felt protected by the rebels.

Of course, when I heard that members of his group wanted to visit the boy with the pet peacock, I couldn't say no. "Mondiant, they want to come this afternoon," a chief from a nearby village informed me, standing in front of my tent, flustered as though he were delivering a message from a king.

"Why?" I asked. I had only heard stories about this man, whose fighters I tried so hard to avoid whenever I left my tent. I felt childish that I had shown off my new companion. I didn't know that Mubarikiwa would attract so much attention.

"I don't know," the chief replied. "They just wanted me to ask when you would be home."

I was still going to school full-time, one of the few refugees remaining, even though my friends were no longer talking to me. "They can come after school," I told the chief.

He nodded and got up to leave. "I'll tell them," he said. "This is an honor for you, Mondiant."

That night, I was too scared to sleep in my tent. I thought about running away, imagining the route I would take from Kitchanga to the border, the lies I would have to tell in order to get through the checkpoints that blocked the roads. Would the border still be open when I got there? How would I get from the border to Gihembe? I left Mubarikiwa and went into the forest, where I found a small flat patch of ground hidden by trees. I lay down, thinking about the rebels, and hours later, I fell asleep.

The next morning in school, I was so scared I couldn't speak. "Mondiant, is everything all right?" my teacher asked. "Are you feeling sick?" I shook my head. After the last bell, I left immediately, walking back to my tent as quickly as possible.

At my tent, I started cleaning. I swept, organized my school materials, and shook dirt off my school uniform. I wiped dust off Mubarikiwa's feathers. I put my school uniform back on—by far my most formal set of clothing—and washed the dirt off my face and hands. Then I put out some chairs and a pitcher of water.

This is my fate, I thought. *If the rebels want to kill me, that's fine. If they want to take me, that's fine, too. I accept it.* At that point in my life, I felt that I had done nothing wrong. If I died, I wouldn't have anything to answer for. I comforted myself with those thoughts as I waited.

I had just started grinding wheat with water for Mubarikiwa's lunch when I heard footsteps on the banana leaves behind my tent. Unlike those of refugees, who walk lightly in bare feet or plastic sandals, these footsteps were so loud that, at first, I thought it was a buffalo or rhinoceros coming out of the forest to attack me. We lived close to Virunga National Park, and sometimes the animals crossed our roads.

Curious, I walked around to the back of my tent. A man in a rebel uniform was walking toward me. He had a machine gun slung over his shoulder and wore military boots that thumped the ground with every step. A moment later, a group of soldiers surrounded my tent. Each one carried an AK-47 or an RPG.

"Don't be afraid," one of the soldiers said. He swung his rifle casually by his side and spoke to me like we were friends. "How are you doing, son?" he asked. "We heard you have a beautiful pet. Can we see it?"

I nodded. "He eats out of my hand," I said, leading them to the front of the tent, where Mubarikiwa was pecking at some ground wheat. I didn't know why I felt the urge to show off. "Mubarikiwa," I called, "come here."

"Wait," the rebel said. "We need to call our commander and let him know it's time to come." He told me his name. "Have you heard of him?" he asked. I shook my head. "That's okay," the rebel said. "He wants to meet you."

The rebel spoke into his radio again, and a few minutes later the commander arrived. He wore the same beret and military-green uniform, and, like the other rebels, he was young and skinny. When the wind blew, his baggy uniform puffed out around him. But when he spoke, the other rebels were quiet. He carried his gun as though at any moment he might need to use it.

The commander smiled at me. "Mondiant, how are you?" he said, introducing himself.

"I'm doing well," I stammered. "Good to meet you."

"Do you know why I am here today?" he asked. I shook my head.

"I wanted to see your home." He gestured to the forest and valleys that lay before the hillside refugee camp. "You have a beautiful view. And I heard you have a bird that is just as beautiful."

"You are welcome in my home," I said. What else could I say?

The commander sat down and started asking me questions. "How many people stay here?" he asked. "Where is your brother? The village chief told me that you live alone."

"I don't," I said. "I live here with my bird."

The commander laughed. "Where is your family?" he asked.

"They are in Gihembe refugee camp in Rwanda," I told him. I explained how I had arrived in Congo. "I came with my father and my brother. I was so excited to see my home," I said. "But it's impossible." I didn't want him to know that my father was in jail or might have been executed already. "He went back to Rwanda with my brother," I lied.

The commander shook his head sadly. "It's unacceptable that Tutsis should be kicked out of our home," he told me. "I want your whole family to come back to Congo, where you belong."

While he talked, I stared at his weapons. The only other times I had seen guns like that up close was when they were being fired at other refugees. "Are you scared, Mondiant?" he asked. I shook my head, but I couldn't speak. I told myself that he was being kind.

"When you saw us coming just now," he continued, "what did you think?" I didn't answer.

"Maybe you thought we were going to hug you!" he joked. His rebels laughed. The commander was always joking, even on the battlefield. When he laughed, so did his fighters.

"The village chief said you wanted to see my bird," I said. "That's what I thought."

"We want to help you," the commander said, leaning forward in his chair. "We want you to be able to go back to your village one day."

"My whole family is waiting for that," I said.

"And if you ever need food, for you or for Mubarikiwa," he continued, "you can come to us. Will you?"

I nodded. "I will."

He smiled. "Good boy," he said. He turned to Mubarikiwa. "Now tell me about this peacock. How did you get him to come home with you?"

I told him the story of the hunt, and of my former friends. I told him how the screams of the bird reminded me of the screams in Mudende. "If the bird could speak," I said, "I think it would have asked me to save its life." I whistled and Mubarikiwa came to me, opening his mouth for the wheat paste I kept in my pocket.

By now, refugees and villagers had gathered in a group around my tent, watching our meeting. The commander reached into his pocket and produced a handful of bills. "Go buy some banana juice and some beer," he said, giving the money to an eager boy in the crowd. Soon, the gathering around my tent became a party. The commander drank beer and made jokes, feeding wheat to Mubarikiwa, who spread his bright feathers in appreciation.

I was happy. That day, people from all tribes, Hutus and Tutsis alike, shared food from the same clay pots, talking to one another as though there were no war. An unfamiliar joyful feeling spread through the camp. People started dancing, and the commander, lively with beer, gave a speech. "We have different cultures," he said. "Not all of us have money. We speak different languages, and we have different jobs. But we are all Congolese." His voice was raised above the crowd, who stopped dancing and talking to listen. "Let's be united," he continued. "Let's fight against the enemies of Congo who want to divide us. It's time for us to love one another and to rebuild our country." I remember that the villagers, and not just the refugees, clapped. I clapped as well. Although I was not drinking, I felt drunk.

The commander turned to me. "Today I heard Mondiant's story," he said. "I heard about how he took this peacock from friends who wanted to eat it. Mondiant was angry. He didn't want this beautiful bird to die. Because of his humanity and his forgiveness, he rescued the bird, and now look at them. They are a family."

Twenty-Three

The rebel group was full of refugees like me, people who had returned to Congo from Rwanda or Uganda and others who had been displaced a day's walk or drive from their home villages. We told ourselves that the rebels were fighting for more than land and power; they were fighting for the very survival of Tutsis in our country. Being a refugee can be radicalizing. We had so little to lose.

The Friday after the commander came to my tent, I visited the rebel base for the first time. My neighbors wished me good luck. No one in the refugee camp cared that I was leaving to see the rebels; almost everyone had a son or an uncle who had become a fighter or knew someone who had died. I left Mubarikiwa in front of my tent and asked Mama Gasana to watch him while I was gone. "If you see Gasana," she said, "tell him to please come visit me."

To get to the rebel base, I had to pass through checkpoints manned by armed fighters who looked like they would use any excuse to kill anyone. I had spent my years in Kitchanga trying to avoid the checkpoints, and now I was voluntarily walking up to one. The rebels stared at me as I approached.

"Do you have any weapons?" they asked me. I shook my head. I carried nothing. My shorts didn't even have pockets.

"Who are you?" they asked, suspicious. "Why are you trying to get to the base?"

"A commander told me to come," I said. "He visited me the other day. I have a bird. . . ." My voice trailed off, as I realized how ridiculous it sounded.

A rebel who had been listening to our conversation walked over. "This is the boy they are expecting," he said. "You're Mondiant, right? With the peacock?" I nodded. "Go ahead," he said. "The commander is waiting for you." They waved me through.

The green army tents and wooden buildings of the rebel camp were surrounded by a trench that, I would soon realize, had been dug mostly by new recruits. They stored supplies like food and water in tents and kept their weapons in a sturdy brick building in the middle of the camp. Someone was usually tasked with guarding that building, which was often the target of theft by other rebel groups.

The rebels prepared their meals over a fire in the open air, protected from the rain by a tin roof. When they cooked, the smell filled the camp. They had beans and corn like we did, as well as other staples they had stolen from villagers or refugees or taken as a kind of tax. "The Congolese government treats you like servants," they would tell us. "We are protecting you. You should help us, too." Sometimes they butchered chickens or cows, which they roasted over the fire, letting the smell roll across through the camp, down the mountainside, and into the village.

Unlike the government soldiers, the rebels lived alone on their base. They thought that separation from their wives and children made them stronger. "We don't have to worry about anyone else," they reasoned. "We can focus on fighting." When Congolese government soldiers went to the base, they were going there to do a job. To a government soldier, his gun was like the farmer's shovel, a tool to do a task. For the rebels, who had left their families behind, fighting wasn't a job, it was their whole life.

I met the commander outside his tent, where he was playing a game. He stared at me as I approached. "Mondiant, you came." He turned to his companion. "This is the boy with the peacock," he said. They offered me some chicken, an astonishing treat. "It's good, isn't it?" The commander watched me eat. Before I left, they gave me some grain to take back for Mubarikiwa.

Back at the refugee camp that evening, I wondered if my image of the rebels had been wrong all along. Maybe they were good, I thought, and maybe they believed in their mission. I had felt at home at their base. The men who gave me chicken were Tutsi, and so was the commander.

I didn't want to care about a person's ethnicity. I was proud to have friends who were Hunde or Bashi, and even Hutu. Until I visited the rebel base, I didn't realize how much the violence had shaped my view of being a Tutsi, and how good it would feel to be surrounded again by people like me.

◆

THE FOLLOWING MONDAY, I started going to the school that was closer to the rebel base. I didn't like it as much as my old school, but I didn't care about studying like I once had. I was almost twelve and felt at once years older and years younger; most of the day, I was distracted by thoughts of my family. I wondered what my mother and siblings in Gihembe were doing, whether they had enough food and whether Asifwe and John would be able to go to school. I thought about my father in jail. Was it possible that he was still alive? After nearly two years in Congo, I longed to see anyone familiar.

At first, I visited the rebel base because I was lonely and hungry. The rebels asked about my bird and would often give me some food to take home to Mubarikiwa. "Keep that bird happy," they would say. "He will bring you luck."

To thank them, I started bringing them a can full of water whenever I visited, detouring to the river and lugging the heavy can past the checkpoints and up the hill. I was proud that I could bring them something they needed before they had to ask for it, and I wanted to be valuable doing other things so that they wouldn't ask me to fight.

Soon, visiting the rebel base became part of my daily routine. In the morning before school, new recruits like me fetched water or carried food from the farms to the base. Sometimes they asked for things while I was at school. "Mondiant, we are hungry," they would say, materializing in the classroom doorway. "Bring us food." One day they started asking us to wash their clothes or boil some water in the kitchen. Eventually they asked me to cook. "You can eat with us if you make the food," they said. I started staying at the rebel base for dinner—the rebels ate rice, potatoes, fruit, sometimes meat—and soon I began sleeping there as well.

Weekends at the base were devoted to learning. Boys my age watched while the rebels cleaned and loaded their rifles, polishing the guns as though they were religious objects. Many children my age fought alongside the older rebels, but I was skinny and malnourished. When I tried to shoot a rifle, the force sent me flying to the ground, and I couldn't help grimacing in pain. The rebels mocked me but made it clear they expected me to improve. "Mondiant, you need to get stronger," they teased me. "We need you to fight."

"Give me another year," I promised. "I'll be stronger." As long as I continued to help them in other ways, they accepted the compromise.

Some of the rebels became my friends. I laughed at their jokes. One of them, a man in his forties named Cyusa, whom the rebels called Kilo Bravo, was a deserter from the Congolese army. He hated the government soldiers the most. "They are weak," he would say. "Spineless and scared." If Cyusa thought anyone was being cowardly, he teased them mercilessly. "Mondiant ran away today," he would say, his shoulders shaking with laughter. "Was it your first time hearing bullets?"

Cyusa carried a handkerchief everywhere he went, tucked into a uniform pocket, which he used to bless his weapons before a fight. "I will send you, my child, to kill ten people," he would say, touching the handkerchief to his rifle or machete. "I send you to kill twenty people." We laughed at his ritual, but Cyusa never missed his target.

I went through a transformation, becoming stronger because of the work they made me do and the food they gave me, and I was in awe of the rebels. The commander became my mentor, letting me sleep in his tent when I stayed in the camp and telling me stories about my own future. "One day, after we've won, you can get your family back from Rwanda," he said. My situation and the situation of all the displaced Congolese made him angry. "No Congolese person should have to live like an exile," he said, shaking his head. "No proud Bagogwe person should have to be like a homeless person."

As I grew stronger, they started asking for more. They asked me to help patrol at night, carrying a gun and walking on the dangerous side of the trench, looking for intruders. One day they asked me to clean the camp, and the next they asked me to clean the battlefield. Soon, I was acting like an assistant during battles, delivering food, loading guns, and helping to plunder villages for clothes and supplies. They issued me an ID, a piece of paper with the name of my battalion and commander. Instead of printing my real name, they wrote the nickname given to most child soldiers, the same slang term often used to call over a servant or a waiter. From that point on I was known only as "Kadogo," or "little soldier."

One day I was in school when the rebels showed up in our doorway. Instead of asking me to leave, they addressed all of us. "Students," they said, "today we fought with the enemy, but the enemy was stronger, they killed many of our people." They indicated for us to stand up. "It is time for you to come with us. Give us your hands to help bring the bodies to be buried." Teachers and students followed them out of the school, working late into the evening carrying what seemed like hundreds of rebel bodies back to the base.

After that, moving the dead rebels for burial became my main job. When a fight ended, while the grass was still wet with blood, I was ordered to the field, where I would help load the bodies onto a truck. It was hard at first. I thought about Patrick and Célestin. I thought about my father.

But soon it became easy. My muscles grew stronger, and I became more tolerant of the smell of blood and rotting flesh. I stopped thinking about my friends and I barely thought about my father. I began to look like a rebel, tattered but confident, walking through villages without fear. It no longer bothered me that people ran away when they saw me. It made me feel powerful. Even animals ran away when they saw me coming, even animals that were much bigger than me, even the dangerous animals from my grandmother's stories.

◆

SOMETIMES MY DREAMS AT NIGHT were so vivid that I woke up thinking that I had lived them. I heard sounds and voices that didn't exist. I heard the frantic beat of drums that refugees used to signal an attack, only to find that the sound was in my head, and I clutched my head, begging it to leave me alone.

To calm myself before I slept, I would sit on a wooden chair outside the tent, counting the stars. I sat and counted and counted and counted until I lost my place, and then I started counting again. It was the only way I could avoid thinking about what I had done all day. If I had dragged bodies from the battlefield, I counted stars. If I couldn't stop thinking about my family in Gihembe, I counted stars. If I imagined myself back in the Congolese jail, I counted stars, sometimes until the rose-pink light of dawn.

My old life was quickly retreating and my life as a soldier came into focus. Soon I was spending almost every night in the rebel camp, eating dinner with other rebels and sharing a tent with boys my age. I still went to school, but instead of returning to the refugee camp in the afternoon, I walked up the mountain. The commander treated me like a son. He teased me and taught me things. He was the only adult in my life helping me think about the future. Now, though, I can see that he saw only one future for me, and that was dying young for his cause.

If, after a big battle, there were a lot of bodies that needed to be moved, he would say, "Kadogo, don't go to school, you need to stay and help your friends clean this up." Some days he made me skip school to cook food or collect water. I did what he said, but every day that I missed school felt like a wasted day. I still thought of education as the only thing that could help me. If the commander had truly been my mentor, he would have understood that.

Still, when I did go to school, at least I went on a full stomach. I was no longer barefoot. I wore heavy military boots and, on cold days, a jacket the commander gave me. Many days I carried a knife or a pistol, and I no longer planned my walks to avoid encountering other fighters.

The other students, even those who had been my friends, began to fear me. They whispered when I passed them on the street and refused to sit next to me in class. They would ask each other questions loud enough that I could hear—"Where did Mondiant get those boots?" or "Why did Mondiant miss school yesterday?"—but were too frightened to ask me themselves. Even the teachers seemed to recoil when I came near.

One day when I was standing in front of the class, a bullet fell out of a hole in my coat pocket, hitting the floor with a loud crack. Recognizing it immediately, the students ran out of the classroom, leaving me alone. Calmly, I picked up the bullet and carried it back to the base. "Did you see, he's carrying weapons," the students whispered as I walked by. "He brought a gun into school."

After that, the only classmates who would talk to me were a few curious boys who looked at the rebels like they were actors in a movie and wanted to interrogate me about what life was like on the base. "Do they have a lot of guns?" they asked. "What do the rebels talk about?"

I told them very little. I didn't want the rebels to accuse me of spying. "I don't think they have too many guns." I shrugged. "I never talk to them," I lied. Although I was embarrassed that my classmates thought I was a killer, I was also too embarrassed to tell them that I hadn't killed anyone yet. Disappointed, they abandoned me as well.

One day I was sitting in front of the commander's tent singing a well-known Congolese song, usually sung on Christmas. "I miss you, my family, I miss you," I sang. "I miss everyone."

A boy just a little bit older than me heard me singing and approached me. "My name is Mihigo," he said. "I think I recognize that song, could you teach me how to sing it?"

"Sure," I said, but after a moment, he laughed. "Actually, I think I know the words after all," he said, and started singing. "I must have heard it a lot when I was a child."

Mihigo became my first friend on the base. Most of our time was spent working together, clearing fields of bodies or getting water from the river. When we weren't working, we walked far away from the camp to the banks of the river and talked. He was the only person on the base who knew anything about my past. "How did you join the rebels?" Mihigo asked me.

I told him the story of being jailed by Congolese soldiers. "The rebels rescued us," I said. "Their base seemed like the safest place to be."

Mihigo was usually very quiet. He was so skinny he had to tie a rope around the waist of his uniform to hold it up. Before he joined the rebels, his life had been good, what my mother might have described as normal. His father, a refugee like mine, owned some cows, and their small fortune meant they could all leave the refugee camp and move to a small village, where my friend had attended high school. "That sounds like my father," I said. "He worked as a veterinarian on farms to make money so we could live in a real house."

Mihigo had lived with his parents and siblings in a nice house, where they pledged to forget their lives in their old village and make a future where they were. One day, while my friend was at school, the village was attacked by government soldiers. "I came home, and our house was on fire," he told me. "The cows were gone. My parents were dead."

Suddenly, Mihigo was an orphan. He was alone and scared. He grew bitter and, as the days went by, angry. "I was the only survivor," he said.

"I thought, I'll join the rebels to pay the government back for what they did to my family."

We became close, but there were limits to what we would tell each other. When intruders were caught in the camp, their executions by knife were quick and brutal and took place in the open as a lesson to anyone watching. Boys like me, who were not yet considered strong enough or tough enough to fight, were made to watch. They wanted us to learn how to kill our enemy, and to think that it was normal. And they wanted us to see what would happen to us if we became spies or tried to run away. I told Mihigo a lot about my life, but I never told him that I wanted to escape, or that I hoped I would never have to fight.

One day we were walking through camp when we heard a commotion. "What's happening?" I asked a man standing nearby.

"There was a thief," he said. "Let's go see."

We followed the shouts to a clearing in the middle of the tents. Approaching it, I could hear both the angry yelling of the rebels and the higher-pitched sobs of the thief. He looked like he was about my age, although he appeared stronger and taller.

"This young man was trying to steal weapons from us," a rebel explained. "We caught him last night. He was sent by our enemy." Which enemy, he didn't say.

Mihigo and I saw other young boys. "Watch," the rebel told us.

They brought the young man into the middle of the crowd. I remember that he spoke really amazing French. He was begging for forgiveness. "Je veux seulement vivre," he cried in his beautiful French. "Je ne le ferai plus, je vais te donner de l'argent." *Wow*, I thought, impressed. *He must have done really well in school.*

We knew that when they brought the long knife up to his neck, we had to watch, and that when they drew it over his neck, no matter how scared we were, we couldn't look away. If they saw that you were scared, they would make you kill the next intruder yourself.

I will tell you the truth: I wanted to be someone who wasn't afraid of killing someone else. I wanted to be like Cyusa—a hulking, confident man blessing his gun in the middle of a fight. I wanted to be like Mihigo, who had found purpose with the rebels, who had a righteous, personal mission against the government soldiers who had killed his family.

But I was afraid. I thought about one of the first battles I had seen with the rebels. Among our enemies were children my age and younger, hundreds of them, and women who were surely their mothers and aunts and sisters. We played our strategy, advancing on the enemy and then, when anyone in the front of our group was killed, replacing them immediately. It gave the impression that we were unstoppable and that we would never die. That day, it worked, and we won. Some of the bodies I cleaned off the battlefield that day were as light as Patrick's; some were bodies that had given birth to babies like Patience. I felt like throwing up.

I didn't think that the young man deserved to die for trying to steal from the rebels. I could have easily been him, sneaking into the base on the order of another rebel group. I knew what it was like to be starving and scared.

Like this boy, I was proud of how well I spoke French. I had studied so hard. Speaking beautiful French didn't matter in this world, though. He was still pleading in perfect French when they killed him. "Watch them," the rebels barked at us, and we turned our heads back to the scene. We would be punished for looking away. But when they drew the knife across his neck, I didn't care who saw me. I closed my eyes and bowed my head.

Twenty-Four

When Faustin and Thomas left Congo, they slipped out of the concrete house early, while it was still dark. Because they were Tutsi, it was particularly dangerous for them to be seen leaving town in the daytime, headed in the direction of the border.

Faustin and Thomas walked through the forest for more than twelve hours, hacking their way through trees and bushes so thick that "a day is a night," Faustin said. My brother later told me he thought about me the whole way. When he now talks about his return to Gihembe, he whispers: "I was so sad leaving Mondiant by himself. But we only had enough money for one person, and he was too young to get himself all the way from Congo to Gihembe." He worried that unless he arranged safe travel for me to Gihembe, I would end up at the rebel base. So many of his friends, like Gasana, had joined. *It's only a matter of time*, he thought to himself. Thinking that, he walked fast and bravely between the trees, as though daring whatever lurked in the forest to confront him.

On the other side of the border, Faustin and Thomas stopped in a small town. They were out of money. "How will we get to Gihembe?" Thomas asked my brother. Exhausted, they found some shade and went to sleep.

Thomas and Faustin lived on the street of that town for a week, delivering bags of food from the market for small tips that they kept hidden in their pockets as they slept. They became street children. When it rained, they sought out an awning or a shop umbrella to sit under until the owner shooed them away. Still, they thanked God for helping them cross safely into Rwanda, and they thanked God that no one was scared of them. Then they asked God to help them find a way back to Gihembe.

There was no way to let my mother know that Faustin was alive, or to get word to me in Kitchanga that he had successfully crossed the border. Thomas and Faustin carried bag after bag of groceries, and when they finally had enough money, they poured it all into the hands of a bus driver and boarded an early-morning bus headed north. My brother watched the Rwandan landscape pass by through the window. He hadn't been on a bus since we returned to Congo with our father. He couldn't believe how excited he was to return to a place he had been so desperate to leave.

At five in the evening, the bus pulled into a depot in a town near Gihembe, and Faustin and Thomas began walking up the hill toward the refugee camp. Little seemed to have changed. The sun still set on one side of the mountain, casting a shadow over the valley. Townspeople still watched him either without interest or with distaste, turning away when he came near. He still lost his breath walking up the hill and felt a familiar sinking in his chest when he walked through Gihembe's gate.

Approaching the camp, Faustin saw that other refugees were whispering about him and Thomas. He had forgotten how shabby they looked, their clothes torn and covered with dirt. Even compared with the boys their age in the camp, they were skinny. Faustin isn't like me; he's never cared what other people thought about him. He walked through the front entrance like a soldier returning home from war, looking for our mother.

When our siblings saw him approaching the tent, they screamed as though seeing a ghost. "Faustin!" Furaha was the first to reach him. "We thought we would never see you again."

"Where's Mama?" he asked, sitting down with them.

"She's getting water," Furaha said. "She'll be back soon." She gave him something to drink. "I can't believe you're back," she said. She didn't ask about me or our father.

News of Faustin's return spread quickly through the camp until it reached my mother. "You saw Faustin?" she asked her friend, who nodded happily, and my mother started running back to our tent, water swishing out of her pot. When she saw him, she immediately started asking questions. She felt in her heart that my father and I were dead.

"Our father tried to go back home, and he was captured," Faustin told our mother. "He wrote to us from jail."

"He's still alive?" my mother asked.

"We don't know," Faustin said.

"What about Mondiant?" my mother asked quietly.

"I left him in Congo," Faustin said. His voice shook. Would she be angry? "I didn't know how dangerous it would be to cross."

At first, my mother didn't believe him. "You can tell me that he died," she said. "It's okay, it's not your fault. You can tell me."

My mother had reason to assume that I was dead. News of other boys who had been recruited and killed fighting with the rebels trickled into the refugee camp, delivered by family members or friends or, sometimes, over the radio. Refugees, with nowhere to go and no way to track down their family, could do nothing but wait. Their families were destroyed. But at least they could start mourning, and stop wondering.

"Mondiant will be fine," Faustin reassured my mother. "He's not with the rebels. He was alive when I left," Faustin said. "I promise. He has people to protect him. He's going to school."

My mother didn't cry. She didn't pretend to be tired. She sat up straighter and took her eldest son's hand, looking him in the eyes. "Faustin," she said, "we have to bring Mondiant back here."

They made a plan, talking through dinner and until it was time to go to sleep. They talked about making our family whole again. Faustin ate all the corn my mother had, and changed into clean clothes, and sat by the fire. He didn't remember Gihembe being this comfortable.

After a few hours, he started yawning. "Good night, my son," my mother said, going outside to sit with friends. Alone, my brother lay down on his mat, his stomach full for the first time since he'd left Rwanda. He listened to the sounds of our siblings sleeping near him and of our mother, sitting in front of our home, talking softly to a neighbor.

Faustin knew he didn't have a future in the refugee camp. Rwanda hadn't granted citizenship to any Congolese refugees, and without it, he couldn't easily work or go to school. It would be a miracle for him to buy a home or raise a family outside Gihembe. He couldn't leave the refugee camp for Kigali, taking advantage of Rwanda's race toward development. Food and clothing, even medicine, would always seem like expensive luxuries. He would probably never get on an airplane. My brother lay there, exhausted. He fell asleep listening to my mother do her nighttime chores, trying to remind himself that he was happy to be home.

◆

MY OWN LONG ESCAPE from Congo began on a Friday after school. I was walking back to the refugee camp with my friend Janvier, carrying a book in my left hand and a book in my right hand, when I saw the figure of a man waiting in front of my tent. I slowed down. The only men who visited me in the refugee camp were rebels, and I had hoped to spend that night away from the base.

The man wore a black coat and boots and carried a walking stick. Unlike a rebel, who always put his strength and power on display, he sat with a slouch as though he was tired.

"Mondiant." He stood up when he saw me. "How are you?"

His voice was familiar and kind. "Alphonse," I said, relieved and amazed. Alphonse was a close friend of my parents. In Gihembe they had often talked together late into the night. He must have been in Kitchanga, a refugee like me. "I am fine." I put down my books and sat down politely, as I had been taught to do around grown-ups.

"Are you doing well at school?" he asked.

"I'm not doing very well right now," I admitted. "This term I was third out of forty-six students."

"That's not too bad." Alphonse smiled. He patted my shoulder affectionately.

"I like being first," I said.

He laughed. "Is that right?" he said. "What happened, then?"

"I don't have enough food," I explained. "It's hard to study." I didn't tell him that the rebels made me skip school to work for them, or that I had been living at their base. "I didn't know that you were in Kitchanga," I said.

"I came from Gihembe," he said. "I have some good news for you. Let's go into your tent so I can tell you." He looked around before he stepped in. I felt ashamed thinking that he was looking for signs of rebels.

In the warmth of my tent, Alphonse told me his story. He had traveled from Gihembe to Kitchanga to rescue his wife and son, who had come on their own years before, hoping to get his son, who had been badly injured during the Mudende massacres, better medical care. But life in Kitchanga was even harder than in Gihembe, and his son had not been able to see a doctor. "Mondiant, do you miss your family?" Alphonse asked.

"I do," I admitted. "I am really lonely." I had begun to long for Gihembe. Even the tiny school in the refugee camp seemed like paradise. I dreamed about playing with my friends in the camp, kicking a soccer ball or throwing marbles. We were refugees, but we had been safe and, at times, happy. I even fantasized about looking for firewood, as though it was a grand adventure that awaited me and not a risky, exhausting chore.

I thought about waking up on Saturdays and putting on my spare shirt to go to church with my mother. We had prayed often for the chance to go home to Congo. "Please, God, bring us back to that lost paradise," we would say, while older people sang about the green fields and beautiful homes they had grown up in, their families and neighbors, the livestock and land and money they had left. "Please, God, we don't want to be refugees anymore," we would say. So much had changed since I left. Now when I prayed, I asked God to bring me back to the refugee camp.

"Your mother and your brother Faustin heard that I was coming here," Alphonse said. "They gave me money to bring you with me. Do you want to come?"

"Yes," I said, immediately. "Please, let me come with you."

Alphonse smiled and patted my shoulder again. "Be ready to go at four in the morning," he said. "I'll come find you."

I couldn't sleep that night. My mind was a thunderstorm of worries. I worried about my friends who were still with the rebels. I worried for Mama Gasana, whom I would be leaving alone in the Kitchanga refugee camp. I was certain that when the rebels realized I hadn't come to the base they would come looking for me. If they didn't find me that night, they would surely track me down the next morning and kill me for trying to desert them. They might kill Alphonse and his family, too, for helping me, or Mama Gasana for lying to them about where I was. I wouldn't be able to tell her I was leaving, I realized. It would be better if she thought I was dead.

Not even the commander, who had let me sleep in his tent and shared his chicken and rice, would have mercy on me if he found out I was trying to leave. He might be the angriest of all. Although I was old enough to know that his offer of friendship was a trick to get me to join him, I still felt a pang of guilt. He trusted me so much and I was breaking that trust.

I worried about the journey. It had been a miracle that I survived fleeing Congo the first time. I didn't expect that God would help me again. The only ID I had was the one issued to me by the rebel group. Would I need to show anyone that, and would they arrest me for showing it? And what if taking me put Alphonse and his family at risk as well?

When I let myself imagine getting back to Gihembe alive, I worried about that too. Would my mother be angry at me for staying away so long? Would my family accept that I had been with the rebels? I sat up with a jolt and suddenly panicked. My school records! They were in Kitchanga. Would I be able to return to the Gihembe school without them?

The wind churned outside my tent. In the forest, palm fronds clapped against one another. I lay there clutching my blanket, watching the sides of my tent breathe in and out with the wind, wondering if each crack or thump I heard was the sound of boots walking over the fallen leaves toward my tent. Long past midnight, I closed my eyes and started counting.

Twenty-Five

It was raining and dark the morning Alphonse and his family arrived to collect me, and I shivered in my tent while we got ready. "Here," Alphonse whispered to me. "Put these on." He held out a yellow wrap skirt and a kitenge. "If they think you are a girl, they will be less likely to stop you."

I put on the skirt and wrapped the kitenge around my head. Once on, the delicate, feminine fabric felt like it had transformed into armor. It wasn't the first time I had disguised myself as a girl in Kitchanga; the rebels often had us dress up when we went to spy for them. I was skinny and young, with a smooth, hairless face and a timid voice. I easily got away with it.

I packed the few things I had into a thin plastic bag, which I looped around my wrist. I left my boots and rebel uniform folded in the corner and tucked my rebel ID into the pile. I never wanted to see it or the nickname Kadogo again.

Alphonse's son was so badly injured that, at first, I found it hard to look at him. His face was snarled with scars and he moved his body clumsily, as though still trying to remember how it worked. Alphonse's son didn't have to wear a skirt. His wounds were so hideous they protected him from suspicious glances. Alphonse's wife was tiny. She smoked cigarettes constantly and spoke very little, but she was kind. Without her we might have drawn more suspicion.

On a dry day and in the daylight, it takes about twenty minutes to walk from the refugee camp to the town, where we hoped to buy seats on trucks heading to the border. We left before sunrise, when the ground was so wet and slippery that rather than walking from the camp to the town, we tripped and slid like newborn calves, our knees buckling with every cautious step.

Slowly, the four of us zigzagged through the forest, hoping to avoid rebels who might be patrolling the area. We crossed swamps, which churned with rainwater, jumping timidly across stones and fallen branches, trying not to land in the frigid water. It was too dangerous to use a flashlight, so we walked in the black darkness, grateful for an occasional flash of lightning and then continuing blind once the lightning stopped.

In the middle of Kitchanga, we cautiously approached a truck that was loading its bed with heaps of supplies to be taken to the border and then on to Goma—sacks of corn and rice, stalks of bamboo and hard bags of coal, even goats and chickens. Alphonse handed the driver some money and then we climbed into the back, perched dangerously on the mountain of food and animals.

Six other people joined us, all heading for Goma. We didn't tell them we were going to the border with the intention of crossing. We tried not to talk at all, not wanting them to know we were Tutsis, grateful for the distracting, relentless rain. When the truck started moving on the bumpy roads, we clung to the slippery railing, trying not to fall out the sides. Only then did I notice that blood was running down my right foot, and when I looked closely, I saw that I was missing a toenail.

The truck was old and moved slowly, weighed down with its goods. Every thirty minutes it broke down and the ten of us climbed out of the back to help get it started again. Alphonse tried to disguise his fear with impatience, but he was more anxious than I had ever seen him. Normally, my parents' friend was jovial, full of jokes. Now he sat rigid atop a sack of rice, his hands clenched tightly. It was his responsibility to get us back safely to Gihembe. He carried the money, and if we met government soldiers who required bribing, he would have to talk to them and pay them. Alphonse was the one who would have to negotiate with rebels who stopped us or explain to the other passengers why we were getting off at the border without revealing to them who we were. Although it was raining, he wore sunglasses to hide his eyes.

The first checkpoint belonged to a Hutu rebel group. The truck stopped, and fighters circled us, asking questions, trying to catch us in a lie.

"You are dressed like a girl, but your eyes look like a boy's," one of the rebels said to me. "Get out, come stand next to me."

Before I could move, Alphonse pulled bills out of his pocket and spoke to them in Lingala. "Fine, go," the rebel said, taking some of the money from Alphonse.

At the second checkpoint, the driver offered the Hutu rebels money before they had a chance to scrutinize us. The bribes working, I started to think we might make it to the border without being caught. I was optimistic enough that I leaned my head against a sack of rice and let the road rock me to sleep.

Two hours after leaving Kitchanga, we came to a government checkpoint. I remember there were guns everywhere, and the blue-and-yellow Congolese flag waved from the tops of the military equipment.

A soldier spoke to the driver in Lingala. He carried a gun with a bayonet on the end and, like all of the soldiers, he screamed when he addressed us. I remember thinking they were roaring like lions. "Who is inside?" He walked around to the back of the truck.

By now, the rain had stopped. We sat on sacks of rice, our clothes soaked and sticking to our bodies, our faces wet and visible. We clung to the truck railings until our knuckles turned white. Alphonse took off his sunglasses and sat up straighter, squaring his shoulders and staring at the soldiers, trying—failing, I thought—to appear unafraid.

The soldier looked directly at Alphonse. "Are you Tutsi?" he asked. "Show me your identification card."

Alphonse passed over his Congolese ID to the soldier, who held it up in front of his face, squinting as though trying to decipher a code. "Where did you get this?" he asked Alphonse.

"The Congolese government," Alphonse said. "It's the same ID as everyone else has."

The soldier looked at him angrily. "You are not Congolese, though," he said, as though he were talking to a child. "No Congolese person has such a long nose or a long face."

"We are Tutsi," Alphonse said. "We are Bagogwe, from North Kivu, and this is my family." He gestured to me, his son, and his wife, all still sitting stiffly in the truck.

"Get out," the soldier said, and we climbed out of the truck. "Stand there." He pointed at the side of the road, a few paces away. Then he gestured to the driver. "Leave," he said. We watched as the truck sputtered down the road away from us.

"Bagogwe Tutsis caused trouble in Congo," the soldier said to Alphonse.

"We didn't," Alphonse said. "We are like everyone else. We love our country."

"Then why are you trying to leave?" the soldier asked.

"We are not," Alphonse said. "We are going to Goma."

"Don't lie," the soldier said. "We know you are going to Rwanda. That's where you're really from." He turned to look at the rest of us. "Is this your son?" he asked, disgusted. "What happened to him?"

"He was hit with machetes in Mudende," Alphonse replied.

"Why didn't he die?" The officer laughed. "I am so sad to see him alive. Look at him." He grimaced. "Where are you going?" he asked again. "Don't lie to me."

Alphonse looked him in the face. "We are going to visit my brother in Goma," he said. "In a few days you'll see us on this road again. I swear."

But the soldier didn't believe us. Before he and his colleagues started beating us, they insulted us some more. We stood there listening and waiting for what came next. "You are liars," he said. "You pretend to be nice people, you pretend to be smart people, but you are not. You are snakes. There is no room for you in Congo." Then he picked up a long iron-tipped pole used by hikers and mountain climbers and raised it above his head.

Just before I passed out, I saw them take money from Alphonse's wife. They stuffed it into their pockets and drove away in their military vehicle. The next thing I knew, I was waking up in a stranger's house.

◆

MY MEMORY IS FRACTURED, but when I think about everything that happened to me and my family, one thing I know for sure is that when we needed help, we somehow found it. There are good people all over Congo, from all of the country's hundreds of communities, who would help each other if they had the chance.

After the soldiers left us for dead on the side of the road, throwing stones at Alphonse's body as they walked away, a pastor and his wife passed by in their truck. They were Bashi and, like most Bashi people we knew, they didn't care that we were Tutsi, or that touching our bodies and helping us might put them at risk if any government soldiers saw. They took us home and let us rest in their own room.

Alphonse was sitting at the end of the bed when I woke up. "Do you know how we got here?" he asked, when he saw that I was awake.

"No," I said. "What happened?" Alphonse's face was swollen and discolored. I thought I must look equally frightening.

"Our brother saved us," he said, gesturing to the pastor, who had appeared in the doorway. "He brought us here, to his home."

The pastor was young and energetic, buoyant and hopeful in spite of what he saw happen in his homeland every day. He smiled at me as I lifted myself out of bed. He was wearing clean shorts and Nike sneakers, and had a neatly trimmed beard.

"How are you feeling?" his wife, a doctor with Médecins Sans Frontières, asked us.

"I'm fine," I said, although my ribs ached as though someone were stabbing my side. "Don't worry."

Their house was huge, with separate rooms for sleeping and an outside bathroom and shower. I thought that they must have some money. They had two young children, who, although they were polite to us, ran away if we tried to hold them or play with them. They were scared of our injuries, and who could blame them?

That afternoon they brought us medicine. The pastor's wife showed us how to apply a salve to our wounds to help them heal and then wrap them in gauze. She measured out pills for the pain. We ate together—mashed ugali and fish. It was only the second time since leaving Bikenke that I had been fed homemade Congolese food. It was so delicious, and eating it so comforting, that I almost allowed myself to cry.

While we ate, the pastor and his wife talked. "I had a friend when I was young," the pastor explained. "He was a Tutsi. He gave me cows, he helped me so much." During the first wave of violence in the early 1990s, the pastor said, this friend's family was attacked. Many of them died. His friend was lucky. "He left and became a refugee, first in Rwanda and now in Europe," he told us. "But he lost so much. And I lost him."

"We hate what is happening in our country," his wife told us. As a doctor with MSF, she had spent a lot of time treating people wounded in massacres. She is the only person I've seen who, meeting Alphonse's son for the first time, didn't gasp or look away. When she talked to him, she looked him in the eyes, and when he stumbled down the hallway, she held his arm to help him walk.

"Congo has become so violent," the pastor continued. "We blame the government, mostly. They encourage us to fight with one another. Instead of helping people survive, they steal for themselves."

"They cannot stand up to the rebels," Alphonse said. "The rebels are stronger than the government in North Kivu."

"That's very true," the pastor's wife said. "In my work, I see sick people and dying people," she said. She stopped eating and looked across the table at us sadly. "I'm used to it. By the time they see me, I am ready to help them. But when I see people like you, left to die outside, not even brought to the hospital . . ." She shook her head. "It's shameful to leave you there."

"We are thinking about leaving ourselves," the pastor said. "We love Congo. But we don't want to raise our kids in this violence." He looked at Alphonse. "We would become refugees if it meant saving our children," he said. "Like you."

We talked for hours after dinner. They asked about my time in Congo, and I told them about school and about my father leaving. I told them about Mubarikiwa. "She was so beautiful, and she ate out of my hand," I said, feeling like I was telling one of my grandmother's stories. I still felt guilty that I had left my beautiful bird at the refugee camp.

I trusted them so much that I told them about my time with the rebels. They listened and didn't judge me. In Congo, almost everyone knew a child soldier. Even in the nice neighborhood where the pastor and the doctor lived, there were probably child soldiers. "Mondiant, we wish you could live in the Congo your parents told you about," they said to me. "You all should rest. Tomorrow we will leave very early for the border."

The next morning, we climbed into the back of a white MSF van, where the pastor's wife covered us with plastic sheets and tried to camouflage us among the medical equipment. I lay with the cold metal of the van against my back and the sheet over my head, feeling the uneven road, and prayed for them. They were two of the best people I had ever met.

At the border, though, I stopped thinking about the pastor and his wife. I thought only about how we were going to cross. I thought it was impossible that the Congolese soldiers would let us leave. I still believe the Congolese government wanted us to die. They didn't want us to be able to tell the story of what was happening to our people.

As long as you had money to bribe them, though, crossing wasn't hard.

Alphonse had hidden small amounts of cash everywhere on his body, in his shoes, his pants cuff, even in his underwear. What the soldiers hadn't stolen from him after they beat us, he gave to the border guards.

Before we crossed, the pastor and his wife hugged us. The wife embraced Alphonse's son like he was her own, and the pastor wrote his phone number on a piece of paper, which he handed to Alphonse. "Call me when you get home," he said.

"I will," Alphonse said, but I don't think he was ever able to.

I wish I could meet them again. I would say thank you for saving us. I would tell them that I know we would have died on the side of the road if it hadn't been for them. If not for the pastor and his wife, I would never have seen my mother again. They risked their lives for four strangers. I would tell them thank you for saving our lives and thank you for reminding me that there are good people in Congo who would help you if they could.

PART THREE

Optimism ornaments our body's organs

We keep our heads up for a better life like others

Come on! Hurry on with standard stamina

Struggle straight until you tie your tie tight

Those we throw away are diamonds

Twenty-Six

The first time I crossed a border I was a little child in the arms of my aunt Florence, a young girl barely strong enough to carry me but someone who would save my life more than once.

The second time, I crossed with my father and Faustin. The bus bound for Congo was alive with gospel songs. I watched my country go by out the window, collecting details that would confirm that I was home.

On my third crossing, walking from Congo to Rwanda with Alphonse and his family, I felt defeated. The border seemed so petty. Why did this unremarkable stretch of dirt and sidewalk, lined with dull concrete buildings flying opposing flags, have so much control over my life? I couldn't accept it.

Belgian and German governments, not the Africans who were born there, had drawn the border long before, like children tasked with dividing their playroom. Europeans drew a line around mountains and volcanoes, beside riverbanks, through farms and villages, schools and markets, taking what they wanted. They sliced families in half and severed centuries-old tribal bonds. They carved out lands full of precious metals and minerals, plotting their excavation by the hands of enslaved Africans and then their profitable export to Europe. After they finished their dissection, the colonists gave themselves control.

Chieftaincies that had existed for generations were chopped up and divided. Colonists took our farmland, redefined our ethnicities, enslaved us, and began pitting neighbor against neighbor. Their border made no sense. Eventually, it made us all refugees in our own homes.

On one side of the border was Congo, where I was born. Congo was vast and varied, rich with resources. I would never think that any place in the world was as beautiful as Congo. But it had been destroyed by generations of violence. It spat me out twice. There was nothing left for me in Congo.

On the other side of the border was Rwanda, a tiny country that, despite its poverty and fresh wounds from genocide, had opened camps for the most traumatized, the weariest, the most fearful. Rwanda offered itself as a safe place, but that offer came with restrictions. No matter how long we lived in the country, no matter how well we spoke Kinyarwanda, no matter if we graduated from Rwandan schools or studied Rwandan history or even if we professed to love Rwanda more than any other place on earth, we would never be truly Rwandan. What the country offered most was pity. It was hard to build a future on pity.

"Do you feel safe now?" some Rwandan soldiers asked us after we crossed. They were kind. Once we explained who we were, they took us to a local restaurant for hot tea and food. "Not a lot of people cross the border the way you did," they said. "We didn't think any Tutsis were still alive in Congo." They asked curiously about our journey. "We are so happy there are people who will do things like that," they said when we told them the story of the pastor and his wife.

Their attention moved us almost to tears. When they asked us if we felt safe, we nodded our heads enthusiastically. "We love Rwanda," we told them. "Rwanda gave us shelter. We live in a refugee camp, but that is okay with us!" Thinking of the rebels and the Congolese soldiers, we meant what we said. We were saved by the ridiculous border.

Coming back to Rwanda this time, I felt like I was a different person. I had experienced loneliness and fear beyond anything I had before. I had bravely said goodbye to Faustin when he returned to Rwanda without me, and I had done my best to be a companion to Mama Gasana in her loneliness, which was even more profound than mine. I had gone to school and studied and now I spoke Swahili as well as my father. I had lost my father.

I had seen more death than I'd ever thought possible. Even though I was only twelve years old, I had carried so many bodies that it seemed to me as though the entire population of Congo could have died on the field in front of me. I learned to spy and keep secrets, even from my friends. I had seen people my age executed just for expressing their desire to leave the rebels. I had watched women be raped and then killed for resisting.

I was a rebel. I had been given a rebel ID and a rebel name and memories of fights that I was sure would give me nightmares for the rest of my life. In Congo, I thought that I would die any minute. I couldn't think about anything else. As soon as we crossed the border into Rwanda, I started to think about my family and my friends. I started to remember my childhood in the refugee camp, both the good and the bad.

While we waited for the Rwandan soldiers to help arrange transportation north for us, the relief subsided, and I began feeling desperately sad. My entire life I had considered Congo my home. When I returned to it, I thought I would shed the label of refugee and become Congolese again. I would become a cattle herder, a veterinarian's son, the teller of my grandmother's stories, as I had been meant to be. I would become someone with a house of my own, an education if I wanted it, and one day, a government ID or even a passport.

Instead, the Congo I had been told about—the Congo I remembered in fragments—was gone. When I was a baby, my family was friends with Hutu, Bashi, Hunde. It didn't matter. The Congo I returned to was only the Congo of war. Neighbors hated neighbors.

The world, I thought, waiting for our bus north, was full of terrible things. I had seen and done terrible things. How could a border keep any of them out?

✦

WE ARRIVED IN GIHEMBE later that afternoon. A lot had changed in the camp since I'd left. The school was now full of students. Most of the tents had been replaced by mud-and-wood structures of different sizes, the UNHCR tents stretched over the top as roofs or hung in doorways or spread over floors. Entrepreneurial refugees set up small stands where they sold candy and cooking oil. Many of those refugees' houses had the more expensive tin roofs.

Our home was now a slightly lopsided cluster of rooms made of mud and reeds collected from the river, with a tin door that swung a few inches above the ground and a UNHCR tent that stretched over the top of the entranceway. The remnants of a fire smoldered in a black circle in the outdoor kitchen. My family was sitting in front talking as I approached.

Faustin had spent every day since he returned trying to reassure our mother that I was still alive. But as the violence intensified in Congo, Gihembe had become a colony of grief. My mother listened to the hushed conversations about boys who had been killed by rebels or government soldiers and watched their mothers collapse. She heard the news on the radio about Congo and imagined her young son caught up in the fighting. She became hopeless. Boys my age, almost as a rule, did not return to Gihembe from Congo.

I can imagine the kind of reunion people will expect, reading this story. Although my mother loves me more than her own life, her tears had dried up long before my return from Congo. Years of war and the hardships of refugee camps can change people, and by the time I returned to Gihembe, her body rarely showed what her heart felt.

When she saw me, she was stunned. For a moment she sat motionless, staring at me, her son who she had accepted was dead in Congo. And when she recovered, she did the best thing she could do to welcome me home. "Are you hungry?" she asked, and she cooked whatever she could find for me to eat. She poured the last bits of shriveled corn and beans into a pot and pounded the last portion of ugali. She borrowed more beans from neighbors and bartered for some sweets from a vendor in Kageyo. She brought precious bottles of banana juice, which she watched me drink until they were empty.

She did this for months. On days when she had nothing to give, she encircled my body with her arms and sang to me. She told me stories like my grandmother had, trying to distract me from my hunger. "I wish I had more to give you," she said.

Because I had returned alive, I became a subject of fascination throughout the camp. "Mondiant, tell us about Congo," my friends would demand. "What does it look like?" They wanted to know if the stories their parents told them about home were true.

"Congo is beautiful," I told them. "It's huge and there are animals everywhere. You can eat fruit off the trees. It's not like here."

What I told them was true. But I felt an obligation to tell them the entire story. "It's very dangerous," I said. "There are people fighting everywhere. It's hard to care about how beautiful a place is when you're hiding in the forest to save your life."

I described the disappointment of living in a refugee camp when we had been promised to return to our villages. I told them about the rebel groups and the Congolese army, how violence choked the people living in North Kivu. "But in Congo, my family was rich," some Gihembe refugees would tell me. "We wouldn't have to live in those places."

"My parents also owned cows," I replied. "They weren't in the refugee camp. Look at how skinny I am. Does it look like I was feasting the whole time I was there?" I held out my thin arm. "I was almost starving." I gestured to my clothes, the same worn shorts and T-shirt that were the uniform of most boys my age. "Look at how I came back to Gihembe," I said. "Does it look like I came back with new shoes or new clothes?" It was exhausting, being the messenger for this failed place.

The hardest questions to answer had to do with the rebels themselves. I wasn't ready to tell other refugees about everything I had been through.

"I've heard that there are people in Congo who are fighting for Tutsis to be able to return," my friends would say. "Did you meet any of them?"

"Some," I replied.

"What are they like?" they asked.

I would shrug. "I don't know," I said. "I went to school. I tried not to talk to them." I knew my answers were disappointing; they were looking for a story of adventure and bravery, one that would make their lives in Gihembe seem connected to something more meaningful than just endless, inexplicable war. But I worried that if camp authorities found out I had been with the rebels, I might no longer be welcome in Gihembe. And I was sure that if anyone knew I had lived with the rebels, I would ruin my family's chance of resettlement outside Rwanda. If we couldn't live in Gihembe, where would we go? "I was scared of the rebels, all of them," I said. "I kept my distance."

When it came to my own family, I didn't know what to say. I worried they would be upset to learn that I had joined the rebels. Even though we had been fighting to protect Tutsis, violence was shameful to Bagogwe. Maybe it would scare them to know what I had seen while I was on the rebel base.

But I wasn't used to keeping anything from my mother, so I revealed my story to her slowly. "When Faustin left, I was so lonely," I told her, describing our concrete house. "It was a really nice place," I said. "But after he left, I moved back to the camp."

She nodded. My mother always tried to understand me. "Were you safer there?" she asked.

"Not safer," I said. "But Gasana's mother was nearby. She was even lonelier than I was."

"What happened to Gasana?" my mother asked. She was preparing beans for dinner, picking out pebbles and dirt, and pouring water through them until it was clear. When she ran her hand through the wet beans it sounded like rain. "Was he killed?" she asked, softly.

I wanted to tell her. My mother knew everything I had been through.

She knew that I had watched killers rape Aunt Florence, and she didn't blame me for hiding and doing nothing. "You were a baby, Mondiant," she said. "Florence would be glad that you stayed safe."

She knew that Célestin, Patrick, and I had hidden beneath dead bodies when the killers had come looking for us. "Some of them were children," I confessed, but my mother didn't think I had a reason to feel ashamed. "Mondiant, that was a smart thing to do," she told me. "It was the only place to hide."

After we were reunited in Gihembe, I described falling in the latrine pit in Mudende and waiting among the dead for someone to rescue me. I told my mother that I hadn't felt grateful for the Red Cross porridge, and that sometimes I resented that organization and all organizations that were supposed to help us. She sighed. "It's natural, Mondiant," she said. "Everyone feels that way sometimes."

I told my mother that I worried I wasn't brave. "No one will ever test me in the forest," I said. "I will never learn how to keep myself safe among the animals in Congo."

"One day you will," she told me then, and she was right. She knew me better than anyone.

"I had a beautiful bird in Kitchanga," I told her that day, watching her wash the beans. "A peacock named Mubarikiwa. But I took it from my friends who were starving and wanted to see if they could eat it."

"You rescued that bird just like the man who pulled you out of the latrine rescued you in Mudende," she said. "You were right to save it."

I told her about carrying the bags of stolen fruit for the rebel soldiers, and how I had spied for the Congolese soldiers when I was in jail even though I knew that they raped many of the girls I told them about.

I told her how grateful I had been to the rebels after they attacked the Congolese base and opened the doors to the jail. "I owed them," I said. "They saved my life."

I told her that in Congo, I felt that I hated Hutus. "Not just the Hutus who attacked us," I said. "All of them."

I told my mother that I hadn't thanked the pastor and his wife when they said goodbye to us at the border, even though they had risked their lives to save us. My mother understood, all of it. "They sound like good people," she said. "They don't need you to say thank you."

Even when Faustin and I shared our father's letter—reciting it to my mother, who had never learned to read—she reassured us, saying there was no way we could have stopped him. "Your father is determined," she said. "He's like his sons. I understand."

But I never felt as much worry over anything as I did over being with the rebels. Even though I didn't have a choice, I felt that if people knew, bad things would happen to my family. People outside the camp—people reading this book—will make assumptions about what I did and what I saw, and I accept that. I know there's a stigma. Only those who have not been to war, who have not experienced anything like what I did, can say, "I would have escaped." But telling my mother filled me with a different kind of dread. I needed her to understand.

After a few days back in Gihembe, I sat with her in front of our home. She was twisting some thread around her finger, getting ready to repair a hole in Baraka's pants. My little brother was growing up and was so active, always into something. I thought about him getting older. If he joined the rebels, I would forgive him, I told myself. I was sure that my mother would forgive him, too. I started talking. "The rebels came to my tent one day in the refugee camp," I told my mother. "They wanted to look at Mubarikiwa."

She put down the pants and turned to look at me. She smiled. "That bird must be so beautiful," she said.

I nodded. "He was. Everyone loved him." My mother waited for me to talk, and when I didn't, she resumed her task. We both listened to the wind whip through the trees that surrounded Gihembe, shaking the roofs.

"There was a rebel commander who was very kind to me," I said. She put down her work. "He offered me food and a place to live. I was so lonely in the refugee camp."

"Go on, Mondiant," she said. "You can tell me anything."

That afternoon, I confessed to my mother. I told her about meeting the commander and how I considered him my mentor, even though I resented that he asked me to miss school to do work for him. I told her about fetching them water and making them food. "They let me eat chicken," I said. My mother would understand as well as any refugee in Gihembe how difficult it would be to turn down a meal of chicken and rice.

My mother listened as I described moving bodies and cleaning weapons. She grimaced when I described in detail being rescued from the Congolese jail. "I was scared of them." I told her. "But the Congolese soldiers were worse."

I must have talked for an hour. It was a relief to finally put everything into words, to turn my trauma into a story. My mother sat calmly, listening to me, Baraka's half-mended pants lying untouched on her lap. She didn't interrupt to ask a question and, although I was watching for it, I didn't see a moment of judgment flicker across her face.

When I had finished, she took my hand. "Mondiant, I am so happy you're here," she said. "None of what happened in Congo matters." She didn't ask whether I had killed anyone. I think she didn't want to know. She sensed my shame at being a part of the rebel group, finding girls for the fighters, picking up human bodies like they were sacks of beans. She was only glad that I was alive. Her heart broke thinking of Gasana's mother, a woman she had never met, alone in her tent in Kitchanga, waiting for a dead boy to come home. "I'm so glad you're back," she said again.

Relieved, I stood up. I decided to look for my friends. "I'm going to play soccer," I told her, running into our home to find the ball that had been entrusted to me. "I'll be back after it gets dark."

But before I left the house my mother asked me to sit down again. She spoke slowly, as though she had spent a lot of time considering what she was about to say. "Mondiant, listen to me," she said. "I understand why you had to be with the rebels. You did nothing wrong." She smiled, and I smiled back at her. "You believe me, right?" I nodded.

"But I have to tell you something that you have to be mature enough to understand," she said. "Will you listen to me?" I nodded again.

"What you went through is difficult," she continued. "I'm glad you told me. But promise me you'll never tell anyone else."

I looked at her solemnly. "I promise," I said. "I'll never tell anyone else." And until now, I've kept my word.

Twenty-Seven

I n Congo, before we became refugees, my father used to love traditional songs and dances called ikinyemera. Some were old and some were new, but each song connected us to one another. We sang about love and families, the land and our heritage. Although by the time I was born, Bagogwe were spread throughout North Kivu and Rwanda, separated by a colonizer's border and the ongoing rotten politics, and living among people of all ethnicities, the ikinyemera kept our culture alive.

Each weekend my father met friends around the fire to sing, talk, and drink beer. After a week of taking care of animals on the farm, my father rested, the ikinyemera circling in the air around him, his neighbors' faces glowing in the firelight. At his house, his children were already asleep, our bellies full. The songs and dances brought peace the way the beer brought sleepiness until my father, groaning with exhaustion, would tell everyone good night, and come home to us.

In the refugee camp, my father forgot about the music. There was no food, so there would be no dancing. There was nowhere for him to go during the day, no work to be done. At night, lying down on his sleeping mat, he didn't know why he was so exhausted.

My father was bothered by a lot of things in the camp. Like everyone else, he missed home. He felt useless. He felt that his life was in ruins behind him, that it had been scrambled by war and displacement and there was nothing he could do to set things right. He had lost his land and his cows. He was powerless listening to his children cry. He heard stories of mothers killing themselves and wished he could help them; he wished he didn't sometimes feel like running away himself. He longed for his old self. He wished that the assured, accomplished leader Sedigi could be summoned with a spell and, like a spirit, reenter his broken body.

For our first few months in Gihembe back in 1998, my father tried to come up with a plan. We hadn't yet lost hope. We assumed that our situation was temporary, and that governments and aid organizations were working to figure out a way to get us home, where we wanted to be and where we would live—we promised—quiet lives. The UN and the Rwandan government encouraged us to feel that way, and my father understood why. We would stay in Gihembe until our wounds had healed. "There is no point in trying to walk before we feel strong enough," my father said. In the meantime, he would find work. People had farms and animals in Rwanda, he reasoned. "Surely someone will hire me to take care of their cows."

But movement out of Gihembe was limited, particularly in those early days. Even if he could have left easily to explore Rwanda on his own, how would he get from Gihembe to the nearest ranch? He spoke Kinyarwanda with a thick accent and a sprinkle of Swahili words, and he had no connections. Job programs for refugees were years away. "I will walk to Kigali and work in a market," my mother said. It was an eleven-hour walk from Gihembe to Kigali, along unfamiliar roads in a foreign country reeling from genocide, among strangers whose language she, like my father, spoke with a telltale accent. My mother's plan was more of a dream.

Steadily, hope of finding work faded. My father stopped trying to come up with a plan. He stayed in the tent all day and all night, ashamed to be wandering around the camp with nothing to do. "When your child asks for something and you can't give it to them, that's the worst feeling," he remembers. He stopped eating his portion of beans and corn so that we could have more, but we were still starving. When the babies started wailing, he sat behind the tent, out of sight. When the older children cried, he walked away into the forest near the camp until our cries faded. He had no money to buy us food and no real idea of how to find work. He felt that he had nothing to give us at all.

I remember that during that time, he was always absent. He rarely had time to sit and talk with me. On days when I brought home my school reports, glowing with pride over my good grades, he would be terse with me. "Mondiant, how did you do?" he asked, already walking toward the entrance to our tent. He knew that I was an excellent student, and he wanted to reward me the way parents should, with a treat or a new notebook, but he couldn't. He felt ashamed of his shortcomings and didn't want to wait for me to ask for things he couldn't give me.

When the representatives from North Kivu came to Gihembe to tell us that it was safe to go home, my father followed their empty promises back to Congo. They were people with high-ranking positions in North Kivu. Why would they lie to us?

"Mondiant and Faustin, you come with me," he said. In our culture, the father tries to teach his sons how to live a good, honorable life. He wanted us to learn to be brave on the journey home, and in Congo, after we had our land and animals back, he planned to put us to work. He imagined raising cattle with his sons beside him, our bodies growing stronger every day that we were back home. He imagined teaching us how to treat sick cows, and how to birth new ones. The idle days of being a refugee would fade into the past and we would become the Bagogwe men we were born to be.

In Kitchanga, when we realized we were not going to be taken back to Bikenke, my father again felt defeated. A familiar sense of depression, one he thought he had left behind in Gihembe, took over. He refused to accept that his land and his cows had been taken from him. This time, he was determined to make a plan. He started working, he made friends. Soon, we were living in the concrete house, surrounded by neighbors willing to protect us, and going to school.

But no amount of money could have kept Faustin and me safe from the rebels who wanted us to join them, or from the other groups who wanted us dead. My father came up with another plan. "We can't stay here forever," he said, packing his few things and leaving us all the money he had saved. "I have to find a way for us to go home to Bikenke or back to Gihembe."

We watched my father walk through the front door of the concrete house. "Faustin, take care of Mondiant," he told my brother. "I'll come back for you both soon. I'll be back in a few days."

✦

WE WOULDN'T SEE my father again until he made it back to Gihembe, months after my return, a journey he attributes to God. After escaping from prison, he returned to Kitchanga, where he begged two priests, men he had known before the war, to take him to Goma. At the border, he leaned heavily on a walking stick. He was so disheveled and dirty, his feet and legs swollen from running, that the border guards assumed he was herding cattle from Congo to Rwanda and let him pass.

"I called your mother from a public phone in Gisenyi," my father says. "She said she would get me back here." My mother sold part of our monthly rations of beans and corn from the World Food Programme and sent the money—around three hundred Rwandan francs, a small fortune— to Gisenyi, where my father boarded a bus and started the trip back to the refugee camp.

When he got to the base of the hill, he stopped. He remembered his torn clothing and dirt-streaked face. His legs were like mine after we arrived at Mudende, swollen to twice their size, the skin stretched and shiny. He felt ashamed. *When I left Gihembe, I said, "I'm going back to my beautiful country,"* he thought. *"I will never come back to this miserable place." Now I said goodbye to Congo. I said I will never come back to Congo.* He didn't want people to see him and ask a lot of questions.

My father waited until the sun set and people went inside their tents. Then he trudged up the hill to find us. We rejoiced that he was home. It was a miracle. My mother cleaned his clothes and the gashes on his legs and feet. When we started asking him questions, she urged us to wait. "Let him rest," she said. And soon enough, he was asleep.

♦

ONCE HE WAS BACK in the refugee camp, we waited for him to feel comfortable enough to tell us more about what he had been through since leaving us in Kitchanga. Slowly, he opened up.

The day my father left us, he walked the many hours from Kitchanga to his family's village, following a route mapped out in his memory. The journey was long but uneventful, and by the time the grass roofs of the village came into focus, my father was newly determined. *I am going to get my land back*, he thought to himself. *I am going to get my family's home back.*

But the village was nothing like my father remembered. When he had left as a young man, it was beautiful. Soft, green fields and dense, dark forests surrounded the tidy mud homes that had been built by patient, attentive hands. Small gardens abutted the homes, growing things that weren't available on the farms or found wild. Every day wives swept the ground in front of the doors for children to play and watch their older siblings return from the farms. People walked from home to home, sharing food and gossip.

Now, like my mother's home village, his village was overgrown and destroyed. It appeared nearly empty as my father approached, slowing down and looking around cautiously. How could a place so alive feel so threatening just a few years later?

He walked over to where two people sat underneath some trees. "Why are you out here?" he asked. "Why don't you repair that home and live in it?" He gestured toward one of the dilapidated mud homes.

"What's the point?" they told him. "War could break out again today or tomorrow. The house would be destroyed as soon as we fixed it, and we are always having to run away into the forest. It's better to sleep underneath the trees."

"Can you tell me where the chief is?" my father asked. They nodded.

"Over there." They pointed deeper into the village. "His house is guarded by Congolese police," they said. "Be careful."

My father was suddenly so sad, he had to stand for a moment underneath a tree to calm himself. He was sure that the chief, even though he was not Tutsi, would understand the injustice of my father's poverty and help him get back what was rightfully his. He told himself that he was only interested in restoring what was fair.

My father slowly approached the Congolese police who surrounded the chief's house, knowing it was a great risk, and asked to see the chief by name. "I've known him since I was a child," he told them. Reluctantly, they let him enter.

"Sedigi, I cannot believe you are alive," the chief exclaimed when he saw my father. He sat in a chair, as though overcome. "I am so glad you are okay."

"I came back to Congo with my sons," my father said. "I returned from Rwanda to get my land, but they took us to the camp in Kitchanga. I need your help."

The chief looked forlorn. How could he explain to his old friend that this simple request was impossible, and that his home was not the home he remembered? It was the kind of story that took more than one person to tell, and he had been alone in his small village fortress for years, thinking only about staying alive. "Sedigi," he said, "the land is gone. I am not telling you this to be cruel, but if you stay here you might die. Try to find a way back to your sons in Kitchanga." Then he opened the door for my father, who left, walking past the police with his head down.

Dejected, my father set off in another direction, toward his father's village. *People will know my family there*, he thought. His father had Hutu friends who he was sure would help him out of an obligation to the family. There, he would be able to sell his family's land and use the money to bring Faustin and me back to Bikenke. Like a character from a folktale, when my father went walking in search of our family's land, he was really searching for our lost Congolese identity.

My father waited for a market day and then set off. It was a long walk and he left early, planning to arrive at midday, when the market would be busiest and he could walk in a crowd, hoping that what we had been told were his Tutsi features—the slender nose and wrists, the long limbs he thought would give him away—would be lost among the strangers. He wore a long coat to disguise his height and mask his thinness, character-istic if not of a Tutsi, then certainly of a refugee. If they saw him as a displaced person, they would ask questions about why he was no longer welcome home.

The walk through the forest was longer and more treacherous than my father had imagined, and it was night by the time he arrived. The streets were empty. As with my mother's village, it was as though the place had been taken over by the forest. Pathways that would have been swept clean and flattened by foot traffic were craggy and overgrown. A sweet, wild smell had taken over, as though animals lived there now instead of people. My father walked as quickly as he could, looking for the familiar house.

His father's friend Gahima opened his door as soon as he knocked. He recognized my father immediately. "Sedigi!" he said. "I thought some-thing terrible had happened to you." He looked over my father's shoulder at the empty street. "Come in," he said. "Where have you come from?"

While my father told him his story, Gahima gave him food and beer. "Where are your sons now?" he asked.

"In Kitchanga," my father answered. "As soon as I sell my land, I'll go get them."

Gahima smiled kindly. Though he knew my father no longer had any land to sell, he would never be the one to tell him. "Sedigi, you can stay here, but you have to hide," he said. "If people know you're here they will kill you and me. They don't want Tutsis in this village." That night, after they had eaten, the friend took my father to a small shed behind the house that they used for grain storage. "Stay here," he said.

Gahima was known for his strength and size. Few people in the vil-lage were brave enough to confront him, but early the next morning when he heard that someone had seen him usher my father into the shed, even Gahima became scared. "Gahima is hiding a Tutsi," they said. The villagers were angry. It was too much of a risk for Gahima to keep my father in his shed. "I'm sorry, Sedigi," he said. "If they know you're here, they'll kill you, and they might hurt my family, too."

That night, out of options, my father hid. He walked into the forest and crouched between the roots of a lombi tree, which grow like walls out of the forest floor, trying to come up with a plan. He couldn't go back to Kitchanga, where Faustin and I were waiting for him to rescue us. He wasn't welcome in his family's villages, and he couldn't go to Bikenke, where, he worried, killers would be waiting for him. After a few hours, he walked to a banana plantation, where he found a hole full of ripening fruit and climbed down into it, falling asleep nearly gagging on the sickly-sweet fumes while villagers searched nearby for the escaped Tutsi refugee.

My father stayed in the hole for three days. For the first time since leaving Gihembe, he admitted to himself that he had no idea what to do. Bananas ripened and softened around him. He knew that soon people would come to collect the fruit and bring it to the market. On the fourth night, Gahima found him.

"Sedigi!" he exclaimed when he saw my father. "I've been looking for you. The village is completely surrounded by people who want to kill you. There is no way to escape. If you come back, we can try to bribe them. Otherwise, you will die here on the banana plantation."

My father, out of ideas, nodded his head and silently followed his friend back to certain death.

◆

HE ENDED UP IN JAIL. That we had known from his letter. "I am very sorry for not coming back to you," he wrote. "There is no chance for me to get out of prison."

He was ashamed to have been caught, and he was ashamed that he had failed Faustin and me, leaving us alone in Kitchanga. No matter how many times we told him it wasn't his fault—"We were fine," we insisted, "we were old enough"—he never accepted that his sons almost died while he was imprisoned only a few hours' walk from where we were.

Every day Faustin, Furaha, and I begged him to tell us more. "What were the villages like?" we asked. "How did you escape?" For weeks he shook his head. "It's not something you want to hear about," he told us. "Let's just focus on the fact that we are all here, safe." But we kept asking until one day, he told us.

"After Gahima found me in the banana plantation, I followed him back to the village," he told us. "I was sure I was going to die. Gahima told me he would try to bribe them, but I didn't believe that it would work."

In the village, a crowd had gathered to watch the fugitive Tutsi be punished. "They told me, 'We are going to kill you,'" my father said. They tied him to a tree, and he waited to be killed. But soon Gahima showed up, holding a fistful of money. The killers contemplated the cash. "We'll take it," they said finally. "But it's not enough to spare him."

"I have goats," Gahima said.

"We'll take the goats," the killers replied, tying them to the tree with my father. "But we still need more."

Gahima brought two rabbits that he was raising as food in his backyard. Finally, the killers were satisfied. "We won't kill him," they said, cutting my father from the tree. "But we will have to take him to jail." The goats, left behind, bleated in panic.

The prison was just a house in the village, abandoned by someone or, most likely, belonging to someone who had been killed or forced to flee. Most of the other prisoners were people who had betrayed the killers; they looked at my father like he was the enemy. Like mine had been, my father's cell was filled with water up to the knees. His hands were cuffed to his ankles, and he had to work hard through his exhaustion not to fall asleep and drown.

"It was terrible," my father told us, sensing our dismay. "But instead of talking about that, let's talk about how I escaped.

"I wrote you a letter," he said. Faustin and I nodded. "I wanted you to be prepared to never see me again. I'm sorry if it upset you. I didn't know what else to do."

"We understood," Faustin said. "You sent us a lot of money, too."

"That was from Gahima," he said. "He didn't want me to worry about you while he tried to get me out of jail," he said. "Every day, he offered the jailers something new—some money or some animals. He never gave up." He reminded us that there are good people in Congo who will help you if they can.

Still today my father can't remember exactly how long he was in jail. "For a year," he sometimes says. "About a month," he says other times. "I think it was only a couple of weeks," he told us. "Gahima finally managed to bribe one of the guards."

Or, he thinks for a moment, maybe something else happened. "My friend was well known in the village," my father said. "He had a gun in his house."

He pauses again, considering. "There was a war going on," he continued. "During a war, when people are starving and fighting, anyone can take a bribe. It meant nothing."

"In any case," my father said, "the guard agreed to open the door for me. At the right hour, I walked through, and I was free. When I got outside, I started running. I had no idea where to go. I found myself back at the banana plantation. I was still in a lot of danger. I knew that if they caught me, they would kill me right away. I hadn't been so scared since we first left Rwanda. It was the same kind of feeling. But I was alone."

He had no hope that he would make it back to us. He kept walking and walking, waiting until it was dark so the killers wouldn't find him. Often, after he had walked for hours in the pitch black, the sun would brighten the banana plantation and my father would realize that he had walked for hours in a circle. "It was like something was keeping me from getting out," he said.

In jail, the killers had taken his shoes and clothes. Gahima gave my father a pair of pants, all he could spare, and my father walked in nothing but his friend's pair of pants, cinched around his skinny waist with a rope. Gahima's kindness still overwhelms him.

He walked for weeks, barefoot, through the forest and the plantation, eating only bananas, until he finally made it to Kitchanga. "When I arrived, I couldn't stand because my feet were swelling," he said. "It was raining so hard it hurt. I trembled like I was dying. I walked in mud up to my knees."

At this point in his story, he usually pauses. He looks at Faustin and me as though checking to make sure we are still there, listening. "In Kitchanga, I asked for my sons," he said. "They said, 'Your sons are gone.' I didn't know if it meant you were dead." He pauses again. "You thought I was dead, and I thought you were dead. I didn't feel normal, emotionally. I couldn't be there without my sons."

My father told us all about his journey and his time in jail, even though he felt ashamed about what had happened to him and what had become of his country. We were amazed at what he had survived. But there were certain things he would never say out loud to us, his children and his wife. There were some things he only thought to himself.

Waking up in the tent the morning after he arrived, my father looked around to see the comforting sight of his family, still asleep, and the familiar contours of the home, the few material things we had tucked away neatly in its corners. He smelled the slightly sour smell that seemed to fill the refugee camp and listened to the wind roll over the tin roofs. He heard refugees stirring just a few feet away in their homes, opening their own improvised doors and starting their own fires for breakfast. He rolled onto his back and saw the sunlight poke through small holes in our roof and thought to himself, "This is it. We are going to die here."

Twenty-Eight

enrolled in school, the youngest student in my class. In spite of the time I had spent away, I wasn't behind the other students, but they still treated me like their little sibling, teasing me for being overly serious about studying and asking me to perform small tasks for them. I didn't know why I seemed so much younger than my classmates, despite what I had been through in Congo. I was desperate to grow up, but I didn't know how.

That year, I shared a desk with three other students: Mutabazi, Innocent, and Fedha. We were crammed together, shoulder to shoulder; when it was time to write, there was never enough room. Our hands and elbows crashed together, making our notes illegible. I never complained in front of my older classmates, but at home I would sit hunched over my writing, crying to my mother that it was impossible to study.

"We need more space," Innocent said one day in class. She was very matter-of-fact. "Someone has to move onto the floor."

"In our culture, young people give up their places for older people," Mutabazi said, looking at me. I was a better student than he was even though he was much bigger and taller, and he disparaged me whenever he could. No one wanted to study on the floor, like a misbehaving child dismissed to the corner to cry.

"No, let's be fair," Fedha, who always defended me, said. "Let's play a game, and whoever loses will sit on the floor."

But I was already moving my slate. I knew that Mutabazi would make my life harder if I protested. "It's fine," I said. "I'm the youngest, I'll sit on the floor." I sat cross-legged beside their desk, propping my book up on my thigh.

"Mondiant is very obedient," Innocent said, smiling at me. I couldn't tell if she was teasing. None of my classmates knew about my experience in Congo. I was certain that if I told them, they would scatter in fear and I would have the entire desk to myself. "I'm sure he really loves his older brother and sister," she said.

Some of my classmates found ways to spend time other than studying. They passed each other love notes, pushing bits of paper across the floor with their feet, giggling at the sight of each other reading their confessions. I was too shy to pass my own notes, but because I wanted the other students to like me, I acted as their courier, carrying the scraps of paper from student to student when the teacher wasn't looking. Sometimes they gave me pieces of candy as payment, which I stuffed quickly into my mouth. I knew this made me seem even more like the classroom's younger sibling, but the candy was so sweet, and normally so unattainable, that I would have done almost anything for it.

The notes became so important that often days passed when other students would forget every part of a lesson but be able to recite entire notes from memory. "Amani told Innocent he wanted to watch soccer with her at Oswaldie's pub," someone said. "Innocent wrote back that she would like that very much." Sometimes girls got angry if the boy they liked passed a note to another girl. Boys who felt slighted by their own object of desire would sulk during lessons. I kept my focus on studying.

One day a much older boy who occasionally came to our class asked me to pass a note to Fedha. It didn't cross my mind that the piece of paper might contain something that Fedha, my constant ally, would find offensive, and I took it from him without question, walking it over to her. "Hey, Fedha," I said. "Someone wanted me to give this to you."

"Who?" she asked. "Is he our classmate?"

"I don't know." I shrugged. "We met outside, and he gave it to me for you."

Fedha opened the note and began to read it. While she read it, I looked for the older boy where he normally sat. He had promised me candy as long as I didn't reveal his identity to Fedha, but he wasn't there.

While I was looking for him, Fedha came up to me. Her face was red with anger. "You said that you don't know the person who gave you this note, right?" she asked, almost shouting. "If you know, you have to tell me, Mondiant."

"I've seen him before," I said. "But I don't know his name." I was trembling with fear. Fedha and I had shared a desk since I had returned to Gihembe the year before and started sixth grade, and I had never seen her angry. When the boy came into the classroom and I pointed him out to her, Fedha slapped me.

For the rest of the day, my face stung. I wondered what had been in the note that made her so upset. I left the classroom fuming that the boy hadn't given me the candy he had promised.

◆

SOON AFTER FEDHA SLAPPED ME for delivering the offensive note, I made the decision that I would be a grown-up. Furaha had gotten married and moved to Nyabiheke, another refugee camp about a day's walk east of Gihembe, and soon Faustin followed her, hoping that he might continue school in that camp, which had more resources for older students. I missed them and I often thought about what their lives might be like outside Gihembe. Did they play mancala now instead of marbles? Would Furaha, who was so angry when my mother announced her pregnancy, have children in the refugee camp herself? I was the oldest boy in our home now. I wanted to shed my youth like a snake sheds its skin.

Instead of playing soccer or hide-and-seek with friends after school, I joined the church choir. Every day I practiced singing in the yard where we held our services, and said a few prayers, most having to do with passing the national exam we would all take, after finishing ninth grade in the camp, to get into a Rwandan high school. And on Saturdays and Sundays, in my greatest rejection of childhood and all the comforts that came with it, I volunteered to collect firewood, joining expeditions of teenagers, including Fedha, Innocent, and Mutabazi, into the land beyond the camp in pursuit of the wood.

Deliveries of firewood to the camp were rare, and when it arrived it was never enough for every family to cook, keep warm, and boil water. We were left to gather what we needed ourselves. Much of Rwanda is lush and wild like Congo, but most of the land around Gihembe is terraced for agriculture or portioned into private farms and plantations. We had to walk for hours to reach a forest big enough to conceal us; all land in Rwanda seemed to belong to someone, in most cases Rwandan farmers who watched with guns for trespassing refugees. Although collecting the wood was dangerous and difficult, the task was generally left to teenagers who could run fast and who did not mind spending the day together, setting out from the camp into unknown parts of the country on what they could pretend was an adventure.

In a refugee camp, being young was a combination of boring and dangerous. Kids I knew died slipping on the wet edges of wells and drowning in the deep water or from drinking tainted water before it had been boiled. Girls who left the camp for school were raped. Girls and boys could be harassed, hurt, or worse.

We caught dysentery and malaria and didn't make it to the town hospital in time. We died of hunger. Boredom could be as dangerous as illness. Kids turned into restless teenagers who found some entertainment in drugs and alcohol. Some had sex too young and got pregnant. Many boys became so bored and hopeless in the camp that, in spite of how many of their friends had already died before them, they left to join the rebels in Congo. There they took up arms, imagining sending part of their salary back to their parents in Gihembe. In Congo it was even easier to die, but at least you could tell yourself you were taking control of your life. If it was shameful to be violent, it was worse to starve. In the refugee camp, many days we were so hungry we couldn't do anything at all.

Even with all the dangers, our parents loved us and tried to keep us safe. My mother made sure I was home every night and filled my stomach with whatever she could just to help me sleep. They made sure we studied, washed our clothes, and went to church.

And even the most worried parents—the ones who kept a supply of herbal remedies in their tents for illnesses and walked their children to the wells—allowed their children to go far away from the camp to find firewood. Without firewood, we would die. The dried beans and corn had to be boiled, as did most of our water. Kids often got hurt or caught and punished by farmers or security guards—the previous weekend a girl named Fifi had torn open her leg after being pushed onto a sharp tea tree by a guard at a tea plantation—but we had to go. So every weekend, our parents, feeling frightened but remaining practical, reluctantly sent a group of older kids out into the known and unknown dangers of the world outside. "Be careful," my mother would tell me, hugging me at the front flap of our tent. "And try to bring back as much as you can."

✦

ONE SATURDAY, I woke up just before dawn and gathered the tools I could. We didn't have proper axes, but anything that could create force and leverage helped—rope, bricks, even cooking pots. Mostly, we had to rely on our own body weight to snap branches, and the nascent strength of our skinny arms to carry them home. Setting off early was important. In the morning we could drink some water and feel close to normal. But soon enough hunger would settle into every part of our bodies, weakening our arms and legs and distracting us from what needed to be done. At least if we were far from Gihembe by the time our empty stomachs started twisting into angry knots, we could use our hunger as motivation to get home faster.

"Come on, get up!" I knocked on Gasengi's door. I relished moments of authority over Gasengi, who, like our other classmates, seemed so much older than me.

"Hi, Mondiant." Gasengi appeared at the tent entrance, bleary-eyed, holding his own assortment of tools. "Are we ready?" He squinted at me. Lately, Gasengi had started wearing a new expression on his face, one he thought made him look like a man. He squinted and frowned slightly, looking just over my shoulder, as though examining the horizon for danger. To grown-ups he must have looked ridiculous—a skinny boy trying on his father's clothes—but to me he looked determined, intimidating, almost manly. I wondered when I might also start to change.

Together, we walked from zone to zone, knocking on doors and trying to get together a big enough group for it to be a successful mission. Eventually, seven boys—Fabrice, Steven, Jeremy, Mutabazi, Gérald, Gisore, and Vincent—awoke slowly and gathered their tools. When their mothers said goodbye, we laughed at their worried expressions. We knew that what we were doing was serious, and like most refugees we remembered the murders we had witnessed, and that we had escaped our own deaths more than once. Still, like teenagers everywhere, we felt invincible. Heaving our ropes over our shoulders, we walked to the edge of camp. "Don't worry!" we shouted to our mothers as we left the tented area. "We'll be back, and we'll all have fire all week!"

At the edge of the camp, we stopped and looked at one another. No one knew where to go. Each direction had its own risks—a particularly cruel landowner; a long, hilly walk; the rumor of animals. "Let's go east," Fabrice suggested, shrugging.

"No, last week we walked east for fifteen miles and there was no wood," Vincent replied. We were silent for a moment, thinking about how disappointed and exhausted we had been, returning to the camp with nothing. Adulthood, we all thought, meant carrying the burden of feeding your family. That week, we had failed.

"North?" Gérald asked. Gérald was young but tall, and braver than almost all of us combined. It was like him to suggest we walk north, where the forest was abundant and owned by a particularly territorial farmer. For a minute, no one spoke. We were all scared thinking about what we might find if we headed north. We thought about Fifi, her white thigh bone exposed under the deep gash, the tea plantation security guard standing over her while she told us to run. Which was worse, getting caught by angry landowners or returning to the camp empty-handed? "It's starting to rain," Gérald pointed out. The longer we waited to leave, the harder gathering wood would become. "Let's go north," I said finally. There was nothing to do but start walking, and even Mutabazi followed me.

✦

SOMETIMES ON THESE WALKS, I could admit that parts of Rwanda were beautiful. The hills around Gihembe were difficult to cross quickly, and the towns felt off-limits and threatening. The camp, meanwhile, had become monotonous and characterized most by the yearning I felt to leave. Although my most recent experiences of Congo were limited to massacres and, later, to collecting bodies for rebels, it was hard to let go of it entirely as the lost paradise my parents once described. I remembered my time with the rebels and how difficult and dangerous it was to escape. I remembered Alphonse trying to hide his fear behind sunglasses, and the government soldiers leaving us for dead on the side of the road.

But refugees in Gihembe still spoke often of the home they had left behind. Every year that passed, Congo grew still more glorious in their memories. Never mind that it had expelled us like a stomach full of rotten food and promised to kill us if we returned; the image of home as a beautiful place you want to return to is hard to give up. If, as a refugee, you let go of that idea, what do you have left? You will have given up.

Rwanda, though, was also an abundant country. Since taking office, President Kagame had been celebrated for easing tensions and helping the nation reconcile, and for helping it to grow economically. Tourists, we heard, even visited for the natural beauty. Inside the camp, nothing had changed, and all this progress sounded like a rumor. In leaving, though, even just on a walk for firewood, it became possible to imagine that people were happy living in Rwanda. Land tamed for agriculture turned into rich, green hills and forests. Animals sprinted in our peripheral vision and fruit trees tempted us with bananas and mangoes. Birds so brightly colored they seemed to glow perched on the high trees.

None of it was ours, though. As hungry as we were, we denied ourselves the bananas, which we knew we could be killed for eating. We put away our tools when we saw an animal that could feed half the camp for a week. Usually our goal outside Gihembe was to be quiet, stay out of trouble, stay out of jail. When it came to firewood, we had to break those rules. We needed the wood, and in order to get it, we had no choice but to be thieves.

After hours of walking, we made it to the forest, soaked but safe, and began breaking apart the wood as quietly as possible. The rain, which by this point was falling heavily on the leaves and ground, masked the sound of our work. We waited for a crack of lightning before snapping off large branches; smaller ones, rubbery with rain, bent quietly before tearing off. Soon we had as much as we could carry. "Let's go," we whispered, exhilarated by the success of our mission and still looking over our shoulders for the owner.

We started on the long walk home. After each mile we became happier, more confident in our success. Our voices grew louder. We felt like the heroes we had pictured when we left the camp that morning. I felt taller, more confident, closer to the man I imagined myself to be. The rain had stopped, and the wood was drying out; it would be easy to burn in big, productive fires. Bundles of branches slid down our backs and shoulders, scraping our arms and legs. We loved the pain of those small cuts. They were trophies that our mothers would lovingly clean and wrap and that we would wear like badges of honor until they healed.

A half hour from the camp we had almost begun to celebrate, when we heard dogs barking. "Stop!" A man approached us, a dog pulling against his leash. He wore military fatigues and civilian pants and led a group of similarly dressed men. They stood in front of us as though manning a checkpoint, although they had seemed to come out of nowhere. "Where did you get that firewood?"

"We got it from the forest over there," Gérald said, pointing west of where we had come from. "We had permission from the owner." He didn't say that we were refugees; he didn't have to. The security guards knew who we were by looking at us and what we carried.

"The wood looks like it came from our forest," one of the men said. They had small guns tucked into their waistbands, reminding us that we were guests in their country. "Don't you think so?" he asked his companion, who nodded.

"How can they tell?" Gasengi whispered to me, and I shook my head. Wood was wood, we thought.

"Put it down," the men said, pointing to a spot between us. "It's not yours, leave it here." There was no way to argue with them. Even Mutabazi had his head turned down and was silent. One by one, we heaved the bundles of wood from our backs and piled it onto the ground. Empty, my arms began to feel sore. I wondered if Gasengi was wearing his new, manly expression, but I was too frightened to turn and look.

By now, the wood was dry. It formed a tall, beautiful pyramid. It was more than enough for refugees in our zone to burn fires all week. It would have kept us dry and cooked our food. It would have kept away mosquitoes and lightened the dark night so that we could stay up later, talking and sharing stories. And since we had found it on a Saturday, the group of us would have been able to spend Sunday playing soccer. I tried to suppress my sorrow and replace it with anger, which seemed more mature, but I felt like crying.

Without saying anything, one of the men took a slim bottle from his pocket and poured clear liquid over the pile. We knew immediately from the poisonous smell that it was kerosene. Once the wood was covered, he lit a match and tossed it on top of the pile. In an instant, our hard work was engulfed by a giant flame. The wood cracked and splintered in the fire, we yelped as the wind blew sparks in our direction, and then, because we felt embarrassed for appearing scared, we crossed our arms in front of our chests and did our best to stay still. We watched the fire burn fiercely through the chemicals.

Satisfied, the men started walking away. "Refugee kids," one said, loud enough for us to hear. "They don't have any manners."

We stayed in a half circle until our wood was ash. Then we walked the rest of the way home, children desperate to see our mothers' forgiving faces.

Twenty-Nine

I
n Gihembe we suffered from many things. We walked into the camp with visible pain—broken limbs, distended bellies, machete wounds—that the aid organizations were equipped to help us overcome. They fed us what they could, wrapped our wounds in gauze, and took us to the doctor when their equipment wasn't sufficient. We survived. Our invisible pain, though, went untreated.

With my father home and me back in school, and all of us focusing on our daily tasks, life began to return to normal. Gihembe, with all its sameness, took over. We stopped talking about what we had been through and started reciting a familiar script: When are the World Food Programme deliveries coming this month? Who will go get water? Did you hear about this boy who went to Congo, the one whose mother hasn't heard from him in two years?

My father and I stopped answering the curious questions about our experiences across the border. We didn't see talking as a step toward becoming whole again, and close as a family. We didn't consider that in order for us to move past what we had been through in Congo, we had to confront it, and there was nothing in the camp that encouraged us, or any refugees, to do so. No one was there to treat our invisible pain.

Instead, we behaved as though honesty itself were a wound that needed healing, and as though our past were a weapon we needed to run from until we could no longer see it. As time went by, we became silent, and soon it felt again that all we had ever known and all we would know was the refugee camp.

We tried to forget our own lives, so is it any wonder that the world forgot about us? For years Bagogwe had lived in Gihembe wondering when we would be offered a way out. The violence we experienced was so tremendous and so life-altering that it was hard to accept that outside the camp, life went on. In Kigali, the Rwandan economy began its celebrated boom years under Kagame; in The Hague, the United Nations decried genocide, and built camp after camp for a world bursting with refugees; in Washington, one president's moral focus was another's forgotten war.

Celebrities came to tour Gihembe. When they did, we tidied up the camp and rushed to greet them. Administrators hung signs and led the celebrities to the school, the church, to visit the smiling woman whose new baby lay peacefully against her chest. We continued to attend events memorializing the Mudende massacre or celebrating the UN on World Refugee Day. We smiled at the camera crews, talked to journalists, imagined our stories being told in newspapers around the world. We did our part, we thought, to make sure people knew who we were and what was continuing to happen to us.

I understand now that Bagogwe are only a tiny portion of the tens of millions of refugees in the world. Maybe that is why it has been so impossible for us to get people's attention. What can we reasonably expect from a world that considers the genocide long in the past?

But we should have kept talking. Of all our invisible pain, our silence is the one that has hurt us the most. In Gihembe, we were told to be quiet. "Don't upset anyone," my mother told me if I got in trouble at school. "Don't talk to him," Faustin said if we passed a government soldier, staring at us from beneath the shade of his hat. "Shhhh," we said to one another when we were looking for firewood. "Whatever you do, be quiet." When some refugee kids tried to steal fruit from a farm and the local forces caned us on the backs of our legs, we tried not to scream or cry. And after they let us go back to Gihembe, we walked stiffly from the entrance to our homes, not uttering a single word to anyone out of shame.

When one of my favorite teachers spoke out against the lower salaries that refugee teachers received compared with Rwandans, he was told by Rwandan camp administrators to stop. "You'll lose your job," they said. And after that same teacher was elected by the camp to be Gihembe's community leader, the same administrators quickly revoked his position. "It's because he talked too much," refugees whispered to one another knowingly. Though we recognized injustice in and out of the camp all the time, we had no way to speak out against it. We worried about what would happen to us—our futures, our citizenship, our resettlement—if we did.

Refugees are told to be quiet, and to be grateful for what we have. But I understand now what we gave up by accepting that bargain. If we don't tell people what our life is like, they are left only to imagine. Do you think that refugees simply leave their homes and stay somewhere temporarily before they are resettled? Do you think everyone in the world has a passport or is a citizen of a country? Do you think that refugees lead easy lives, collecting food or money we don't have to work for, living happily off the generosity of the UN and our host nations?

Silence is a disease. I started writing my book because I wanted to reach other people—people who had no connection to us, who were not from Congo or Rwanda, not from Africa, who had never met a refugee or thought about what a refugee camp might be like. I want to reach them and let them know that we are still here. In spite of our silence, we have a lot to say about the way the world works. That world can seem very remote to us in our refugee camp, but we are learning more about it and our place in it every day. For example, when I lived in Gihembe, I thought that being a citizen of a country was a present given to you by a kind leader, showing you mercy. Now I know that having citizenship is a human right. Being heard is a human right.

✦

WHILE WE WERE COMPELLED to stay silent, Rwanda was actively trying to come to terms with what had happened during the genocide. Radio shows were devoted to people talking about what they had been through; in the afternoons we listened to gruesome stories and calls for reconciliation. In 2005, the country instituted a system of community justice known as gacaca courts. While the leaders of the genocide were prosecuted internationally, foot soldiers would be brought to justice in Rwanda by Rwandans. That justice could be a jail sentence or community service, but Kagame's government also encouraged forgiveness as a way to move forward. So much of the small country had participated in the killing and destruction, it was hard to imagine rebuilding if everyone was sentenced to life. Already the country's jails were bursting with those accused of participating in the genocide against the Tutsis.

Near Gihembe, gacaca hearings were held on Mondays and Wednesdays for five years. They drew huge crowds. If it was nice out, villagers packed the streets, verandas, and playgrounds close to where the hearings would take place, talking and angling for a view of the murderers and rapists who would be tearfully confessing to their victims and the families of their victims. These trials became as common a sight as the weekly markets.

The first time I saw one, I was fourteen years old, and I stumbled upon it by accident. It was a beautiful spring day after a rainy week and I left Gihembe with some friends for Kageyo, where we liked to play soccer on a wide, flat field that was better suited to the game than anything in cramped Gihembe. As we approached the field, though, we noticed that it was full of people, most of them sitting and facing a small clearing where a group of men and women were in conversation behind long folding tables. "Let's go listen," I said to my friends.

At the front of the crowd a man sat between local leaders. Police stood at either side of the table, watching the man and watching the crowd. I recognized him immediately, although I didn't know his name. He was well known in the town, a loud voice at all the sports games. After long nights drinking beer and eating kebabs at Oswaldie's pub, he would stumble back to his house, amiably waving at his neighbors. He couldn't have been more than thirty years old, making him a young man when the genocide happened. What could he possibly have done?

Once the crowd was quiet, the man stood up and began talking. "Back when I was a boy, I used to help feed cows that belonged to a family that lived in this village," he said. "The family were Tutsis, and they were my neighbors. One night I met with other Hutus and I told them I wanted my neighbor's cows. You should kill them, they told me. So I did. I killed seven of them. One of them escaped."

"Where did you bury them?" one of the other men sitting at the table asked.

"I threw their bodies into the latrine ditch," he said. He folded his arms in front of his stomach and shrugged like a child. "I wish it had never happened."

When he had finished, another person stood up. He appeared to be only a bit older than me, and his voice quivered when he spoke. He sounded nervous. "I am the only person who survived from that family," he said, addressing the murderer. After his family was killed, he fled to a refugee camp in Uganda, and the life he described was eerily similar to mine. "I was a child, and I hid from this man and the other murderers the best I could," he said. "For the past twelve years I have been living as an orphan in a refugee camp, wishing that I could return home and at least bury my family properly."

Around me, some people were weeping. Others were watching in silence, expressionless. The refugee approached his family's killer. "I forgive you," he said. He offered the killer a cow, an act of extraordinary generosity from anyone, and particularly a young orphan. "I give you this cow to show you that I forgive you in my heart." Then it was over. If it was any more complicated than that, as a teenager, wide-eyed at the spectacle, I didn't know.

Forgiveness wasn't always given so easily. At another trial, I saw a Tutsi survivor stand up in the crowd and point at a Hutu woman. "This woman was my friend," she said. "When I fled, I gave her all of my money and my baby. She promised to keep the baby safe, and if I survived, she would give the baby back to me. But now she denies even knowing me." They screamed at each other, each certain they would lose the child they both loved, until the police came to separate them.

In another village, a group of seven rapists was confronted by one of their victims. She was six years old when they raped her, and she had contracted HIV. Now all she tried to do was forget about what had happened to her, but the fragments of memories were like shrapnel, slowly killing her. Standing in front of her rapists, she was so traumatized she was almost mute, and the crowd was so angry that the seven men who raped her had to be taken away by police after they confessed.

I thought they sounded truly sorry. It sounded like they were confessing to God, asking for forgiveness. But what did I know? No one questioned the methods of the gacaca courts, which seemed to be lifting Rwandans out of the hell of their own history. At the same time, the gulf between many Hutus and Tutsis widened. One could forget that not every Hutu had participated in the genocide, and that some Tutsis would have once told you about their Hutu neighbors who had saved their lives.

Our experience as Congolese refugees was not part of the gacaca courts. In Rwanda, we were spectators only. But we still sometimes came face-to-face with the people who had killed our loved ones. One night in Kitchanga, the men who had attacked us in Mudende visited our concrete house. Upon hearing from a friend that they were on their way, my father ran to a UN phone in the middle of the town to call my mother. "Don't let them in," my mother begged him from Gihembe. "They tried to kill you before and they will kill you now."

My father, though, wanted the chance to forgive them. Even when

Faustin and I were young and fought, he would first come to us and sit us down like we were much older than we were, giving us the chance to resolve our issues. "Before I punish you," he would say, "you have to ask forgiveness from each other." Because we wanted to please him more than we wanted to punish each other, we always did.

The killers came carrying metal drums of beer on their heads, and my father left our front door open for them. Villagers joined, drinking and talking. It was like a party. They didn't mention how they knew us, or why they were there.

"Have you ever been to Rwanda?" my father asked. If they were there to admit what they had done, he wanted them to confess and then leave. If they were there to kill him, he wanted them to do it quickly.

"Yes, we've been to Gisenyi," they said, referring to the part where Mudende was established.

"Wow, interesting," my father said. "Why did you go there?"

"We went to visit a friend," they said, looking my father in the eyes.

After they left, my father sat at our table drinking the last bit of beer. "They think we don't know who they are," he said to Faustin and me. He wasn't angry. He accepted it and moved on.

I don't know how I would feel if they had confessed that night, or if refugees had been given their own gacaca trials. If the men who raped my aunt Florence and killed my grandmother, who beat my mother and father until they were almost dead, told me they were sorry, would I forgive them? Would I give them a cow, so they believed that I truly forgave them? It's a very hard question. For me, it's almost beyond my imagination.

I remember that Faustin and I did not drink the beer the killers brought, although we were old enough that our father offered us a little. We were certain our father would be poisoned. And later, in Gihembe, I eventually had to stop going to the gacaca trials. Even with their offer of resolution, they frightened me. The trials made me feel that I was surrounded by killers, that at any moment our neighbors could snap and kill me, too.

After watching the gacaca trials, anytime I was outside Gihembe, I would run from anyone I saw, thinking of the violence that person might be capable of. When Bitege, a knock-kneed man, chased us through Kageyo, screaming at us for looking through his windows, I wondered if he had once confessed in a gacaca court, and if so, what horrible things he had done.

People wept that day on our soccer field when the young Tutsi man, the sole survivor of the massacre of his family, gave the Hutu murderer a cow. I felt that his forgiveness was real, and I also believed that the killer regretted what he had done. But still, as a kid, when I heard that he killed seven people, I became scared of the affable young man who drank beer at Oswaldie's and shouted at the soccer game. It didn't matter that he confessed and was sorry. I knew that if I met him during the night, I would run.

Thirty

I didn't see any way out of Gihembe other than school, and so I became
obsessed with being the top of my class. Besides collecting firewood and
the occasional soccer game, I did nothing but study. In the refugee camp,
school was more than a place to learn; it was an escape hatch.

The refugee school had come a long way since its days in a tent. We
no longer studied only the Congolese curriculum, and we met in a proper
packed-mud-and-wood building with a tin roof. But our resources were
still limited. Students shared supplies and desks. We had no internet to
reference. At night, when we were hungry, it was hard to think about
grades.

Most important, the refugee school didn't extend past ninth grade.
Refugee students who wanted to continue their education had to earn a
place in a Rwandan public school by passing a national exam and finding
a sponsor willing to buy uniforms and supplies, as well as pay the school
fees. These modest expenses were, for us, completely out of reach without
help and so, on most days, leaving the camp and going to high school
with Rwandans felt like an unattainable dream. Still, I knew very few
refugee students who didn't share that dream.

Growing up in a refugee camp teaches you to be resourceful. Before
anyone had money for a real soccer ball, we kicked around whatever
we could. Cheap plastic balls collapsed after half an hour, and wads of

banana leaves instantly flew apart with our kicks. We watched movies through windows in Kageyo, making up the dialogue we couldn't hear. We learned how to build fires with wet, dead kindling; walk quickly through streets glutted with mud; and build roofs and doors out of materials most people would have thrown away.

Every day we proved ourselves to one another in the camp. Our teachers asked us question after question, testing how much we had learned, and clapped for us when we got the answers right. "You are the smartest group in all of Gihembe," they would tell us, smiling like aunts and uncles. "You all will be whatever you want, one day." We left school glowing with our achievements, forgetting for a moment that so much of the world was beyond our reach.

We had few opportunities to show Rwandans how smart or how ambitious we were. Our achievements inside the refugee camp were like secrets. The national exam, though, was available to any student regardless of where they were born or where they lived or what kind of identification card they carried. It was respected by everyone in the country. If you passed, it didn't matter if you were a refugee or someone who could trace your family back generations in Rwanda, you were granted a position at a public school. You learned the same things as Rwandan students, and were taught by the same teachers. People admired you. At least, that's what I imagined late at night when I thought about leaving the refugee camp. I let myself think, *Wow.*

If you didn't pass, though, your life was over. You had to study and retake the test or, more likely for refugee students with limited resources, drop out of school altogether. Rwandan citizens with money could enroll in a private school, but for refugees, at least all the refugees I knew, that was not an option. The national exam was the only way we could get out of Gihembe. I wanted to do something with my life. I should have died so many times—in Gihembe, in Mudende, in Kitchanga—that if I wasted my life, I would be dishonoring the people I loved who had been killed. And in order to do anything at all, I needed to pass that exam.

The national exam was very difficult. It lasted a full week and covered things I felt prepared for, like physics and chemistry, as well as subjects that seemed out of my grasp as a refugee, like computer science. We took solace in the fact that most of it was based on rote memorization. "As long as we can recite the information, we can pass," we said to one another. "We don't have to really understand it."

Still, in Gihembe we were at a disadvantage. We didn't have access to the same study material as most of the Rwandan students, and because we didn't have the internet, we couldn't access practice exams. Our teachers, as wonderful as they were, struggled to prepare us for an exam few of them had taken themselves. We realized quickly that, as with most things in the refugee camp, if we wanted to pass the national exam, we would have to improvise.

My friend Gasengi and I were the best students in our class. "Gasengi, let's start a study group for the exam," I said, seizing an opportunity to show that I had grown up since the incident with Fedha. "Anyone who wants to can come study with us. We will all try to pass the national exam together." The more refugees who passed the exam, I thought, the stronger our message would be to the outside world. "They would have to accept that we are as smart as Rwandan students," I told Gasengi, who agreed. "If there were hundreds of us graduating from Rwandan schools, they would have to take us seriously," he said. "They would have to help us go to university."

For weeks, Gasengi and I collected tiny amounts of money—one hundred Rwandan francs, just pennies—from as many families as we could and used it to buy a small blackboard and some chalk and kerosene. Even the poorest parents in the camp contributed whatever they could, because it was for school. They would have done anything to help. I don't think there were any parents in the entire refugee camp who didn't dream about their children one day going to a Rwandan school outside Gihembe.

Ameh, an orphan in ninth grade, opened up his tent to the group for the lessons. Every evening between school and dinner, Gasengi and I strung a kerosene lamp across the top of the tent and studied, along with whoever from the school wanted to join us, from a few old national exams we had begged our teachers to find for us. A Catholic aid organization that had worked in Rwanda since 1995 promised they would try to sponsor students from Gihembe to go to high school. With their support we would be able to afford transportation, the small school fees, uniforms that consisted of long pants rather than shorts. After we learned that, we started meeting twice a day, once after school and once in the predawn hours before school began.

Dozens of refugee students attended our study sessions, including Mutabazi, Innocent, and Fedha, who by then had forgiven me for delivering the offensive note. Because so many of the boys had been killed in Congo, there were more girls in our study group. Their presence sent another message. Girls our age could be raped when they left the camp, but they were willing to take any risk in order to go to school.

In the study group, we shared the same fantasy. "One day we will all be in high school together," Gasengi said. "Then we will go to university in Kigali, and after that, who knows." Compared with Célestin and Patrick, who each coped with the boredom in Mudende by developing wild aspirations to be a pilot or a doctor, children my age in Gihembe weren't open about wanting so much. We were less naïve. Or maybe we didn't dare to think that far beyond our tents and the small school we attended every day. Maybe we were tired; it takes energy to want things beyond what you have.

Once we started studying for the national exam, though, our dreams bubbled to the surface. Gasengi said that he wanted to be a doctor, and I confessed that I dreamed about more than being a teacher. "I want to change education in refugee camps forever," I said. "I want to make sure that refugees get the best education in the world."

Students dreamed of being aid workers and university professors. We wanted to make movies like the ones we saw occasionally in Kageyo. We imagined ourselves working the jobs of the characters in those movies, being spies or high-powered lawyers or race car drivers or, in one particularly appealing instance, becoming a scientist who studies the animals in Congo.

We all wanted to leave Gihembe. "Maybe we will live in Kigali one day," we said to one another. "Or Europe, or America." While we studied, the world suddenly seemed open to us. All we had to do was pass one test.

◆

IN NOVEMBER, we woke up early and walked down the hill to the school in Kageyo. Some of us were nervous and quiet. Others bubbled over with excitement. "I can't believe it's today," Fedha said. As was required by the school of all girls, her hair had been cut close to her scalp. At first, she had worried that it would make her ugly. I thought, but was too shy to say, that it made her even prettier. Without hair her eyes looked enormous, as though she could see something coming from miles away, as though she were superhuman.

Many of us, being teenagers, were grumpy, desperate to go back to sleep. "Gasengi, did we study enough African geography?" I asked, panicked. My friend smiled and nodded. "Mondiant, we studied everything," he said. "There was nothing more that we could do. Don't worry."

The Rwandan school was modest, built of wood and bricks and surrounded by a small yard for playing. Classrooms were decorated with faded maps and posters about handwashing. We sat in long rows, side by side with the Rwandan students, monitored by local authorities who were there to make sure no one cheated. When the sun went behind a cloud, the police turned on fluorescent lights that made the white walls glow a sickly yellow.

The Rwandan students stared at us. They were curious, I thought, but not suspicious, and if it mattered to the students that we were refugees, they didn't show it. They looked like anthropologists, making note of our differences. Waiting for the exams, we did the same.

We wore cheap sandals made out of recycled tires, or walked barefoot, but the Rwandan students had on real shoes. Their clothes were cleaner and newer, but otherwise the same as ours. At midday, when there was a break from the exam, the Rwandan students ate food they had brought with them or went home for lunch, while we sat on the playground, talking and ignoring our familiar pangs of hunger, going over the exam and trying to guess what came next. I sat on the bottom of a slide, the cold of the metal seeping through my pants, closing my eyes and trying to picture our study materials and the practice tests.

Every morning of the test week, we walked down the hill, a parade of desperate, determined students, and every evening we retraced our steps, rehashing that day's portion of the test. "Did you get the entire periodic table?" I asked Fedha. "What did you say about why tea is important to Rwanda's economy?" she asked Gasengi. "Did you find that the value of x for question twenty was six?" Innocent asked no one in particular.

Before the exam we might have obsessed about the Rwandan students, discussing what they wore and ate, whose parents came to pick them up in a car and who walked, like we did. Did they look at us with acceptance or distaste? When they laughed, were they laughing at us? But now there was no room in our conversation for those students. We hoped for their sake that they had studied as much as we had. We were all certain that we had done well and that soon we would be leaving the camp.

◆

IN JANUARY, two months after we had walked as a group down the hill to the school in Kageyo to take the national exam, the Rwandan Ministry of Education released the results of the exam. Because we didn't have internet in the camp, we had to walk to Kageyo, where they were posted on a board outside the local school.

As soon as school let out in Gihembe, we ran to the town. Dozens of us crushed together outside the school, searching for our names. When I found my name, I immediately went home running, celebrating and jumping with my classmates who had also passed. Out of over two hundred fifty refugee students who had taken the exam, fifty-two had passed, and over half of our study group, more than any other year.

My mother was sitting in front of our home washing beans for dinner. "Why are you so happy, Mondiant?" she asked, smiling herself at my enthusiasm. I hadn't told her that the exam results had been posted. If my name wasn't on the list, I wanted to be able to be alone and not have to answer any of her questions.

"I passed the exam," I told her. "I'm going to study outside of Gihembe."

"Mondiant, that's wonderful," she said. "Ibyo ni byiza cyane." Here, again, her words mean the most to me in Kinyarwanda. She seemed relieved; my mother knew that the only way out of the refugee camp was to get an education. I couldn't believe that all my hard work had paid off.

◆

THE CATHOLIC ORGANIZATION that would sponsor me and other refugee students had done a lot of work in Rwanda since the genocide. It was one of many organizations that tried to help in refugee camps, whether by sending food or money or school supplies, or helping to build homes to replace tents or systems for fresh water. Sometimes these organizations offered exposure to the world, sending photographers who documented us in front of our homes or studying in the one-room school, children reaching their hands out toward the camera. After every visit, every photography session, every delivery of goods, we waited hopefully for something big to change, but it never did.

I understood why outsiders were interested in witnessing life in the camp and helping if they could. When the fighting first started in Rwanda, most countries ignored the violence. As the number of deaths began to multiply and whole cities of refugees grew in remote parts of the country, those countries felt guilty. They sent money, medicine, kind words. Individuals who were shocked by the level of violence also donated to relief funds. For the people who felt they had let the violence happen, refugee camps were a good place to atone. They recognized that the scale of the violence was not mere war, that it was the attempt to extinguish a population on the basis of ethnicity, and they began using the term *genocide* as though it were a validation for all we had been through, or a reward for our suffering.

I was so grateful for the help we received in Gihembe, whether from the Rwandan government, the UN, or smaller aid organizations. Without them we would surely be dead. But it's not enough to sustain someone's bare existence in a refugee camp. As the years went by and I grew older and smarter and more curious, I began to question what these organizations and celebrities and researchers wanted when they came.

Why did we clean up the camp and wash our clothes in preparation for a visit from an outsider? Why did we laugh and smile for the cameras? Why did kids start singing "Food is coming, we're going to eat" when we saw the World Food Programme trucks pass by our classroom window? When organizations suggested decreasing the amount of money we received each month or insisted on paying refugee teachers less than Rwandan teachers, why did we accept it, complaining only in our tents? It is disorienting to feel so hopeful upon seeing well-wishers or aid workers one moment, and so crushed the next moment when they are gone, the dirt curling around their back tires as they drive back to their Kigali hotel. It is impossible to live your life on hope alone.

It had been more than ten years since Congolese refugees arrived in Rwanda. Although we spent every day watching for the approach of these aid trucks like farmers during a drought watching the clear sky for rain, we didn't realize that our helpers were growing weary of us.

Two weeks after we learned who had passed the exam, the Catholic organization announced that in fact it wouldn't be funding refugee students that year. It was as though a foot had come out of heaven to crush us. I heard that we'd been in the camp for so many years that donors no longer wanted to sponsor us. Instead, they were going to sponsor other refugees from other countries where the number of displaced was increasing. It made no sense. Just because you're in a refugee camp for a long time doesn't mean you give up your dreams. For me, at that moment all the joy left Gihembe.

Thirty-One

I spent the next few weeks hiding in our tent, feeling sorry for myself. I was barely able to drag myself to school. I was so upset, my family didn't ask me to collect firewood or water. They were scared to talk to me. I was as fragile as an egg.

The tent became like the cave had been in Congo. It served only to hide me while I waited for my terrible fate to track me down. I worried I would never be able to leave. I worried that one day I would walk in a depressed fourteen-year-old and the next day I would walk out a grown-up with a wasted life and no future outside the refugee camp. When Faustin and his friend Fabien told me about a construction job ten miles away from the camp, I asked if I could go with them. "Sure," Faustin said, his calm voice hiding the relief he felt at seeing me get up and show interest in something.

The next morning, we rode on a truck to the construction site, where a huge building was being erected beside a tall hill. The developers needed as much labor as possible to get the job done quickly, and the builders recognized that refugees were a good resource. Rwanda had instituted work programs for refugees, but it had been hard to persuade locals, who were mostly very poor, to hire us, and so job opportunities like this were still very rare. We jumped at the chance to make money, which was the only way to break the pattern of dependence encouraged by life in a refugee camp. I planned to save what I could and buy my own school supplies and uniforms. I was still determined to take my rightful place at the Rwandan high school.

We lined up with other men, waiting for our assignment. Most of the work was hard physical labor—unloading building materials from trucks, carrying steel rods and concrete blocks. When it was my turn to talk to the human resources manager, he looked at me and laughed.

"What are you doing here?" he asked me. "You're a little boy."

"I can work," I said. "I'm nearly fifteen."

"Are you a student?" he asked.

"I am," I said. "I need to buy books, pens, and shoes before school starts."

The manager sighed. "Are you able to lift heavy things?" he asked. "Can you carry steel and concrete?"

"I am sure I could," I said, although I wasn't sure.

He shook his head and wrote something down in the large notebook he kept on the desk in front of him. "Go stand over there," he said, pointing to a group of older boys. "You're too scrawny to lift the steel. If I see you trying, I'll fire you."

I was assigned to carry concrete blocks from one part of the building site to another. Because we had built most things in Gihembe using pressed mud and plastic for a roof, I had never carried the gray blocks. They were heavy and uniform, and the structure was sleek and well built. It looked sturdy, like it would last forever.

Work began at six thirty in the morning and ended at five thirty, with a thirty-minute lunch break during which I normally sat, scanning the crowd for my brother. My hands blistered and bled, and my back hurt. I stayed quiet; if I admitted that I was in pain, I would be admitting that I was too young and weak to do the work, and I wanted the money.

I didn't see Faustin and Fabien all day, and when we met to walk back to Gihembe together, I asked them where they had been. They looked at each other and laughed.

"We were painting inside," they said, giggling together.

"How did you get to paint the rooms while I was carrying concrete?" I asked. "You both are bigger than me."

"We told the manager we were trained painters," Faustin said. "We didn't think he would believe us, but he did. Do your hands hurt?" He and Fabien burst out laughing again.

Faustin was staying with us in Gihembe that night, and he and Fabien gloated about their victory the entire walk home, teasing me for not being smart or daring enough to pull off the same trick. "We are masterminds!" They laughed with each other. "All we had to lift was a paintbrush while you had to lug stones and blocks."

At first, I fumed at them. My legs and arms were so sore I felt like they might fall off. I resented my brother for being bigger and stronger, and now I resented him for also being smarter. The specks of white paint on his T-shirt and pants infuriated me.

But we returned day after day, and every day I felt stronger and faster. I no longer ached on the way home. By the end of the tenth day, I was carrying almost twice what I could the first day and I had the equivalent of ten dollars to spend. I went to the market and, for the first time in my life, presented a vendor with my own money, which I used to buy a new pair of shoes and pants. It would take a while before I had what I needed for school, but I was getting closer. I started to see the humor in my brother's trickery. It was lucky to be assigned to paint while everyone else toiled around you, and my brother didn't have a lot of luck in his life.

◆

WITH THE PROMISE OF SCHOOL FADING, young people were trying to figure out other ways to leave Gihembe. Boys like me and Faustin looked for work, doing whatever we could for a small amount of money. Girls my age took on greater responsibility doing chores outside the camp, even though for them the risk of being assaulted or raped increased with every step they took away from the entrance.

For some of the older girls, their best option was to find a husband. Sometimes, this was a cause for celebration. If a girl's family in Gihembe found the man suitable, they would do whatever they could to throw a small party. Women wore their most beautiful Congolese kitenges and men spent what they could on beer. After it was over, we all wished we could have moments of joy like this every day; they were the only thing that truly distracted us from hunger or anxiety about our future.

When Bagogwe girls chose local Hutu men as husbands, though, their families didn't throw parties. They gossiped and shook their heads; some mothers cried. "It will never last," they whispered. "Hutu and Tutsi people don't get along together." They theorized about why a girl would marry the Hutu man in the first place. "Is it just to move to Kigali?" they wondered. "Is it because he has some money?" Although the people in the camp would never be actively cruel toward a Bagogwe girl—many remembered back in Congo when, for generations, intermarriage was normal— her family would act as though it was their duty to feel shame for the entire community. One young woman I know was cut off by her family when she married a Hutu man, she said, out of love. "Don't call us if he hurts you," they told her. Their reaction angered me, but I tried to understand. If all Hutus weren't monsters, then who were we hiding from inside Gihembe?

Boys my age continued leaving to go fight in Congo. My friend Claver, who had been a geography teacher, was given thirty dollars by a rebel to leave Gihembe and join their ranks. "I have no future here," he told me before he left. Still despondent at the prospect of not continuing my education, I couldn't argue with him.

By that time the UN had distributed mobile phones to refugees, and Claver often called me over the weekend from the rebel base asking me how the camp was and sending messages to his mother. "Have you gone to high school yet, Mondiant?" he would ask. "Don't forget the most important subject, geography!" he teased. One day someone else called from his number with news that Claver had been killed while on patrol.

I heard about the death of Mihigo, my only rebel friend in Kitchanga, on the radio. My friend who became a rebel after his entire family burned to death in their home was shot by Congolese soldiers while they flew above him in a military helicopter.

But boys kept leaving to join the rebels. They were angered by news reports, and they left to take back their homeland. They saw their parents retreat into a dreamworld, and they left to provide for their families. They couldn't turn down the small amount of money that a recruiter, waiting by Gihembe's gates, offered to them. Their schooling was over, their future was in a trap. And so they disappeared and were killed. Life was slowly leaving the camp, like gas leaking out of a rusty pipe.

On a Thursday afternoon before a handful of my friends left Gihembe for Congo, never to be seen again, I was sitting in our kitchen boiling ground corn to prepare it for bread. My legs, folded beneath me, were stuck to the floor, muddy after a night's rain, and smoke billowed off the damp wood into my face, making me cough and squint as I stirred, annoyed.

A pair of eyes watched me through a gap in the bricks. "Go away," I said. "This isn't your kitchen." Wanting to be alone, I walked over to the wall and stuffed a piece of paper into the gap.

"Mondiant, what are you doing?" My friend Amani walked to the front door. "Sorry, I wasn't spying. I was just wondering if you were cooking food." He looked toward the pot hungrily.

"Corn bread," I told him. I softened, seeing how hungry he was. "Do you want some when it's ready?"

Ten minutes later, I called out to my siblings who were playing mancala in front of the kitchen. Amani came with them and we all shared a plate of corn bread and beans. We ate in silence until all that was left were some crumbs and drops of murky, salty water. Like me, Amani had passed the national exam but lost his sponsorship. With our schooling nearly over, we had little left to talk about.

After we had finished eating, Amani led me to a tree behind the kitchen. "Mondiant," he whispered excitedly, "I have some big news. I am going to Congo tomorrow night."

I tried to hide my shock. Amani was sweet and soft-spoken, the kind of person who would peer through a hole in a kitchen wall before asking someone directly for food. He was a teenager but still looked like a child. He wasn't a rebel. "Did you decide already, or are you still thinking about it?" I asked him, trying to keep my voice neutral.

"I've decided," he said. "I'm going with four other boys from this zone." He listed their names. They were all classmates, also denied sponsorship to high school. I played soccer with them almost every day. These were boys I shared every aspect of my childhood with. When I had returned from Congo, they had asked me dozens of questions, and I thought they had understood me when I warned them never to go home.

"Let's all talk tomorrow after school lets out," I said. Amani agreed.

The next day it was my turn to help clean the classroom. I waited for Amani and his friends to join me and then we swept and mopped, wiping down the desks and chalkboard and taking the trash to the dumpsters nearby. We worked in silence and walked home together. "Let's wait to talk until we get there," I said. Once we were together in relative privacy, I started to ask them questions.

"How will you get to Congo?" I asked.

"People came and parked their car outside the camp," they told me. "They will take us."

"How do you know these people?" I asked. "Who are they?"

"They come into the camp a lot," Amani said. "They told us that if we are willing to go to Congo, they will give us money."

"How much money did they promise you?" I asked.

"Three thousand five hundred francs," Amani answered. It was the equivalent of about five American dollars, less than the money we received from the UN every month. I seethed, thinking of these recruiters. It was easy to manipulate young, starving people.

"But why do you want to go to Congo?" I asked. "It's very, very dangerous there. And your families are here."

"Congo has a lot of treasure," the boys told me, echoing the stories about a lost paradise they had heard from their parents their entire lives. "It has copper and diamonds, gold and silver. People go there to become rich."

"I've been there," I said. "It's not like that at all. People are poor just like they are here, and starving just like they are here. But there's also fighting everywhere. Do you remember the war?" The boys had never left Gihembe; all they knew of Congo was the stories their parents told. They were more naive than I had been, and they shook their heads. "Do your parents talk about the war?" They shook their heads again. "Did you lose family members in Congo or Mudende before you came here?" I asked.

This time, they all nodded yes. "My aunts and uncles were killed," Amani said. Others had lost siblings and parents. Some had scars of their own, visible around their calves and ankles, or on their cheeks.

"But that's another reason I want to go," Amani said softly. "We can help our parents get their land and their old lives back."

"That's why my father said he was going," I told them. "But we ended up in a refugee camp that was much worse than Gihembe." I told them about how hopeful we had been, crossing the border, and the heartbreak of being taken to Kitchanga instead of Bikenke. "I cannot explain to you how scary it was," I said. "It was like Rwanda right after the genocide. I saw bodies every day."

We talked for hours. My mother brought us small cups of banana juice, which the boys accepted eagerly and drank in an instant. I told them what the villages in Congo looked like, and how my lessons were often interrupted by rebels asking students to clean up battlefields. But I didn't tell them that I had been recruited by the rebels. I remembered my promise to my mother.

"The rebels are fighting for us," they said. I just shrugged. "I don't think they will win," I told them. "I don't think that fighting is the way for us to leave Gihembe."

By the time Amani and his friends went home, they told me they had changed their minds. "I don't want to go through what you went through, Mondiant," Amani said. "You're right, it's a bad idea." I remember that he shook my hand, as though we had made a deal.

After Amani left, I went to bed satisfied. I thought I had saved their lives and saved their families from mourning. But on Sunday before I went to church, their parents came to our home. "Mondiant, do you know where our children are?" they asked. "It's time to go to church and we can't find them anywhere."

When a Bagogwe is killed, the whole community mourns together for a full week. We light fires outside their home and sing to comfort the family. With thousands of Congolese boys dying with the rebels, most of them still children, it was hard to keep up our mourning rituals. Our throats became raw with singing; the camp smelled permanently of smoldering fire. People stopped crying; it was as though they had forgotten how.

In Gihembe, we didn't even wait to hear that the boys had been killed before we started. Amani's family knew to light the mourning fire as soon as they realized their boy had left.

Thirty-Two

While I studied for what I assumed would be my last month of school, I started asking myself questions that I had never dared to contemplate. Why am I a refugee? I asked myself this over and over, lying on my mat at night trying to sleep. Why me and not someone else? Why Bagogwe? Why Rwanda, and why Congo?

Although I tried to come up with a plan, I was still fighting waves of depression. Sitting on the hill in front of our home, I could see the long paved road connecting Kageyo to the national school. I imagined students boarding the bus to school in new uniforms and shoes, their supplies wrapped tightly in pieces of cloth by worried mothers the night before. In my head it was a war between hope and despair. It was hard to ignore the feeling that my future was in Gihembe. I felt like my body was breaking down.

On Mondays we studied chemistry, physics, and biology, my favorite subjects. One day, during physics, I started to feel dizzy. My eyes began to lose focus until I couldn't read what was written on the chalkboard, even though I was sitting in the front row. My stomach hardened into concrete.

"Mondiant, what is happening to you?" Safuki, the physics teacher, asked. "Are you ill? If you're ill, you should go home."

I shook my head. I didn't want to go back to my home and sit on my mat with nothing to do. "Just let me go outside," I told the teacher. "I'll feel better if I get some air, and then I'll be right back."

Outside the classroom there was no garden or playground. There wasn't a bench where someone could sit if they felt sick. Surrounding the classroom was just the refugee camp, with its mishmash of brick structures and tents built alongside winding, narrow pathways carved like a wide staircase up the Rwandan hillside.

I leaned my back against a brick wall and then slid down against it until I was sitting on the ground. My head felt like it might float off my body. I breathed for a moment, putting my head in my hands. After things stopped spinning, I stood up carefully and went back into the classroom, silently taking my place at my desk. There was no way I was missing one of my last physics classes.

A few minutes later, I closed my eyes. Flames were painted on the insides of my eyelids, blindingly bright. The next thing I knew, I was at home lying on my woven eucalyptus mat. My mother and her friend were sitting beside me, weeping as though someone had died.

"What's going on?" I asked. "How did I get here? I am supposed to be in physics class."

My mother put her hand on my forehead. "Shhhh, Mondiant," she said. "You need to rest. You came back from very far away."

"What does that mean?" I was confused. My head hurt. "What happened?"

"You lost consciousness in class," my mother said. "Your classmates brought you here. They thought you were dead."

"What happened, Mondiant?" her friend asked. "Your eyes rolled back, and we thought you had taken your last breath."

I was about to tell her that it was because we hadn't eaten for three days, when I felt my mother flick her fingernail against mine. When she did that, it meant be quiet. She didn't want anyone to know that I was hungry.

My mother wasn't the only one who stopped her children from talking about their empty, aching stomachs. Hunger was common in Gihembe, but it was shameful. When children got sick or died, their families often denied that it was because of malnutrition. We died of malaria or cancer, car accidents or snakebites, but never of hunger.

People used to whisper that camp authorities wanted it this way, too. "If no one ever admits to dying of starvation, they don't have to admit how bad things are in the refugee camps," they said. In Gihembe we had a clinic where people were given simple medicines for headaches and fevers, but it took a long time to be transferred to a big hospital and, without good diets, people remained weak. Our monthly rations of corn and beans were never enough, and neither was the seven dollars—or one month, eight; the next month, six—that replaced them. I think if we'd simply had sufficient food, a lot of refugees would still be alive.

Hiding our hunger was part of the campaign of silence. In Gihembe, no one admitted to being ill. I have friends whose bodies are covered with machete scars, but I still don't know exactly how they got those scars. We pretended that their skin was smooth, or that they were born with them. We never mentioned them, even when the scars were on their faces. Those same friends would have not eaten for two days, but if you asked them to share your lunch they would say, "No, I'm full." We lied to ourselves and one another about our own pain so that we didn't feel ashamed of our own weaknesses and our parents' deficiencies. Amani must have been particularly desperate to lurk around our kitchen, asking for corn bread.

My mother kept flicking her fingernail against mine until I pulled my hand away. "I have a really bad headache," I told her friend. "I don't think I slept very well."

◆

STUDYING FOR THE NATIONAL EXAM, I could forget that I hadn't eaten for days. With my dreams of high school in ruins, that hunger seemed permanent and impossible to ignore.

The first time I stole, I took some money from my mother so that I could watch the Champions League in Kageyo. I still feel guilty for doing that. I remember the disappointed look my mother gave me, and the desperate one she gave my father when she realized we had nothing to eat because of my selfishness.

The second time, I stole out of hunger. I was walking with a dozen friends to the forest to gather firewood, close to fainting. It had been two days since I had eaten anything, and I was sure that for most of my friends, it was the same. We barely talked on the way to the forest.

On the way back we passed some passion fruit vines. Normally, we walked by the vines, which we knew belonged to a Rwandan farmer, and tried not to think about them. We joked and told stories and did whatever we could to distract ourselves from the food hanging within reach. Stealing was shameful, and we didn't want to upset our parents.

That day, though, I was so hungry that I felt dizzy. I remembered fainting during physics class and wondered what would happen if I collapsed outside the camp. Would my friends have to leave behind their bundles of wood in order to carry me? I didn't want them to have to. I stopped in front of one of the trees. My heart beat fast with the thought of taking something that wasn't mine. But in my head, it was simple. *Instead of dying*, I thought, *let me go and steal.*

I didn't have to say it out loud. As soon as I stopped in front of the passion fruit vines, other kids stopped as well. "Is there anyone around?" Mutabazi asked, looking over his shoulder. The same local security forces that burned our firewood would beat us if they caught us stealing the farmer's fruit.

I shrugged my shoulders. "Some of us will keep watch," I said. "Maybe they are all at home because of the weather." It was raining so hard I could barely see my hands. If security guards did discover us, it might take them longer than usual to recognize the figures of refugee children snatching the fruit. Maybe in the extra moment, we could pluck something off the tree and eat it. Nevertheless, we would have to be careful. "Be quiet," we said. "If you see someone coming, run."

Because the boys in our group were faster than the girls, we decided that the boys would take the passion fruit while the girls stood watch. If they saw anyone approaching, they would yell at us to run, and then start running themselves. We parted ways like thieves in a movie, girls trotting off to stand beside the fence that surrounded the farm and boys wading into the mud, where we began wrenching the brown spheres from their vines. We planned to take only as much as we could eat right there. If we brought any home to our families, they would punish us for stealing.

We worked quickly under the cover of rain. Unlike the Rwandans, who lived under proper roofs and wore regular shoes, we were used to living our lives pummeled by the Rwandan rainstorms. We routinely excavated our plastic sandals out of knee-deep mud, and we were accustomed to falling asleep with water dripping onto our arms. We collected firewood, cooked, and studied, damp from rain. Now it would hide us.

But the farm was bigger than we realized, and therefore more profitable and heavily guarded. Passion fruit vines had been knit loosely together over dozens of poles; they were a reliable source of income for the farmer, who was so certain that refugees like us would ruin his crops if we could that he employed dozens of men to watch for us day and night. The farm was only fifteen minutes from Gihembe, and very close to the main road and the office of a local leader in Kageyo, situated at the base of a giant upward slope and otherwise surrounded by high fences topped with barbed wire.

Before we had a chance to crack open even one passion fruit, we heard dogs. "Run, run!" The girls' shouts were muffled by the rain, and stopped as soon as the local security forces came into view. "What are you doing!" they shouted. We dropped the fruit and started running.

Local security are nominated by townspeople to patrol places like private farms. They aren't police, but they are trained by the police and paid by the government. They wear uniforms, and when they see something happening, they are responsible for detaining people until the police arrive to arrest them. Because they were recruited from surrounding towns, we usually recognized their faces. That familiarity, though, rarely protected us. If they thought it was necessary, local security alerted the Rwandan police or military after they'd caught someone. With refugees, they almost always thought it was necessary.

The guards chased us all the way to the fence. We were faster than them, but the fence was impossible to climb. Barbed wire tore through our legs and hands, caught on our shorts, and stopped us from jumping to the other side. It cut a gash in my palm so deep that I still have a scar, which, like the scar on my chin, I tell people I got playing soccer.

"Why are you stealing?" they screamed at us, pulling us down to the ground and immediately beginning to cane our legs and arms. "You steal every day!"

When I had a chance to catch my breath, I shook my head. "I'm sorry," I said. "We don't, we really don't. This is the first time we've been here."

"Every day there is some fruit missing," the security guard shouted at me. "You come here every day, and every day somehow you get away. But not today." He started hitting me again.

I don't know if Rwandan citizens are caned by local security. I never saw it happen. The local forces aren't supposed to beat the people they find, and I only ever saw them hurt refugees. They wouldn't stop no matter how loudly we protested. "We haven't been here before," we insisted, our faces pressed against the mud.

"We saw you running, and we saw you taking fruit," they said. "We saw you." We curled our bodies as tightly as we could and let them hit us. I was relieved to see that most of the girls seemed to have gotten away.

Suddenly, my friend Saza began to shake. Saza had epilepsy and often had seizures in class. That's how he had gotten his nickname; Saza means "old man" in Kinyarwanda. In Gihembe, we knew how to help him, placing a stick in his mouth to stop him from biting his tongue, giving him space, and taking him to the clinic after he had recovered. The guards, though, stepped back, alarmed.

"What's happening to him?" One of the guards put down his cane. For a moment we only heard the rain, now at a slow drip, falling on the leaves. Saza kept shaking, his legs and arms splayed stiffly out from his body, his head lurching backward. The guard turned to look at his colleague who had been beating Saza. "What did you do?" he yelled. They would get into trouble if one of us died. "Pick him up, let's take them to the office." Two of the guards picked up Saza, stiff and traumatized, and carried him through the farm in the direction of their office. After a minute, my friend stopped shaking and swung limply between them like a hammock, quietly crying.

We were detained in a small white house on the edge of Kageyo. We waited there for two hours, sitting on the cold concrete floor while they caned us and threw water on us, accusing us of weeks of theft. Saza lay quiet in the corner, wet and still.

We tried to defend ourselves. "We are students," we told them. "We have never taken a single thing from the farm before." I knew they were right, though, to call us thieves. I was so ashamed that I prayed that I would be able to escape.

"Why were you stealing?" they asked us.

None of us answered him. I imagined my mother flicking my fingernail with hers, reminding me to keep our family's shortcomings private. If we told them, "We didn't eat," what would they think of refugees? "They can't even feed their children," they might say. It wouldn't have stopped them from beating us.

I don't know what would have happened to us if Saza hadn't had a seizure. After they beat and interrogated us, they decided to let us go. One of the men called the community leader in Gihembe. "We have your children," he said angrily. "They were stealing fruit. Come and get them."

Representatives from the refugee camp eventually arrived at the house to get us. We looked at the floor when they came in, too ashamed to make eye contact. They didn't care that we had been beaten. That was normal. They only wanted to stop the guards from calling the police.

"Please, we will take them," they said. "We will make sure they never steal again."

"Go," they said. "Take them. But if we see them again, we are calling the police." We helped Saza walk to the door, our beaten bodies like crutches for his broken one.

In Gihembe, our families immediately began rewriting what happened so that no one would know we had been starving. Our attempted theft, the running, the gash in my hand, our battered and swollen legs, our shame and guilt—it wasn't about the lengths people will go to when they are hungry, or the desperation refugees in Gihembe felt every month waiting for more money or more food. "The kids have to be more careful when they go look for firewood," people said. "They stopped at the farm. They were caught on private land."

We became trespassers, lost children beaten by guards when they discovered us walking aimlessly through the private farm. "Saza is sick, you know," our parents said. "He has seizures all the time." There was no mention of why we would have been risking our lives for a few bites of fruit. In Gihembe, children were killed for trespassing; we did not die of hunger.

Thirty-Three

At night, Gihembe is quiet. Without a reason to be outside, or many lights to help play endless games of mancala, and because hunger makes you sleepy, most people retreat into their homes and tents early. It's warm inside, and relatively dry when it rains. When the wind rushes through the camp, rattling the tin and plastic roofs, inflating the tents, you feel safe inside. Your family is there, and if you're lucky you can dream of Congo before the war.

Inside our homes, we can be honest with one another. We don't have to worry about word getting back to camp administrators that we were complaining. When there is a dispute in the camp, we wait to talk about it until we're inside together. If people feel betrayed by the camp authorities, we watch the sun disappear over the mountain and then meet in the privacy of our homes, talking softly about the unfairness. "We can't be expected to live off seven dollars a month," my mother will say. "Shhh, Eugenie," my father tells her. "Let's not let the neighbors hear." He says this knowing that the neighbors are probably saying the same thing in their own homes to their own nervous spouses.

In Gihembe, we are forever grateful and forever frustrated. We are grateful because we are alive. We are frustrated because that's all we are. When we try to push back or to ask for more, it never seems to work.

Gihembe had its own informal political structure. Every two years we elected the camp's leadership, including a community leader whose job was mainly to send messages from the camp to representatives from aid organizations and the Rwandan government. There was a limit to what the leader could say, though, and more than once someone who appeared to be a troublemaker would lose the support of the UN. The most outspoken refugees never seemed to last as leaders, no matter how much we supported them.

I looked up to these leaders, particularly the ones who caused trouble. One of them, Ndayisaba, had been my math teacher in middle school. He was young and not afraid of anyone, but because he wasn't well known outside the camp, the officials thought he would be a safe choice for community leader and allowed us to put him in charge.

In school, though, Ndayisaba spoke all the time about how unfair it was that refugee teachers were paid significantly less than Rwandan teachers, in spite of the extra work they had to do, writing curriculums suited for refugee students who were still catching up, or staying late when we needed extra help. Rwandan teachers were required, like all visitors, to leave Gihembe at five, after the camp had closed its gates. "Those are the rules," the principal would tell Ndayisaba. "They have to leave early. No one is allowed to be here in the evening. What am I supposed to do about it?"

But Ndayisaba wasn't satisfied with that answer. He explained to us how unfair the arrangement was. "Just because we are refugees, it doesn't mean we have to accept less money," he told us. When our food rations were rotten or so old the beans were inedible even after they were boiled for days, he refused them. He would stand up to the people distributing the food and say, "We are not taking it."

After the UN suggested decreasing the amount of money refugees received per month, he protested, writing letters to the representatives and spreading word around the camp. "We don't have to just take whatever they give us," he would say. "We are human beings. They have to treat us like human beings."

Because he spoke up, Ndayisaba was removed from his position by the camp authorities. They did it quietly, sending a communiqué one morning to the camp letting us know that we would have to elect a new community leader. Refugees were confused and angry. "He was fired because they want to continue to give us rotten food," we whispered to one another inside our tents. "Life here is so unfair and no one will listen to us." But as furious as we were, we never said anything except late at night, in the privacy of our own homes after all the camp outsiders were long gone. The message from the camp administrators was clear: If you speak out, we will punish you.

Ndayisaba's firing was an awakening for me. I learned that if your leader is quiet, you will be quiet. If your leader speaks out, it gives you the confidence to speak out. If they fight for you, it gives you the confidence to fight.

Because of him, I recovered from my depression. I climbed out of my tent into a new world. It was possible, I realized, to speak your mind if you wanted to, and to fight for what you wanted in life. Maybe very few people would listen, and maybe you would be punished, but pointing out injustice mattered to those who were suffering. Just because the camps had become permanent fixtures in the Rwandan countryside, it didn't mean that our suffering had to be permanent.

◆

SOMETIMES WHEN I FELT STRESSED, I sat outside at night, just like I had in Kitchanga. I enjoyed the stillness of the camp, listening to the wind through the trees and the occasional cry of a baby. Trying to leave my depression behind me, I made plans. I had bought some shoes and pants with the money I made from working construction jobs, but I still needed someone to pay my school fees. Although I had avoided asking my mother for things for years, knowing how desperately sad she became when she was unable to provide them, I decided to try. "Do we know anyone outside the camp?" I asked her.

"We have a friend who works in a bank in Kigali," my mother said after a moment. "I speak to her every once in a while, she's very kind." She hated to admit how much we needed in Gihembe. Had it been for food, she would have told me no. Feeding us was her responsibility. But she had watched me surrender to depression, and now she was willing to try anything to get me to high school.

I borrowed a mobile phone from a neighbor and called my mother's friend. She picked up after a couple of rings. "Hello, Aunt," I said, using a friendly term. "This is Mondiant."

"Mondiant," she said happily. "It has been so long since I heard from you. How are you doing? How is your school going?"

I paused, wondering what I should say. Why did I think I would be luckier than Gasengi, who still hadn't found a sponsor, or Fedha, who had done even better than I had on the national exam? I took a deep breath and told her. "I am not a student anymore, Aunt," I said. "I passed the national exam and was supposed to go to a school in eastern Rwanda, but my family can't afford the school fees."

"What have you been doing, then?" she asked.

I described to her the job at the construction site. "Mostly, though, once school ended, I stayed home," I said. "To tell you the truth, I don't know what to do."

"How much are your school fees?" she asked.

My mother's friend had a good job, but she wasn't rich. Still, she offered me the money. "Mondiant, I can pay for your first year," she said. "After that, you will have to find someone else. But I am happy to do it while I can."

I couldn't believe it. I hung up the phone and started singing gospel songs so loud I thought for sure the walls of our house were shaking. I was going to high school! And my luck didn't end there. My brother Faustin and sister Furaha gave some money as well, even though it meant they would have to put off their own dreams. My father used the small amount of money he had saved to buy me clothes and supplies. My mother, who had been putting aside tiny amounts of money from our monthly stipend, also contributed every penny she could.

Even with all the support, I didn't have money for transportation to the school, which was over forty miles away through a difficult stretch of Rwanda that could be dangerous for a boy alone. My mother, always faithful, offered a solution. "I'll walk you halfway, Mondiant," she said. "We can carry your things together."

A week later, we packed everything I needed: some clothes, a little bit of food and water, and the school supplies I had managed to collect over the years. It was a boarding school and students were responsible for bringing their own bedding. All I had was the thin woven mat I had slept on since arriving in Gihembe, but I was too elated to worry about what the Rwandan students would think of me when they saw it.

My mother and I woke up early on Sunday morning. I slung my bag over my shoulder, and she rolled my mat tightly and placed it on top of her head. Then we started walking.

Since the day I became old enough to leave the camp without her, my mother used to wait anxiously for me to return. She knew how long it would take me to gather firewood or fill cans with water, and she would distract herself for as long as she could, cleaning or talking with neighbors or trying to devise ways to establish a small business in Gihembe like the one she'd had in Bikenke. She would do these things for as long as she was able, and then she would sit on a familiar, worn patch of dirt in front of our home and watch the horizon for a sign of my T-shirt. Only after she saw the red speck getting bigger as it moved slowly toward the camp did she stop worrying.

Now she was leading me away from Gihembe. We walked in silence, stopping occasionally for water or to rest. We joked when we felt tired. That night, my mother and I stopped in Nyabiheke refugee camp, a half day's walk east, where Furaha gave us dinner and a place to sleep. The next morning, we started walking again.

About halfway there, my mother handed me the mat. The rest of the journey would be along a busy road, through towns and markets. She didn't have to worry that I would lose my way. "Mondiant, I'll leave you here," she said. We hugged. Then she turned and walked away from me. I watched her until the bright color of her clothing disappeared into the hills, and then I continued on my own.

◆

FOR THE FIRST TIME I saw how people outside the refugee camp really lived. Students at my high school had families with cars, and money for extra clothes. Their parents drove them to school and left them with large packages of food, which the students unwrapped to reveal whole feasts that they ate only for lunch. When parents visited in the middle of the day or during breaks, they brought treats like juice and cookies, sacks of fruit, new shoes. When the students went home, they went home to electricity. Some even had televisions.

Rwanda was a poor country before the genocide, but the violence completely destroyed the economy. After the genocide, the hundreds of millions of dollars of aid that poured into the country went mostly to refugee camps and to trying to rebuild from the scraps of a country, and most people remained poor. Somehow, Kagame led the country into an economic boom. Farms began producing profitable and exportable crops like coffee. Cities like Kigali exploded and were industrialized. Even around Gihembe, the government paved roads and built schools. More houses in Kageyo glowed with electricity at night. When I started high school in the mid-2000s, the country was considered a success story. I now know that the students were far from wealthy, but to me they seemed rich beyond my imagination.

Refugees benefited from the early aid, but once we were considered safe, that aid began to drop. Because of this perceived stability, and the sheer number of years that refugee camps had existed in the country, authorities announced their intentions to reduce the amount of money we received monthly, which most of us were barely able to survive on. Even though it was Kagame's government building the infrastructure like roads and schools, refugees looked closer to home to explain the shortcomings in the camp, and to many the UN became a foe. "I don't have a husband, I am married to the UNHCR," women used to say, only half joking, blaming the UN for all their problems. By the time I went to high school, the differences between me and my Rwandan classmates had to do with more than just nationality or ethnicity; they were people the country had invested in and believed in, whereas I was forgotten.

Six other refugees from Gihembe had managed to get funding to go to school. We stuck together. That first night, worried that our accents and our clothing gave us away as refugees, we didn't join the other students for dinner, even though we were hungry. We studied hard to catch up. Eventually, all of the other refugee students left school, some because their funding ran out and others because they couldn't keep up with their subjects. I was alone but determined to stay. When my mother's friend's money ran out, Faustin, who was by then teaching in the Nyabiheke refugee camp, asked for the rest of the semester's pay in advance, which he sent to me so I could continue my schooling. My brother worked for four months without collecting a cent, so that I could study.

I excelled in high school. On the first test I placed fourth in a class of fifty-three students, in spite of it being on literature, then my worst subject. I was proud of my hard work. But still, I was beginning to build a cocoon of shame around myself. I forgot the spirit of my teacher who had protested a refugee's low wages, and I even forgot about my mother's selflessness walking me to school. I was relieved that the journey from Gihembe was too long and arduous on foot and too expensive by bus for my parents to visit. I didn't want my parents, who I loved more than anything, to confirm what I was by showing up, skinny and disheveled. Did I truly deserve a place in the school? I wasn't really Rwandan. I had lived off the goodwill of the state and the UN for more than ten years without contributing anything.

Students, not realizing that I was from Gihembe, whispered viciously about refugees at night while we were supposed to be asleep in our dorm. They wondered if we had diseases, why we complained so much when our families had food delivered to us every month without paying for it. "Refugees are all on drugs," they said. "They are drunk all the time. They are like homeless people living in our country." Students in Rwanda had been raised to speak about the genocide with respect, but many of them had not been told to treat refugees with the same sensitivity.

My bunkmate, Jadot, heard something in my voice that made him suspicious.

"Mondiant," he said, "are you from the Congolese refugee camp?"

"No." I pretended to be surprised. "Why would you ask me that?"

"You speak Kinyarwanda like a Congolese person," he said. "I'm from the same district as the Congolese refugee camp. When you speak, it reminds me of how the refugees sound."

"What Congolese camp are you talking about?" I asked, trying to act innocent.

"It's called Gihembe," he said.

"This is the first time I'm hearing that name," I insisted. "I've only ever seen refugees in movies."

This made Jadot, who did worse than I did in school, feel superior to me. Finally, here was something he knew more about. "Interesting!" he said, sitting up on his bed mat, which was newer than mine and probably made in a factory. "Let me tell you about refugees," he said. "I have friends who live in that camp. Some of them have been living in the camp for fifteen years."

Friends? I thought to myself.

"Those refugees have nothing," Jadot said. "They live in tents and the UN gives them beans and sometimes vegetables. They are so desperate and hungry that if you have five hundred francs you can go and sleep with any girl that you want."

I didn't say anything, but Jadot kept talking. "Be careful, though," he said excitedly. "Those Congolese girls are very beautiful, but ninety-five percent of them are HIV positive and they'll sleep with anyone who gives them money, they are so poor."

He stopped and turned to me. "Did you hear what I said, Mondiant?" he asked. He expected a reaction.

I didn't know what to say. I wanted to run away. I wanted to hit him. Maybe if I had been brave, I would have stood up and declared to him, "Stop talking like that. You don't know what you're talking about. I am Congolese, I live in Gihembe. You are an idiot, you are a liar. None of those girls would ever touch you."

I could have reported him to the school principal. Maybe they would have expelled him for being lewd and saying terrible things about refugees. Maybe he would have apologized and felt horrible, and never said any of those things again. Who knows, maybe what he said was illegal and he would have been put in jail.

I didn't do any of those things. Instead, I turned away from him and stood up. "Jadot," I said, "thanks for telling me about the Congolese refugees. I have an exam tomorrow. I have to go to a review session." I left the bunk and sat outside by myself all night, not sleeping.

Thirty-Four

The first person I knew of who was resettled by a refugee agency outside Gihembe was Sadiki, a fourteen-year-old orphan who had been so injured and ill after the Mudende massacre that although he lived alone, he couldn't take care of himself. Sadiki was like the camp's son; everyone's mother made sure his food was cooked and his clothes were washed, but at night he had no one to talk to, and in the morning he had no one to wake him up for school. Scars from burns and machetes covered much of his body, and when he walked, one leg dragged behind the other.

Because of his injuries, Sadiki qualified for a medical resettlement program in Europe, and when we found out he had been accepted and would live in Holland, we celebrated for him. Life was difficult for everyone in Gihembe, but for Sadiki it was almost impossible. "Where is Holland?" we asked one of our teachers. Some of us had seen the Holland national team play soccer, and we could picture their bright orange uniforms, but we had never seen Holland come to life in a movie like cities in America, so we didn't know whether it was beautiful. We were happy for him, but we weren't jealous.

When I say that the refugees in Gihembe are like diamonds, I am thinking about so many people—the students who studied day and night for the national exam; parents who scraped together pennies to buy extra food for their hungry children; teachers who slept in the classroom so no one would steal the chalk.

I am thinking about refugees like Sadiki, who probably would have died young in the camp but who, when he called me after some years in Holland, sounded like a new person. "I use crutches now," he said. "I'm really fast on them!" He spoke Dutch, had graduated from college, and now works at a bank. He hoped to get married. He was crazy about the Dutch soccer team and wore orange on the days they played. "Mondiant, I am so happy," he told me. "I am so happy."

◆

IN 2008, WHEN BARACK OBAMA was elected president of the United States, Gihembe celebrated. Most of us didn't know a lot about American politics, but we weren't naive. We knew that American presidents, even one with African heritage like Obama, would act first in their country's best interests, and that accepting refugees was a controversial idea to many Americans. Still, Obama was Black and had an African father, and we hoped that meant he would be more open to taking people who looked like us, from a place close to that of his ancestors. For the first time, I allowed myself to dream about a life outside Rwanda.

The US ambassador to Rwanda visited Gihembe and encouraged us to work for what we wanted. "Don't lose hope," he said. He knew a lot about the situation of Congolese refugees around the world. "We remember the massacres in Mudende," he told us. Some people cried, hearing him talk about Mudende. We thought that no one cared about those massacres. All we wanted from presidents was empathy. "See, the Americans haven't forgotten about us," we said to each other.

We gathered eagerly around the ambassador, asking question after question. If we applied for a visa, how long would we have to wait at the embassy to talk to someone? Would our UN refugee identity card be enough if we didn't have a passport? What kinds of shots would we need, how many, and how much did they cost? Each question was a little hopeful balloon we let go into the sky. It was the refugee who didn't ask questions when the ambassador came, who sat sullenly by his tent or insisted on finishing a game or a bottle of beer before strolling listlessly to the meeting, that we worried about. That refugee had given up.

Obama's focus on Congo and Rwanda wasn't very different from that of US presidents who came before him. He pressured Kabila to give up power in Congo but was unsuccessful; the dictator had no intention of leaving. Unlike Bush or Clinton, Obama criticized Kagame in Rwanda, but not too much.

Still, when Obama's ambassador told us, with what sounded like genuine feeling, that the administration still cared about what had happened to us at Mudende, we felt rediscovered. America was so far away, and yet the idea of America defined so much of our lives in Gihembe, and we pinned all our hopes on Obama bringing us to the United States as refugees. We had never been to America, but a collage of images from the television shows and movies we watched in Kageyo unfurled in our heads. We pretended to learn from the fast-paced, outrageously plotted thrillers, as though they could provide a guidebook for when we first moved there. "New York is crazy, it's so crowded!" we would say. "Remember to stay off the subways at night."

We listened to the somber reporters on Voice of America tell us about the conflict in Congo, sighing about never being able to go home. Our clothing was donated to us by American organizations, and we held on to it for years until it fell around us in rags. I wore a T-shirt decorated with a black-and-orange tiger, the logo of the Cincinnati Bengals, even though I had never been to Ohio and had never watched a game of American football. My friend Gérald had a baseball hat with the logo of a Texas college team, and my brother John wore a T-shirt on which *Utah*, a word none of us could define or pronounce, was printed in bright colors in front of a snowy mountain.

After Obama was elected, we renamed neighborhoods in the refugee camp after US states. Rwerere was now called Michigan; others were called Arizona and Kentucky. We liked the way these states' names sounded, how substantial they felt when we spoke them. We wanted desperately to live in those words.

When I was in high school, my mother began applying for resettlement, filling out paperwork at the local UN office. It was an arduous process, and often bewildering. At every step, we did what we were told, and yet it often felt like we were swimming in the open ocean with no direction to land. There were papers about our family history on which we narrated our lives as though suffering were a competition; papers asking us about criminal records; endless shots and vaccinations. My mother traveled from Gihembe to the local UN office by herself, carrying our papers and IDs, waiting in endless lines and answering endless questions, all to begin a process that felt so random it might as well have been a lottery, to receive a future that, other than being outside Rwanda, was completely unknown.

A few weeks after she started the process, my mother took me aside. "Mondiant, there is a problem with your papers," she said. "They say you can't be part of our application." Worrying that I would be punished for joining the rebel group, I had lied to the UN people when I returned from Congo, telling them that I had been in a refugee camp in Uganda and that I had lost all my documentation. They had accepted my story—it wasn't outlandish—and given me new papers, with the name I gave them: "Dogon," a name I invented based on "Kadogo," the nickname given to me by the rebels. Because of that, there was no record of me at the UN office. As far as they were concerned, Mondiant didn't exist. "If we want to continue with our application, we have to leave you off of it," my mother said. I gave her my permission. After all she had done for me, how could I deny her the chance to resettle somewhere else with my younger siblings? "I don't want you to stay in Gihembe because of me," I said. "I'll figure out a way to get out of here on my own." I think she trusted that I would.

With Obama as president, going to America didn't seem impossible. Throughout the camp, refugees worked and hoped and followed the rules, dreaming of leaving Gihembe. When someone was finally granted official resettlement, the camp exploded in celebration. We set up long tables with beer and mancala. Women put on colorful dresses and sang traditional Bagogwe songs, and men played music. If we were envious or worried that we would never see the family again, we didn't show it. We didn't ask them for anything, although we needed everything, and when we thought of where they were going—Germany! America! Canada!—we imagined, naively, I now know, a blissful existence, with all they could dream of at their fingertips. We hugged them, patting their backs and congratulating them. We concealed our sorrow until their airplanes were far above the clouds.

One of our neighbors, Lumumba, filled out paperwork for years, dragging his wife and children to Kigali for endless rounds of shots and meetings with the UNHCR office, and praying every day at the outdoor church for it all to amount to something. Returning from Kigali or from the church, Lumumba had a wide, hopeful grin on his face. "One step closer!" he would say, waving a form or showing off the bandaged spot on his arm where he had been vaccinated.

Lumumba was a tall, energetic man. When he was on a mission, as he often seemed to be, he walked between tents so quickly that his sandals kicked up clouds of dust. Although he had lived in Gihembe for over fifteen years, he hadn't lost hope that he would one day leave. It made sense to me that he shared a name with our revolutionary leader. I think he was a hero, like all the parents who resisted suicide.

As his children grew up, Lumumba told them stories about what he imagined life in America would be like. "There will be parks for you to play in, and a big house with rooms for each of you to sleep in," he'd say as they fell asleep, writing his own cradle songs. "There will be school as long as you want to go," he continued, to himself. "College, even." Lumumba made a career of planning for his family's future outside the camp. His tent filled with papers, and he worked through them with the diligence of someone studying for a PhD.

In reality, though, our chances for resettlement seemed to rest entirely on the whims and politics of world leaders—not just Obama, but the prime ministers of Canada, Australia, and the UK, the presidents of France and Germany—these larger-than-life figures we would never meet but who could determine our future with the casual flick of a pen. One day we could be visited by an American ambassador who assured us that his country hadn't forgotten the Mudende massacre, and that his president was determined to help us reach better lives. The next day another leader could turn away from the refugee camp and never think about us again. They were elected officials, just people, but to us they had so much power they were almost gods.

I revered these leaders, just as I revered President Kagame, in part because they held so much more power than I did to change my own life. I saw a lot of my own story in the life of the Rwandan president. He had fled his home when Hutus began attacking Tutsis during the Rwandan revolution in the late 1950s; he was very young, even younger than I had been when I left Bikenke. His family had first stayed in northern Rwanda before crossing the border into Uganda, where he would live near the border until he was a teenager. Like me, Kagame flourished in school and, like me, he became emotional when he heard his Ugandan classmates disparage Rwandans. But while I ran away in sorrow when Jadot insulted Congolese refugees, Kagame became resolved to fight for Tutsis, first in Uganda and later joining rebels in Rwanda determined to retake control of the country. In the disarray of the genocide, they were successful.

That this man, tall and skinny as a reed, and a former forever refugee, had become the most powerful man in Rwanda seemed to contradict all that we refugees in Gihembe thought we had learned about the world. Kagame filled us with hope, and he became admired around the world. His affable, pensive face was often in magazines and newspapers accompanying stories about how he had lifted Rwanda out of the ruins of the genocide. He was a refugee, like us, and he understood what we were going through.

Now, though, we needed Kagame's help again. We needed the same opportunitites as all Rwandans. The country, we heard, was in the middle of an economic renaissance. It was evident even in Kageyo, where new roads connected the town to the rest of the country and where even the poorest residents now seemed to have electricity. Refugees, however, remained stuck and hungry, living off handouts. We dreamed about going to school, getting married, and leaving the camp. We yearned to become Rwandan citizens and forge real lives in Rwanda, where we felt safe, but we had to fight for everything. We needed more from the leader who had saved us. We needed Kagame to give us citizenship. Until we had that, as much as Rwanda had become our home, we could only dream of leaving.

I read somewhere that if you see only one color for a long time, it can create or exacerbate trauma. For so long, all I saw were hundreds of white tents, each with a plastic roof and the UN logo on the side. Rows and rows of white tents as far as you could see. White blocks concealing thousands of stalled lives. White that even when it glowed inside from the morning sun or became smeared with mud during the rainy season remained blank.

Even when the tents were replaced with mud-and-wood structures, the plastic tarps were repurposed as temporary roofs or walls, or slung over the side to catch rainwater, or laid on the ground in front to sit on. We smoothed out walkways, built small shops to sell food or tailor clothing, went to school, but we could never get rid of those white tents. Now my home in Gihembe is made of sturdy mud walls, reinforced with wood and straw, with a proper swinging door and a small front area where we play games. And yet, I still refer to it as a tent. When I think of that home, I picture the thick plastic, puffed out with the strong Rwandan wind, stark white against the green country. That's what I looked at every day for twenty years, those white tents, that nothing color.

When we sang and danced for people leaving Gihembe, it was because we wanted them to remember Africa as home, not as a difficult place that didn't want them. We wanted them to remember the Bagogwe people as united, and our culture for being celebratory. We wanted them to picture us in colorful dresses like the ones our grandparents wore. Then maybe they could forget the white tents and let go of their trauma.

✦

BY THE TIME Lumumba and his family were granted resettlement in the United States, I was already in New York, working toward my master's degree. My own escape from Gihembe was so beyond my imagination that it seemed like it had to be a folktale passed down and exaggerated from generation to generation until it resembled reality the way that pure gold resembled a dull rock. In Gihembe, my suffering and my longing had been universal; almost everyone I knew had survived the Mudende massacre, and almost everyone I knew dreamed of a better life. But my escape was wholly unique, so like a dream that I often still feel I might wake up back in Gihembe. Lumumba's escape, however, was proof that, sometimes, the system worked.

My mother called early one morning while I was at NYU. "Lumumba has been accepted to resettle in the United States," she told me, ecstatic. Lumumba was like a brother to her, and she wanted to see him and his family start a new life.

"After everything they went through," I said. "That's amazing. Tell them I said so. When do they get here?"

"First, they'll go to Germany to meet with the resettlement agency there," my mother said. "There are a few more steps, but they are so close. There will be a party for them tomorrow night in Gihembe." She sounded almost wistful. "Lumumba has worked so hard," my mother said. "He deserves this."

That day I felt happy. Maybe it wasn't the swift emptying of the camp like I imagined in my dreams, but every Bagogwe family who made it out was a victory for all of us. Each of them represented a new hope for the whole community. They could speak for us and help others back in the camp. Lumumba's success followed a comforting logic; he had worked hard, followed all the rules, and now he and his family were being rewarded. Life as a refugee can often feel unfair to the point of chaotic. But that day, the world made sense.

It was 2017 and Donald Trump was president. My new American friends at school had wept after the election. I felt a sense of doom, too, in America, although I didn't know what was to come. I didn't know what would happen to refugees. I didn't know how difficult it would be now to come to America, and how impossible my dream—persuading the American president to care about a group of African refugees halfway across the world—would come to seem. I didn't know that the story of Central American refugees pouring across the border with Mexico would include images of children in cages, or that all people of a certain religion or nationality would be banned from the United States. And I couldn't have predicted that the next time I visited Gihembe, I would find a despondent Lumumba and his whole family sitting in unbearable silence in their old white tent, defeated, after nearly a decade of hard work, by the stroke of a president's bitter pen.

Thirty-Five

I spent every year at the Rwandan high school ashamed that I was a refugee. While other students' parents picked them up before breaks in cars, I walked by myself for days back to Gihembe, my belongings expertly balanced on my head, stopping in Nyabiheke camp for a night with Faustin and Furaha. My parents couldn't even afford the five dollars for a bus.

Jadot kept telling stories about refugees. He was short and small, but his family had some money. He wore stylish clothes and his parents picked him up for holidays in a Suzuki. In my high school, if your family had a car, it meant you were rich and had authority. Jadot was used to people listening when he spoke.

Even after that first night, I had tried to be his friend. I sat next to him in class and laughed at his jokes. One day I took him to Nyabiheke camp to play soccer. When we arrived he leaned over to me and whispered, "Be careful, Mondiant. There is another refugee camp close to here where almost everyone is HIV positive." After that, we drifted apart. "I'm really busy with school, man," I would tell him when he asked if I wanted to play soccer. "Okay," he would say. "I understand." But he looked sad. I almost felt sorry for him.

As unhappy as I was, I excelled at school. Every semester I was ranked among the top three students in the class. I was particularly good at science, but as the months went by, I also started to do well in literature. What had previously seemed frivolous compared with other subjects like science and math began to seem vital. At night, willing myself to fall asleep before Jadot could say anything bad about refugees—the other students loved hearing salacious stories from Gihembe, a place as exotic to them as Kigali was to me—I thought about the poems we had read in class.

I started writing my own poetry, pouring my insecurity about being a refugee into the pages of a notebook I kept close to me at all times. Writing about my own life made being a refugee seem less of a threat to my position in the school, and more a feature of my own identity, like a thread in one of my mother's scarves, no more or less important than all the other threads that made up the whole. "Those we throw away are diamonds," I wrote, thinking of the people I knew in Gihembe, whose lives depended on people outside refugee camps recognizing that they were people, too.

Although I still refused to admit to any of my classmates that I was a Congolese person from Gihembe camp, I did my best to make life easier for myself and for any other refugees who might enroll in the school after me. I started an organization called I Am You, which was meant to highlight and celebrate the school as a place for people of all ethnicities, tribes, genders, and cultures. I believed in the organization's mission, but I also used it as a shield. If I led a group based on inclusion, then no one would question my own right to be included.

I Am You was so successful it was expanded into other Rwandan schools. Still, I never talked about my own background. Many students thought that refugees were leeches in Rwanda, unable to contribute to the country. I didn't want them to think that about me.

I should have been ecstatic to be at school. Finally, I had been given the chance to leave Gihembe and prove that I was capable of building a life outside the refugee camp. So many people—my mother's friend in

Kigali, my own parents, my siblings—had sacrificed so much for me to be there. And yet, I was miserable.

One summer, on break before my final semester of high school, I again found myself in a deep depression. Gihembe hadn't changed at all. The home we lived in would never get bigger or nicer. The wind would continue to shake the roof off above us during a storm so that we woke up to leaves crashing down on us. We would never get citizenship or passports or proper jobs. No country would take us. Everyone had already forgotten about us.

Back in the refugee camp, my enthusiasm drained out of me. I lay on my mat at night, thinking about what would happen after high school. Would I be able to get a job? Would I ever become a citizen of any country? I wondered if high school, and all the work it took to get there, would be just for show. Gihembe was like the center of a whirlpool, pulling me back no matter how hard I tried. At the end of all this schooling, even if I were the best in the class, would I end up still a refugee? Why, then, had God spared me in Mudende?

It was almost time for our fasting holiday, which lasted four days, but even praying felt as hard as climbing a mountain. I pictured my father thumbing through his Bible, the only book he owned. Reading it transformed him. When he sat with his Bible, so worn it lay flat in his hands, he was no longer a cattle rancher or a refugee. He wasn't a father failing his children in the refugee camp, a hopeful immigrant denied admission to the United States or Europe, or a bitter returnee from the forced repatriation. He was a scholar.

Like my father had so many times before me, I took our Bible outside and sat beneath a huge tree next to the main walkway through Gihembe. The weather was mild, and the sun felt good, warm but not too hot. My T-shirt blew around me in the gentle wind. I turned to Ecclesiastes, chapter 7, verse 10, and read it softly to myself. "Do not say, 'Why were the old days better than these?'" I read. "For it is not wise to ask such questions."

✦

THE CHURCH IN GIHEMBE sat in the shade of a circle of trees. On hot days, we worshipped outside. During our days of fasting we lived at the church, singing and praying, thanking God for helping refugees around the world. Unlike at school, where I couldn't admit who I was, in Gihembe I prayed because I was a refugee. I thought about all the times in my life I had been saved while others were killed. No one on earth was luckier than I was.

On the fourth day of the fast, an old woman came to preach in the church. She was a well-respected religious scholar from the south of Rwanda, who also liked to predict the future. She made her living traveling from church to church, but it was her first time in Gihembe. "God sent me north," she told the congregation of refugees. "He told me to come to a refugee camp called Gihembe. He said that when I got here, he would give me a message and show me who the message was for."

I was sitting in the front of the congregation, faint with hunger. Although I had heard of the woman and was eager to hear what she had to say, I couldn't focus. Instead of watching her, my eyes were turned down toward the ground, where tiny black ants swarmed over a small pile of sand. I was wondering whether to poke at the ants when my neighbor jabbed me in the ribs. "She's pointing at you," he said.

"Stand up, please," the woman told me. I stood, my legs shaking with hunger. She looked at me kindly. "God has a message for you," she told me. "Are you ready to listen?"

My cheeks burned with embarrassment. In Gihembe, and at school, we were rarely singled out except when we had done something wrong. Everyone was silent, waiting for me to answer. "Sure," I said. "I'm ready." I thought I heard someone, maybe a friend of mine, giggle.

"Before I say anything, you have to tell me, have you ever seen me before?" the woman asked. I thought that her face was angry, as though she was ready to hit me. "Have we ever met before?"

I shook my head. "No," I said. "This is the first time I've seen you."

With that, she began shouting, raising her arms toward me. "You have been in the darkness for a long time," she yelled. "You have been hungry, thirsty, poor. You have been traumatized and you have felt remorse about the things you did and didn't do." Around me, refugees began to murmur their agreement. They felt moved by her power and authority, but I was frightened and embarrassed. I wished she would finish her speech and give me permission to sit down again and fade back into the crowd.

But as I stood there her words began to take root inside me. My stomach was empty in reverence to God, and not because of poverty. My head was light because of my devotion, not because of illness. I was standing and being singled out because this religious woman, revered throughout Rwanda, wanted to address me, not because I was in trouble. I began to feel strong, as powerful as the words she spoke, and started to really listen. "God told me the dawn is going to break," she said. Her tone had softened, and she smiled at me and at the congregation. "God knows your commitment, your hard work, your ambition. God will send someone from far away to help you."

I nodded and smiled back. So many people had helped me already.

"I see you at the airport," she told me. "I see you flying abroad for school. I see you helping people. You will no longer be hungry. People will help you with everything they have." She stopped talking. Sweat ran down my back, and I looked out of the corners of my eyes at my friends and family seated near me. I felt self-conscious again. "Sit down," she told me. "I'll come back next year to check on this prophecy. By then, you will be studying in college."

The service ended and we began going home. Now that we were allowed to eat, our hunger started to feel like a drug. People dragged their feet and rubbed their eyes, as though waking up from a long sleep. I stayed sitting, unable to move, thinking about what I had just heard, when the woman approached me again. "What's your name?" she asked. Up close she was just as intimidating as she had been in front of the crowd.

"Mondiant," I told her. I was embarrassed that she was talking to me, and wished she would go away.

"Mondiant," she said. "You don't believe what I told you?" I shrugged. I didn't want to offend her.

"I don't know," I said. "It's hard to believe it."

"Why?" she asked. I shrugged again. How could I explain how impossible it was to imagine flying on an airplane when I had barely managed to go to high school? "It's hard to imagine that those things would happen to me," I said.

"Let me tell you some things about your life," the woman said. "And then maybe you'll believe me." She leaned close to me and began to whisper. She knew things that were secrets in my family. "I know that you tried to steal fruit when you were looking for firewood," she said. She knew things I had never told a single soul. "I know that you considered killing yourself," she said in a sad, intimate whisper that made my skin feel cold.

She knew about my life in Kitchanga, and my time with the rebels. "You did what you had to do," she said. "And when you couldn't take it anymore, some kind people found you and helped you escape. Isn't that true?" I nodded. I couldn't speak.

"Don't worry so much, Mondiant," the woman told me. A crowd had gathered around us, straining to hear what she was saying to me, the young refugee who had been chosen out of everyone to receive her promises. "God protected you in Mudende and He will protect you again," she said. She smiled and walked away, greeting the people who had gathered nearby waiting for her to finish talking to me.

When my friends saw me, they laughed. "Good for you!" Gasengi teased. "Tomorrow you'll get on an airplane and study in the United States. You've never even been to college, but soon you'll have a PhD." I laughed along with them, agreeing that what the woman had told me was absurd.

At home, though, when I was alone, I started to think about her predictions, and I felt unsettled. Was it possible she was right? Would I go to college and leave Rwanda? To calm myself, I returned to the church and fasted for one more day. I prayed, watching the sunlight fall behind the hills around the refugee camp at night and rise above them again in the morning. I stared into the wind until my eyes watered.

I thought about my future. How much control did I have over my own life? I had once assumed that everything that happened to me was a script laid out for all Congolese refugees. My "moment," when my father showed up at our front door, his head bleeding, set my life in motion, and after that I had little say in what happened to me. I had spent so much time fixated on that moment, and on the trauma of my past, that I had never really considered how much of my life still lay ahead of me. Was it possible I had no idea what my life would be like? Was it possible I was waiting for another moment, a better one, that would set in motion a better future?

◆

WHEN MY DAY OF FASTING WAS OVER, I went home and ate from a bowl of warm beans and corn. "Mondiant, are you all right?" my mother asked, concerned. "I'm fine," I said. "Just hungry and tired." I wasn't ready to talk.

After I had eaten, I sat by myself outside our home and thought about what the woman had told me. I longed for what she said to be true. But it seemed selfish to want all of that, and blasphemous to pray for it. Why, out of all the students who had passed the national exam, would I be the one to leave Rwanda? Why not Gasengi, who was as devoted a student as I was, and even smarter? Why not Faustin, who had sacrificed his teacher's salary to send me to school, or Furaha, who now had a young family of her own? Why not Célestin and Patrick? Why did my friends die in Mudende when I was destined to move so far away from the refugee camp that I would need an airplane to get there?

Finally, I forced myself to stop thinking about her words. *If what she says happens, that will be great,* I told myself. *But if not, that's fine, too.* As desperate as I was for the fulfillment of all of her predictions, I knew that to believe her would be to continue handing my life over to some unseen, uncontrollable force. And I was tired of fate, and the longing for some lost paradise that came with believing in its power. I wanted control.

✦

BEFORE I LEFT GIHEMBE, my life existed for me mostly as a series of stories, half remembered and half told to me. Some stories helped me understand the world around me, while others I used to distance myself from what I learned. Some were given to me, a gift or a curse, while others I invented to protect myself from what I half remembered really happening. In stories, tragedies were lessons. In stories, miracles happened.

When I was a child in Bikenke, they were the stories my grandmother told to keep me from putting my hand in the fire or wandering into the forest by myself. They were the stories I told myself about watching my father and Faustin return home from the ranch, hungry and tired, and about feeling my mother's arms as they lifted me from the shade of the mango tree as it started to get dark. Then, in an instant, they became the stories I tried to forget but couldn't, of us fleeing Bikenke and hiding in the cave, about machetes and fire and Patience dying, of Bikenke getting smaller and smaller as we walked farther and farther away, becoming refugees.

While those early stories in Congo were motivated by fear and by love, my stories from Gihembe were stories of waiting and wishing. I found school and friends while my parents struggled to keep our family together, all the while longing for lives that had become as real as a folktale. My brother and I followed my father back to Congo and two years later returned to Rwanda. Everything that happened in between those border crossings became its own violent, hopeful, disappointing, half-remembered, timidly recounted volume.

Refugees are usually written about. Our lives are evidence of the human toll of war or famine or prejudice or climate change. When we pass away on desperate journeys across frigid bodies of water or along uninhabitable stretches of desert, our deaths highlight the impact of failed immigration policies or harsh border policies. Politicians campaign on us, whether for or against letting us into their countries; sometimes the same images and the same stories are used to argue completely opposite points. Nations use our existence within their borders to demonstrate their own generosity. Journalists report on us again and again, asking the same questions and getting the same answers and writing the same sad dispatches. We rarely get to tell our own story. I only really started to live my life—to escape the stories that made up my life—when I was able to take control of how people saw me.

After our fasting holiday, I returned to school, finishing at the top of my class. At our graduation ceremony, students were given a chance to speak. Uplifted by the praise from my teachers, I stood up and raised my voice so that even the students in the back became quiet. "We are finishing high school now," I said. "The world outside is waiting for us. Let's be light for the people who are lost in this unfair place we call the world."

I looked around. Outside, Rwanda was quiet. Dust swirled in the beams of afternoon light that came in through our classroom windows, gathering at the feet of my classmates. I was surprised that they were quiet as well, their heads turned toward me as though what I said was important. Even Jadot, my former friend, sat quietly, listening as I spoke.

"I was born in the Democratic Republic of Congo," I said. "When I was three years old the war broke out. I became a refugee." Jadot looked down; later he would apologize to me, admitting that he had never set foot in Gihembe. "I have been a refugee since 1996 and I am still a refugee," I continued. "But I have hope. We all have the power to say, This is not how my story is going to end." After the ceremony, I packed my things and began my long walk toward home.

Epilogue

Every year that passed after my high school graduation from the Rwandan national school, I grew stronger and more confident in who I was and what I wanted out of my life. Still, I had to work hard to prove myself.

In 2011, when our high school scores were announced, my grades were good enough to enroll at the University of Rwanda in Kigali, the best school in the country. Attending college was a struggle; I applied for and received a scholarship that was taken away from me when it was discovered that I was a refugee.

I remember that conversation like it was yesterday. I remember that the scholarship administrator's office in Kigali was small and stuffy, and that he looked at me suspiciously from behind his desk. "Where are you from?" he asked.

"Forty-five minutes from here," I stammered. I wasn't familiar with the geography of Rwanda beyond what lay between Gihembe, nearby forests, Faustin's house in his refugee camp, and my high school.

"There is no town there," he said. "Where are you really from?" When I told him, he denied me the money.

Nevertheless, I enrolled in the university. That first year, without a way to support myself in Kigali while I studied, I took my books back to Gihembe. *I can learn on my own,* I thought, *and return to Kigali for the exams.* When that didn't work—"Mondiant, you have never been in class," a teacher said to me. "I'm sorry, but I can't pass you"—I left school for a year and became a teacher in Gihembe, where I led a protest for higher wages and learned the value, and the dangers, of speaking up. No one is worth less because of where they are born or where they live. When I saved enough money, I went back to Kigali, intent on graduating.

In college, I was surrounded by Jadots. "Refugees are filthy," they whispered. "Look, there is Mondiant, he is so puny!" They laughed. "Mondiant, I thought you would be big, but you are no bigger than a kid." This time, though, I didn't care. I proudly acknowledged who I was. I taunted them back. "Sure, I am a refugee," I said. "So how shameful is it that I am so much better at school than you?" Most of the time, that shut them up.

◆

AFTER COLLEGE I moved back to Gihembe, where I again began teaching. Now, I thought, finished with school, I wanted to try to make an impact in the lives of refugees around me. I couldn't pay for them to go to school like I had or figure out the magic right answers to grant them resettlement in Europe or the United States. But I could listen to them and help them tell their stories.

I founded Seed of Hope, an organization devoted to collecting the stories of refugees, particularly women. We hoped to heal and connect refugees between Rwanda's five camps. Through my work with Seed of Hope, I started spending time in each of the camps, learning about the lives of refugees, most from Congo or Burundi. I realized that we had so much in common, and that our shared experience is what makes us strong.

I also made friends with an American student who traveled to Gihembe for research. Unlike other observers, this student wanted to sleep in the camp, which made me nervous. What would he think about the way we lived? My mother obsessed over what to feed our visitor. "He's not from the camp, Mondiant," she said. "Go to the market, buy some tomatoes at least." But when the student showed up, he asked such open-minded and honest questions that not even the small heartbreak I felt watching my mother work through her embarrassment took away from my pride in showing him Gihembe. He didn't look at the camp with pity or disgust. He looked at it as though it was important, and as though he could learn something from the refugees who lived there. He understood how far we had come since the day we arrived, survivors of the Mudende massacres.

When would Congo look at us the way the American student did? A few years after we arrived in Gihembe, some Bagogwe elders wrote to President Kabila to tell him we wanted to be repatriated. "Dear Sir," they wrote. "We are ready to come home." But Kabila never replied, and neither did anyone else in the government. It appeared that we were forgotten.

✦

MY LIFE'S STORY is the story of so many refugees who shared hardships, ambitions, loss, and hope. But at a certain point my story begins to diverge. My life was changed by a miracle, and miracles are difficult to explain.

In October 2016, I met, via video call, an American businessman named Tim Armstrong. While he was CEO at AOL, he and the company had done a lot of charitable work. For fifteen minutes Tim and his staff listened to me talk about Rwanda, Congo, and Gihembe. "Nice to meet you," Tim said when our time was up, and I said the same. Although we exchanged phone numbers, I did not expect to hear from him again.

Instead, Tim called me all the time. We talked about life in Gihembe, the violence in Congo, and what I wanted most. "Citizenship," I told him, again and again. "Of any country," I said. "I just want to belong." One day while I was helping my father repair the roof of our house in Gihembe, Tim phoned.

"What are you doing now?" he asked.

"I'm working on our roof," I told him. "It rained last night, and we didn't sleep at all."

"Mondiant, do you want to go to graduate school?" Tim asked. "Is that something you think about?"

"All the time," I said. After becoming a citizen of a country, continuing my education was all I ever thought about.

"Where do you want to go?" Tim asked.

I put down my tools and sat on the grass by our house. I wasn't sure what to tell him. No one had asked me that question before, as though where I went in the world was a choice I could make and not a decision made for me by world leaders or by war.

"I don't know," I said. "Maybe Kenya? I heard that there are great universities in Nairobi."

"Kenya is a possibility," Tim said. "But when you dream of leaving Gihembe, where do you dream of going?"

"New York," I answered quickly, almost laughing. "But that's impossible."

"Why?" Tim asked. "Why is that impossible?" A few months after that phone call, I was accepted into NYU. Tim Armstrong was the first person in my life aside from my family who believed in me. He paid for my education, and he and his family accepted me like a son.

The night before I left Rwanda for New York, the camp threw a party in my honor. Men set up tables with beer and mancala, and women put on traditional celebratory dresses, and we all danced. It was rare for happiness to spread throughout the entire camp at once. I felt gigantic with pride that I had caused it.

"Mondiant, write and tell us all about New York!" they said. Close friends, looking a little sheepish, would say, "Tell us, when you can, how to get there ourselves." An older man, a leader in Congo, stood up and addressed me. "Mondiant," he said, "we did not get a chance to go to school. But your generation is smart. When you repatriate to Congo, make sure no one is left behind."

The next day friends drove me to the airport. I protested when one of them picked up my suitcase, but he laughed. "There's nothing in it," he said. "It's easy. Don't worry." They reminded me to write them letters and emails. If they were envious or worried that they wouldn't see me again, they didn't show it. They didn't ask for anything.

I spent the first few months in New York trying to adjust to the different world while stubbornly pretending that I already knew everything. Tim's children, Jack, Hope, and Summer, are younger than me, but they became my teachers, helping me navigate American culture so that I wouldn't feel like such an outsider when I started school at NYU. They took me to restaurants and helped me decipher the menus, and when I complained afterward that the food hurt my stomach, Tim's wife, Nancy, brought me water. We watched the kids' favorite movies together, and when I met my classmates in New York I would tell them, *These are my favorite movies.* Even today, Tim and his family are my lifelines in New York.

◆

AT NYU, everything reminded me of Gihembe. I couldn't believe how much the students had available to eat, what variety of food they had, and how few of my classmates seemed to ever consider that it might be taken away from them. It wasn't me, exactly, who was eating this food, but the American version of me. In America I was more optimistic, I was fatter. I walked down the busy Manhattan streets dodging people because I had somewhere to be. In classes I tried to be a good student. Outside, I tried to be a good friend. My homesickness was surprising but crippling.

It wasn't until I arrived at NYU that I realized how most people my age looked at the world, not as a heavy door to pound on until it opened, but as a gift waiting to be unwrapped, full of possibility. Other students talked about their early lives as though they were prologues to incredible adult lives. They shared their dreams with anyone who would listen.

I discovered the books written by other survivors of the Rwandan genocide and devoured them. In the camp, no one knew that these books existed. It was encouraging to discover that people cared enough about us to pay attention and publish our stories. I made a note to bring some copies with me to the camp when I returned to visit that summer. Although none of them were about Bagogwe specifically, I thought it would make people feel less alone if they knew those books existed.

On good nights, alone in my dorm room, I imagined myself the Bagogwe ambassador to the world. I would tell everyone who would listen—presidents, journalists, academics—about the plight of Gihembe refugee camp and they would listen, amazed. "We thought the genocide was over," they would say, shaking their heads. "It's not fair, all the refugees who don't have a chance." Then I would tell them how they could help, and they would.

Soon, if I kept up my campaign, Gihembe camp would cease to exist, the hundreds of makeshift homes empty, maybe dismantled and removed, and Bagogwe, if not returned to Congo—even I knew this was too far-fetched of a dream—settled in a new country, with passports and identities. Refugee camps around the world would follow, their residents finding new homes and meaningful lives in countries that wanted them. All major governments would realize that resettlement was not only the humane thing to do, it was smart; who knew what we could contribute to Germany, or America, if given the chance.

On bad nights, though, when guilt about my free education overwhelmed me like a migraine, I yelled at myself. *How can you tell leaders and journalists about the Bagogwe people?* I would think. *You haven't even told your friends at NYU. You're a traitor.* I dreamed that I went back to the camp and others called me the same. "You betrayed us, Mondiant," they would say. "And you betrayed your family, you betrayed Congo, you betrayed all refugees."

I worried that after I graduated, my degree from NYU would mean nothing. I would end up back in Gihembe. I imagined the disappointment on my friends' faces; the disappointment on Tim's face. I thought about rain leaking through our roof onto my paper diploma, ruining it. I felt that I had no home. I had once visited the Congolese mission in New York, looking to connect with other Congolese people, but there I had been greeted with disdain. "Where did you grow up?" they asked. "Gihembe?" They shook their heads. "Oh, so you are Rwandan." No matter what I achieved, I was still a refugee. We would all be refugees our entire lives.

✦

PAUL KAGAME HAD ONCE BEEN a refugee himself, so when I found out that I was going to meet him face-to-face I was sure that he would listen to me, even though I was just a graduate student and he was the president of Rwanda. Kagame was scheduled to speak at the Nantucket Project, where Tim, who is an investor and occasional participant, had arranged for us to share a table with the president at dinner. All day I rehearsed what I would say to him, even though I had had a lifetime to memorize it.

I would tell President Kagame about the struggles refugees still endured while in camps, and how difficult it was for us to go to school, raise families, and get jobs. I would tell him that we were grateful for his help— without him leading Rwanda and opening refugee camps, my family would probably be dead—but that now we needed something beyond safety. We needed a real home.

But how honest could I be? Would I tell President Kagame about how much we all wanted to go back to Congo, even after all we had been through? Would he understand our desire to go home, or would he be insulted that we were so eager to leave the home he had given us?

Shortly before dinner was scheduled to begin, Tim led me to a room in the back of the restaurant, where Kagame was waiting with two of his staffers. The president sat next to me at the small table. He looked like his photos, thin and tall with a contemplative and inviting expression. He wore a black suit and the black-frame glasses that made him look like a college professor as much as a president. In his speech at the festival, he had talked about forgiveness and rebuilding. "We were a country that lost everything," he said. Rwanda was so wounded it was hard to see that it would survive. "Rwandans looked each other in the eyes," President Kagame said onstage. "How do we reconcile? We had to make a choice."

I looked the president in the eyes and introduced myself. "I am Mondiant," I said. "I was born in eastern Congo. When I was three years old, some of our Hutu neighbors attacked my father while he was watching our cows, and we fled to the Gihembe refugee camp. We've lived there ever since."

President Kagame looked at me kindly. "Very nice to meet you," he said. He offered his hand for me to shake. "How long have you been living in Gihembe?"

"Twenty years," I replied. I worried my honesty would come across as critical. To compensate, I smiled. "On behalf of my people," I told Kagame, "thank you for keeping us safe."

"That's a long time," Kagame said. "I grew up in a refugee camp, too. Mine was in Uganda."

I nodded. I knew his story.

"How did you make it to the United States?" the president asked.

I told him about pushing my way through university in Kigali, and the disappointment of realizing that no matter how hard a refugee worked, he didn't have the same opportunities as a Rwandan citizen. "I put my energy into the organizations I founded," I told him. "But I lost hope that I would end up living anywhere but Gihembe."

"And now you're at NYU?" he asked.

"Because of Tim," I told him. "I want to use my opportunity to help the people who are still in Gihembe."

No one else in Gihembe had a person like Tim to step in and help them. Was it right for me to present my case to the president as an example of a refugee eager to make the world better, if only given the chance? Me, whose life is a crazy miracle?

It was a short meeting. My stomach rumbled with hunger. The next day I would go back to NYU and my classes, gifts given to me by Tim and his family. I would study hard, write letters to my family and friends in Gihembe, and return every night to my dorm room, trying to plan for the future while not dwelling on it so much I couldn't sleep.

"Mondiant," the president said, "how can Rwanda help?"

"First," I said, "we need to be citizens. Without that, we can't do anything." I told him about leaving Rwanda for New York, how even though I had a visa, UN travel papers, and documents proving that I had been accepted into NYU, I was still detained at every step. "Without a passport, we can't travel easily," I explained. "If we can't travel, we are trapped."

I remember that the president was kind and that he listened. I think I remember a look on his face that suggested he was sifting through his own memories of being a refugee, and that those memories were like a thread connecting us. "That can happen, Mondiant," he said. "You can be a Rwandan citizen, if you want." I took a deep breath.

Dinner took place at a large round table covered in a white tablecloth. Tim pointed out some celebrities I didn't recognize. I wasn't sure what to eat so I copied Tim and orderd a lobster, my first. The muffled conversations at other tables throughout the busy restaurant started to sound like the waves outside our window.

I was eating lobster. I was thinking about what had just happened. President Kagame offered me all I had thought I ever wanted. With Rwandan citizenship I could get a Rwandan passport and a well-paying job, travel freely, buy a house, marry. I could do anything. I could finish my book with a happy ending, then lock away the manuscript and never think of it again. But if I wrote that book, what would be the meaning of my story?

I was a young Congolese Tutsi who had escaped death with my family and grown up in a refugee camp. By age twelve, I was retrieving bodies from battlefields, eager to please the rebel commander who had taken the place of my father, who was missing. When I was older and back in

Rwanda, I pushed my way into high school and then college, even though I had no money and even though other students mocked and disparaged refugees. I hid who I was until I decided not to be ashamed, and I kept trying. Just like other refugees my age, I refused to give up. Unlike a lot of them, I never had to.

One day I was plucked from the camp and offered a chance to study in New York City at one of the best universities in the world by a man who barely knew me but who thought that I could do wonderful things if given the opportunity. Would you believe that story, if you read it? Would you believe that a Congolese boy who grew up stateless, surrounded by stateless people, was on his way to graduating from NYU? Would you believe that a few months later, as if by a miracle, I was being offered citizenship by the president of Rwanda himself?

In our meeting, I thanked President Kagame, and I meant it. He was offering to fulfill a dream I'd had since childhood. But it wasn't the ending I was looking for.

"There are so many others like me," I told him. "Everyone in Gihembe needs a home like I do." I said no. I said thank you. I told the president, "Everyone has a story, there is a lot of work for us to do," and I thought to myself, *Get back to work.*

Visiting Nyabiheke primary school.

Hope, me, Jack, and Summer.

Tim, Sedigi, Eugenie, me, and Nancy.

My older brother, Faustin (left), and younger brother John.

My first day at New York University.

With Rwandan president Paul Kagame and Tim Armstrong.

Getting ready to speak at the United Nations on World Refugee Day.

Playing mancala with my community elders and peers in Gihembe.

ACKNOWLEDGMENTS

Thank you to my family and friends who have been with me throughout my journey, and to those we had to say goodbye to along the way. To my parents, Eugenie and Sedigi; my brothers, Faustin, John, and Baraka; and my sisters, Furaha, Patience, Asifwe, and Mukeshema: Your love and support, as well as your sacrifices and perseverance in the face of incredible challenges, made this book possible.

Thank you from the bottom of my heart to Tim and Nancy Armstrong, my mentors and my American parents. I can't fully express how grateful I am to have been welcomed as a part of your family. To my American sisters, Summer and Hope, and my American brother, Jack: You can't imagine how much you have helped me. I learned so much from all of you.

Thank you to Shared Studios, whose portal project in Kigali first connected me to Tim, and to AOL, which gave me a stepping-stone to my new life and showed the world that refugee camps are not simply rows of tents but communities filled with people longing to change their countries and the world.

I will always be grateful to President Paul Kagame for saving my life and the lives of other Congolese Tutsis after the massacres in eastern Congo and in the Mudende refugee camp, and to the United States for welcoming me as an adult.

New York University helped me find hope and a new perspective on life. Everyone at NYU—from the cafeteria workers to the professors who knew about my background and provided me with extra resources—contributed to my graduation. Special thanks to my professors Dana Burde, Elisabeth King, Carol Anne Spreen, Hua-Yu Sebastian Cherng, and Dominic Brewer, as well as my academic adviser, Jamie Baldwin. Alexandria Martinez and her husband, Kerry Meier, helped me navigate school and the city; I will never forget taking the ferry to the Statue of Liberty with them, or getting lost on the subway and ending up in the Bronx instead of JFK Airport.

It was at the offices of Flowcode (formerly the dtx company) that Jenna Krajeski, my coauthor, and I spent hours talking for this book. Without the understanding of my coworkers, the book could never have been written.

Virginia Smith and Caroline Sydney listened to me and cared about my story before I ever imagined it could truly be a book. Their intelligence and empathy, and their patience, made the manuscript infinitely better. Without Amanda Urban, I don't know when my dream of writing my own story would have become a reality. Special thanks to Jenna, who has been a blessing to me. The time she devoted to this project and her professionalism are incalculable.

In Gihembe, too many people to name here helped me. They are my neighbors, friends, and classmates. Their lives are what this book is about. I'm also thankful for Sybil Miller, and Scott and Rachel Baker. Your encouragement and support strengthened my belief that although I was a refugee, I shouldn't give up on my dreams.

I will forever be grateful to the United Nations, as well as Alight, World Vision, Plan International, World Relief, Save the Children, and the Red Cross, who provided relief to us for decades. These are the organizations whose logos appeared on the blankets that covered my thin body, on the cans I used to fetch water, on the books I read at school, even on my shoes and the plastic roof that covered my head. Without these organizations I would be dead. But the greatest gift they gave me is the ability to pursue an independent life, free of those logos.